Musicals, Marigolds & Me

Paul takes us on a journey through his long and varied career from his beginnings in the sixties to the present day. Having shared the stage on numerous occasions, it certainly brought back a 'Memory' or two for me. If you love entertainment you'll love this!

– Elaine Paige

Paul is one of the funniest gentlemen I have ever worked or played with. We mastered mono waterskis together. And he was the first to play the title role of *Jesus Christ Superstar* in the West End. Nobody did it better.

– Sir Tim Rice

A terrific book full of details of a long and varied career.

– David Essex

From Andrew Lloyd Webber to the Bee Gees, from Gielgud to the Krankies – Paul Nicholas has worked with them all. Actor, writer, director, pop star… like Paul himself, this funny, heart-warming and truthful book is a rollercoaster ride through an incredible career. I consider myself blessed to have been a part of it.

– David Ian

Musicals, Marigolds & Me

Paul Nicholas

with Douglas Thompson

fantom
publishing

First published in 2021 by Fantom Publishing, an imprint of Fantom Films
fantompublishing.co.uk

Copyright © Paul Nicholas 2021

The right of Paul Nicholas to be identified as the author of this work has been asserted in accordance with Section 78 of the Copyright, Designs and Patents Act 1988.

A catalogue record for this book is available from the British Library.

ISBN: 978-1-78196-376-0

Typeset by Phil Reynolds Media Services, Leamington Spa
Printed and bound by CPI Group (UK) Ltd, Croydon, CR0 4YY

Jacket design by Stuart Manning

Contents

Preface

I N 1999 MY AUTOBIOGRAPHY *Behind the Smile* was published. I had just turned fifty-five and felt it was probably a good time to have a look back on my life thus far. Although it documented my career as a performer, it was interspersed with personal recollections of a more private nature. Now, more than two decades on at seventy-six, I've written another book. Only this time I've focused more on my professional life as a performer and producer.

In 1968 I was involved with the beginning of the upsurge in popularity of musical theatre in the UK with my first show *Hair*.

In 1972 I was cast as Jesus in the original West End production of *Jesus Christ Superstar*. Following *Superstar*, Elaine Paige and I were the first English Danny and Sandy in the original West End production of *Grease*.

I've walked the tightrope as P. T. Barnum, swashed my buckle as the Pirate King in *The Pirates of Penzance*, and achieved a childhood ambition of playing the Gene Kelly part (Don Lockwood) in *Singin' in the Rain* directed by another musical legend, Tommy Steele.

In 1981, Andrew Lloyd Webber invited me to do the workshop of his new musical *Cats* and thereafter play the role of Rum Tum Tugger in the original West End production.

I've co-produced *Grease* in London and on Broadway, *Saturday Night Fever* at the London Palladium, and many other musicals with the inevitable hits and misses that come with producing shows. I've appeared in the musical films *Tommy* and *Sgt. Pepper's Lonely Hearts Club Band*.

I enjoyed a brief but successful pop career as well as appearing as Vince in the BBC's BAFTA-winning sitcom *Just Good Friends*. More recently I played the evil Gavin Sullivan in the long-running soap *EastEnders* and appeared as myself in the popular reality series *The Real Marigold Hotel*. This was the show where a group of mature celebrities visited exotic locations around the world, hence the 'Marigolds' in the book's title.

Other than a few mentions of my flamboyant father – the entertainment lawyer, Oscar Beuselinck – and my ever-loving wife of fifty-two years, Linzi ('I think I'm starting to get on her nerves…'), there is little or no mention (much to their relief) of my six children and thirteen (and counting) grandchildren and great-grandchildren.

This book is about the beginning of my professional journey as a sixteen-year-old singer from north London and where that journey has taken me over the last sixty years.

I hope you like reading the book and enjoy the trip.

CHAPTER ONE

Have Talent, Will Travel

'Music I can wish ya
Merry music while you're young
And wisdom when your hair has turned to grey'
  – Arvide Abernathy, *Guys and Dolls*

I'VE WORKED WITH the legendary knights of theatre – Olivier, Richardson and Gielgud. Sung with David Bowie, topped the pop charts, the television ratings, made Hollywood movies and was the first British *Jesus Christ Superstar*; but for a moment there in 2017, I appeared to be better known for trying to find a pair of underpants in India. Which as it turned out became one of the highlights of the television series *The Real Marigold Hotel*…

When my agent called me in 2018 and said they wanted me for *Guys and Dolls* at the Royal Albert Hall in London, my mind immediately jumped to the 1955 movie.

'Ah yes. That would be for the Marlon Brando part, Sky Masterson?'

'Err… no.'

'Then it must be the Frank Sinatra role, Nathan Detroit.'

'No...'

'Then it's Nicely-Nicely Johnson, who has the big show-stopping number, "Sit Down You're Rockin' the Boat"?'

'Err – no!'

'Well, *what is it then?*'

'The grandfather.'

'The grandfather! What does he do?'

'He's the leader of the Salvation Army Band and has one song...'

'Okay, I'll do it!'

So, in 2018, I became Arvide Abernathy, leader of the Save-a-Soul Mission band in *Guys and Dolls*. He might not be the best known of Damon Runyon's characters but, as my agent said, he has one great song – 'More I Cannot Wish You'.

Sometimes, it's easy to forget I'm seventy-six going on twelve and those leading man roles aren't going to be as frequent as they once were. It seems like five minutes but I'm heading towards more than sixty years in show business, and the desire to perform and to succeed is still as strong as when I started in the early 1960s as a rock-'n'-roll pianist for 'Screaming Lord Sutch' as one of his 'Savages'.

It's in the blood, which is a bit of a cliché but it's true. You just want to keep doing it. When you're young, you have insecurities about what you can achieve as a performer; with time, you learn what your strengths and weaknesses are. You go through a lot of highs and lows and there are times when you begin to doubt your ability as an artist. In my experience the most enduring quality that every performer needs, and which has certainly served me well over the years, is tenacity.

Today I am looked on by some as a voice of experience. During a rehearsal of *Guys and Dolls*, after I'd just performed the grandfather's song 'More I Cannot Wish You', one of the young cast members came up to me. He was fresh out of drama school and said, 'It's great to hear you sing in person. I'm a great lover of *Cats* and play the album all the time. I love your performance of the "Rum Tum Tugger".' I thanked him. I was chuffed.

The West End cast album of *Cats* was recorded in 1981 which is a very long time ago. When I started in show business in the early 1960s, aspiring performers were separated into three categories: actors acted, dancers danced and singers sang. Today, young performers are trained in all three disciplines. They all sing, dance and act to a very high standard and many of them – particularly those strong in dance – regard *Cats* as a show they would like to be in. I doubt they've even heard of Screaming Lord Sutch, founder of the Monster Raving Loony Party (who I must say in passing had a marvellous defence policy – 'No one must sit on de-fence').

I'm always happy to talk about musical theatre and the magic conjured when all the elements of storytelling and music come together. As I explained, I've been around quite a time and in many cases I truly do have the T-shirt – and of course the underpants, following my adventures in India with *The Real Marigold Hotel*. That's the BBC reality series based loosely on the 2011 film *The Best Exotic Marigold Hotel* which is about British pensioners enjoying themselves, finding personal fulfilment and happiness in India. The TV show inspired by it is a travelogue with familiar faces who are getting on a bit in age but are up for new experiences. Not many people get that opportunity and I think that's what makes the series so popular. 'What if?' That's where we 'Marigolds' come in. We test drive the exotic spots, not just to visit but to retire to.

I'd never done a reality show other than *Only Fools on Horses* for the BBC's Sports Relief, where a group of celebrities learn the art of show jumping… but that's another, somewhat painful, story for later. The great thing about *Marigold* is that you can't be voted off, unlike some other celebrity TV shows. It's not a competition, so you're not under any pressure to win. It's that lack of rivalry that people enjoy, seeing how faces they've known on TV react to challenging situations but without some of the more extreme forms of behaviour that happen in the jungle or on romantic islands.

I liked the idea behind it of older people travelling somewhere new and possibly retiring there. For instance, I'd never been to India and probably would never have gone. However, opportunities like that don't come along every day and it seemed like an adventure that was too good to miss. It's one of the plusses of being a performer that one day your agent calls and asks you if you fancy a trip to India. Why not? We all wonder how we'd react, survive, if suddenly asked to cope half a world away dealing with different languages and cultures, particularly with seven other celebrities.

It was an inspiring show to be in and it showed life doesn't have to stop because you're older. In many ways it's better because a lot of the expectations placed on you when you are young quietly go away. I used to dread getting old but actually I'm enjoying it. Getting older is very liberating because you don't give a hoot.

For that first series I did in 2017, I would be staying at a hotel in Kochi, which is in the tropical state of Kerala in southern India, along with my fellow 'Marigold' travellers: the dancer-entertainer Lionel Blair, former snooker world champion Dennis Taylor, comedian and 'birder' Bill Oddie, actress Amanda Barrie, singer Sheila Ferguson, TV chef Rustie Lee and agony aunt Miriam Stoppard. It was a properly diverse mix. I wasn't really sure how I would react to the group.

We arrived at the hotel to be greeted by ladies dancing in traditional outfits and scattering flower petals which was a lovely welcome.

The first decision that we had to make as a group was where everyone was going to sleep. Obviously the ladies – along with Lionel, being eighty-seven – should have first choice of the available rooms. Trying to be courteous, I let everyone else choose first and so consequently I ended up with the worst room. It was a tiny room above the kitchen overlooking an old bath in the garden. Above me was the air-conditioning unit and outside was a busy road and a noisy electric generator. Not ideal. Apparently this was the overflow room if the hotel was overbooked. The only thing that it had in its favour was a four-poster bed which meant I was able to rig up my mosquito net.

We all met the next morning for breakfast. What you don't realise if you've never done a reality show is that the camera is with you twenty-four hours a day. Obviously when there are seven or eight of us, they use a couple of camera crews. They want to see you unpack. They want to see you do all the things one normally does when arriving at a hotel. They film you in the mornings as you get up, when you're washing, showering and shaving. All sorts of personal stuff.

6

We're all artists and if you're an artist you want to be seen. It's a natural thing as it's who we are. Subsequently, there was always a bit of competition for camera time. Pointless really because you never know what will end up being shown. No matter how interesting you think you are or how witty, it all comes down to how the director edits the show.

My search for underpants ultimately seemed to be of interest. One woman wrote in saying the funniest thing she ever saw was me trying to buy underpants in India. Simply, the underwear I'd originally packed had vanished from my suitcase; it turned out I'd left it all at the hotel during our stop-over in Mumbai. There weren't any branches of Marks and Sparks near the hotel in Kochi; so that's when the search began, trying to find a month's supply in India.

It got a lot of laughs but for me it became a mission. I didn't contrive to make it a story; it became a story because it was real. I had to find some underpants so that became my story. All of us needed stories. Most of the ladies in the series are searching for love which was the original *Marigold* movie plotline.

The first episode pretty much centred on my nail-biting quest for pants, which of course the producers filmed as if it was the hunt for the Holy Grail. Bill Oddie, Dennis and the others joined in the search and it made good TV, but for a time there I thought I might be going commando for the duration. I was surprised how difficult it was. Most of the men wear the traditional *kaupina* which is similar to a loincloth and would have been very difficult to wear under my chinos. When I finally found some underpants, the only sort that were available were a brand called 'Playboy'. I initially bought six pairs but then thought, this is India, better make it eight.

Some of my fellow Marigolders I had met before. I wasn't sure how I would feel living with seven people who were not strangers but were not close friends or family. However, on *Marigold*, I found we all just mucked in.

The very nature of the series meant we were able to experience the traditional Indian culture, the people, the dancing and music which I loved and of course the food which I found a little challenging. It was a bit too spicy for me. I think my lack of interest with food comes from my mum who wasn't interested in food either and brought me up eating eggs and bacon and that's about as exotic as it got. Even adding a bit of brown sauce was pushing the envelope… so the spicy stuff was off my menu. While the others were tucking into a chicken biryani – one of Dennis's favourites – I was feasting on a mushroom omelette.

Dennis Taylor and I got on like a house on fire. One of the highlights of the trip was when Dennis and I visited the birthplace of snooker, the Ooty Colonial Club in southern India. The great bonus of *Marigold* is meeting people and Dennis Taylor was a bit of a hero of mine. The 'black ball final' of the World Snooker Championships in 1985 when Dennis took the title from Steve Davis was really something and a sporting event that so many still remember. There are a few moments like that that do stick in your mind, so meeting Dennis and then going to the home of snooker in India was one such moment for me. It was a real thrill for Dennis to play on the table where the game was invented.

In the nineteenth century, billiards was a popular pastime among the British Army in India: two of the most popular games were black pool and pyramid pool, and in 1875 at the British Army Officers' Mess in Jabalpur in the Central Provinces, Colonel Sir Neville Francis Fitzgerald Chamberlain suggested combining the two games which was the birth of snooker.

The name 'snooker' comes from a comment Chamberlain made about a player who missed a shot. He called him 'a real snooker' referring to his lack of experience; 'snooker' was slang for a first-year cadet.

In 1885 when billiards champion John Robert went to India, he met Colonel Chamberlain and brought the game back to Britain; so for us, playing on the original table was something special.

We were met by Jimmy, the current president of the Ooty Colonial Club; and following a lovely lunch, Jimmy allowed us to play on the original 1875 table which was still in mint condition. I could see how moved Dennis was by the experience, and he said to Jimmy, 'What a great honour it is and a lifetime dream to be here. I would think I'm the first world champion to come to the club. You don't know what that means to me.' It brought a tear to my eye but Dennis still didn't let me win.

The producers of the show had arranged for all of us to attend a traditional Hindu wedding, which meant we had to find suitable Indian clothes to be part of the special day. I managed to find a traditional red outfit complete with turban. The music, colour and tradition made it a beautiful ceremony and a wonderful day.

Indian people are very family-orientated and have a lot of time and respect for the older members of society. You won't find many elderly in care homes in India as they remain an integral part of the family and continue to be involved with all aspects of family life.

If you're ever in Kochi, the train trip to Madurai and the Pudu Mandapa Temple are worth a visit. We all caught the overnight train to Madurai so we weren't sure what to expect. Although the train was very crowded with limited compartments, the production team had booked us sleeping accommodation. Dennis and I were assigned a compartment with four bunks: one for Dennis, one for me, and another was occupied by a mother and her young child. The lady didn't seem to mind that she was sharing with us, and the child was very well behaved.

In the morning we were given breakfast, and on arrival were taken in taxis to see the Meenakshi Temple, situated in the heart of historic Madurai City. It is the most impressive and important of south India's temples and dates back to the twelfth century – that's nearly as old as the combined ages of us Marigolds. The temple complex covers fourteen acres and houses 4,500 pillars and fourteen towers. It's enormous!

The sheer size of the temple means that it's easy to get lost inside, and there's so much to see and marvel over that you could easily spend a few days there. It is a 'living' temple, full of industry and a constant stream of couples who are waiting to be married in its corridors. Although non-Hindus can wander around inside the temple, they can't enter the shrines.

I was amazed by the energy of the older members of our group; Lionel at the time was eighty-seven, Miriam eighty-two and Amanda eighty-one during filming. I felt like the teenager at seventy-one and Dennis, Rustie, Sheila and Bill were even younger and barely out of nappies. They were up for everything and like all performers, adored being on camera and being the centre of attention, me included.

9

On our last night in Kochi, the producers arranged a party for us and we were asked if we would like to perform. Sheila, who was the lead singer with the Three Degrees, sang her worldwide hit 'When Will I See You Again' which was received enthusiastically by the partygoers. Lionel opted to do a bit of a soft-shoe shuffle to 'Me and My Shadow' and showed that he was as nimble as ever. He finished his number with a flourish and a twirl at which point his trousers fell to his ankles. This was met by laughter and wild applause from the assembled audience.

When he came off stage, I said, 'Lionel, I loved your routine, and the comedy ending when your trousers fell down was brilliant!'

He looked at me slightly embarrassed and said, 'It wasn't rehearsed. I forgot to wear a belt.'

I paused. 'Well, keep it in Lionel. It was hilarious.'

Following my trip to India, I was invited to take part in a spin-off show called *The Real Marigold on Tour*, which also involved Sheila, Rustie and Dennis; so off we went to Iceland. As a result of our trip to India, Dennis and I were apparently having a 'bromance' so the producers thought it would be a good idea for us to share a flat together. Sheila and Rustie were also staying together in another flat a mile away.

Iceland is a magical place, known as the 'Land of Fire and Ice', and is situated a few degrees south of the Arctic Circle. It has some of the largest glaciers in Europe and also the most active volcanoes. It has a rich history of folklore and legends and is known for its tales of strange creatures, elves, trolls and monsters. Apparently eighty per cent of the Icelandic people believe in such creatures. Dennis, being Irish and a leprechaun, felt perfectly at home.

We were filming during the summer months which meant there were only three hours of semi-darkness each night. It never gets completely dark in the summer in Iceland. It's not unusual for people to start playing golf around midnight, and on one occasion I was woken up at three a.m. by someone mowing their lawn.

With such television shows there has to be an element of theatricality. Dennis and I joined an Icelandic male choir who travelled all over the country singing for the locals in natural beauty spots. The song Dennis and I sang was in Icelandic but they gave us copies of the music so it wasn't difficult to follow. We sang in a beautiful setting, surrounded by mountains. It really was 'the sound of music'.

You have to have your highlights and our visit to Iceland had several of them, notably the dramatic waterfalls and hot springs which included a trip to the 'Blue Lagoon'. This is a geothermal spa where people go to soak up the rich minerals found in the sea waters which, it is said, help psoriasis. Sheila and I took a dip and felt invigorated by the experience. I think Sheila was further revitalised by the prospect of meeting a Viking. Sheila is still a very attractive lady and she did meet her Viking who took her out for a romantic dinner; I believe they are still in touch.

Iceland has become a very fashionable destination for tourists, and the 350,000 inhabitants enjoy the commerce that tourism brings to the country. However, they are also very protective of their country's natural beauty. Many Icelandic people are concerned that too many tourists may harm the country's natural beauty.

Following our stay in Iceland, our next port of call was Thailand. For this trip we had a change of cast. Rustie Lee couldn't join us and so she was replaced by Rosemary Shrager, the celebrity chef. Rosemary had appeared in the first series of *Marigold*.

Dennis, Sheila and I met Rosemary for the first time at Heathrow Airport and I was immediately struck by her warmth and personality. It must have been a little bit strange for her to join a new group of Marigolds but it didn't take long for all of us to relax with each other.

During the long flight to Bangkok, Rosemary and I got chatting and discovered that in 1978 she and I had been bidding for the purchase of the same house in north London. She knew the layout inside out and had obviously been very keen to buy it. Unfortunately for her and luckily for me, I pipped her to the post and still live in the same house to this day.

We finally landed in Bangkok and the following day flew to Chiang Mai where we were to share a house for the duration of the trip. Chiang Mai is the largest city in northern Thailand and the capital of Chiang Mai Province. It is the second city and the spiritual heart of the country. It is smaller than Bangkok and less frenetic. It is a big draw for travellers, backpackers and the elderly who enjoy its spiritual atmosphere.

The house we were sharing was self-catering so we had to do our own cooking. It was immediately clear that Rosemary and Dennis enjoyed their food, particularly curries. They were happy to sample the local fare, no matter how many legs it had. I was of course less adventurous but did manage to find a very good local restaurant that did a wonderful take-away pizza.

There are over two hundred Buddhist temples in Chiang Mai, one of which is the 'Wat Prathat Doi Suthep Temple' which is a sacred site for the Thai people. 'Doi Suthep' is the name of the mountain atop which it sits. There are plenty of Buddhist monks who mostly speak English and are happy to show you around the temple.

Before I arrived in Thailand there were two things I knew I wanted to see. The first was the railway built between Burma and Thailand by the British POWs for the Japanese during WW2. As a boy, I remember seeing the David Lean film *The Bridge on the River Kwai* starring Alec Guinness, a film that has always stayed with me. Unfortunately the railway wasn't on our schedule.

The other was to see the famous 'ladyboys' of Bangkok, and they were scheduled for the end of our trip, the day before we left for home. We were taken to a club where the ladyboys were performing. It was a fabulous show and Dennis, Sheila, Rosemary and I lapped it up. Suddenly to our surprise Dennis and I were plucked from our seats along with two other unsuspecting audience members and taken backstage. We were handed a dress and a wig while a couple of ladyboys helped with our make-up. We were led to the stage; suddenly the curtain went up and we danced for the audience. Dennis looked like a girl you wouldn't take home to meet your mother but clearly loved it. I loved it too, but was a little miffed because my wig was blue and I so wanted to be blonde… Well, they have more fun. The audience whistled and cheered. We were a triumph!

After the show we had drinks with the ladyboys and I had a chat with their very talented leading girl. She told me she had just broken up with her boyfriend. Apparently he felt he couldn't continue with the relation-ship because his parents disapproved of her being a he. As a transsexual she had been through a lot, both emotionally and physically, so to then lose an important relationship was very sad.

I don't know why but it made me think of all of the performers I'd worked with over the years. All of whom start out with hopes and dreams only to have them shattered. It's a tough business, this business they call show.

My penultimate *Marigold on Tour* destination was Buenos Aires, Argentina. Again four of us were invited to take part: Sheila, Jan Leeming (who is still a very smart and attractive lady), me, and my old dancing partner from *Cats*, Wayne Sleep. Both Wayne and Jan had done the very first series of *The Real Marigold Hotel* and the first trip to India. I was looking forward to Argentina, and the idea of spending time with Wayne whom I hadn't seen for many years was a bonus. When we all met at Heathrow, Wayne and I chatted as if we'd last seen each other the day before.

l knew very little about Argentina other than what I'd read on the internet and also learnt from the Rice/Lloyd Webber musical *Evita* which tells the story of Eva Perón, the wife of Juan Perón, the dictator of Argentina during the 1940s and fifties.

On the drive to the flat where we were staying in Buenos Aires, we saw a huge billboard of Eva Perón. It had been erected on the front of the Ministry of Health building by the once President of Argentina Christina Kircher in 2011. Eva had been a champion of women and workers' rights, and she was still much loved and celebrated by the Argentinean people.

I was surprised by Buenos Aires as the city reminded me very much of Paris with wide boulevards, elegant shops and fashionable restaurants. Our accommodation was a spacious flat at the top of a large apartment block in the centre of the city.

The first day's filming began the following morning with a visit to the presidential mansion, Casa Rosada (The Pink Palace). It was here on the balcony, on 17th October 1951 ('Loyalty Day'), where Eva made her famous speech to the people in celebration of Juan Perón being released from imprisonment at the hands of fellow officers who were then ruling Argentina. His freedom set him along the road that would eventually lead to his election to the presidency. Eva had recently been diagnosed with the cancer that would eventually kill her. It wasn't difficult to picture her standing on the balcony; the moment has been beautifully captured in the well-known song from the musical *Evita*, 'Don't Cry for Me Argentina'.

I discovered that Eva's family tomb wasn't very far from our flat, so I went to the La Recoleta Cemetery to have a look. It's a very large cemetery with many imposing tombs. Eva's Duarte family tomb was relatively simple compared to some of the rather grandiose ones nearby. There was a line of people waiting to pay their respects, some with floral tributes that they laid in her honour. She remains a revered figure for many Argentineans some seventy years after her death.

I'm always struck when visiting different countries by the diversity of the music. Argentina was no exception. Yes, there's a lot of American music, but you still hear the traditional music of the country.

I was really looking forward to hearing and perhaps dancing to the music of the tango, so it was no surprise that the director had lined up some lessons for us. It would seem that the dance is very much led by one partner, usually the male, who controls the movement and direction of the dance. In other words the man leads while the woman follows.

The idea was that, with some basic tuition under our belts, we would spend the evening in an Argentinean tango night club – a 'milonga' – on talent night where various performers get up and do their bit. Sheila and I were asked if we could learn a traditional Argentine song that we could perform with a young local singer. So we met him and started to learn the song we were to sing. Sheila had lived for many years in Majorca, so she spoke Spanish, and I found that following the melody in Spanish was easier than speaking it.

We arrived at the milonga and our tango teacher was already there and invited me to dance. After we'd finished, we sat down and a young man came over to our table and asked me to dance. I was a little surprised but of course, being an actor, extremely flattered and said, 'Oh yes of course. Thank you.' With that he took my hand and off we went with him leading and me following.

This is not so unusual in Argentina as the dance originated with men dancing together. It seems the tango began in the working-class tenements of Buenos Aires and Montevideo as the men's fantasy dance.

They had arrived from Europe and at first there were very few women so the men learnt to dance together. The risqué thing that made the tango different from other dances is that the men put their legs in the space between the women's legs as this was something the men wanted to do to them. After the dance ended, I thanked the handsome young man – who I might add didn't offer to buy me a drink.

A little later Sheila and I sang our duet with the young guitarist and the locals seemed to enjoy the song as they all joined in and sang along with us.

Thinking that this was all going rather well and a good idea, the director, a lovely chap called Nic Patten, suggested that as part of the talent night Wayne and I should recreate our 1982 version of 'Mr Mistoffelees' from *Cats*.

I said, 'We don't have any music.'

'That doesn't matter,' said Nick.

'Okay,' I said as I'd had a couple of beers.

Suddenly we were on and I started singing, 'Oh well I never, was there ever a cat so clever as magical Mr Mistoffelees?' with Wayne at sixty-nine leaping around like a young gazelle. I don't think the locals in the club quite knew what to make of us or what the hell we were doing. Still, we were enjoying ourselves until midway through the second chorus when I looked down and saw that Wayne was splayed out on the floor like a dead cat. I think this was probably the result of one jeté and three double vodkas too many. Anyway he eventually got up and we completed the number. It was never shown. I think Wayne had a quiet word, which on reflection was probably a good thing for both our reputations. However, looking back, performing with Wayne again, albeit forty years on from our first performance in *Cats*, is a memory I will always treasure.

Overall, what I most enjoyed about Argentina were the people and their love and passion for the romance and rhythm of the tango. It's a shame we don't have that kind of traditional music, as morris dancing doesn't really do it for me.

My final *Marigold on Tour* trip was to Mexico with Rosemary Shrager and two performers I had enjoyed working with many years before in panto: Ian and Janette Tough, otherwise known as 'The Krankies'. It was a joy to see them again. They are both friendly and jolly and are still a wonderful comedy duo. They'd already filmed *The Real Marigold Hotel* in India and proved very popular with the public. Ian loves food and cooking, and both of them are very down to earth and not remotely grand. Ian's love of food meant that he and Rosemary had a lot in common.

We were staying in Guadalajara, famous for being the land of tequila and mariachi, a traditional Mexican folk music performed by small groups of strolling musicians. Guadalajara is also known as 'the Mexican Silicon Valley'. Our accommodation was at a guest house run by two lovely chaps, one American and the other Mexican.

Part of the show's remit is to demonstrate the ways in which older people's circumstances differ from country to country. With this in mind, we were taken to a complex dedicated solely to activities for older people: volleyball, table tennis, arts and crafts, social events, art classes, keep-fit classes and more. It was basically a youth club for the elderly; somewhere they could interact, have fun and still be involved in life despite their advancing years – which was how we felt being in the *Marigold* show. We were able to take part in a number of activities while in Mexico, everything from canoeing with expat Americans to being serenaded by a mariachi band.

One of the more unusual experiences was a ritual cleansing ceremony conducted in a 'temazcal' by a Mexican Indian, who was a descendent of the original Maya people. He was called a 'curandero', a healer or medicine man. A temazcal is a traditional Mexican steam bath, not unlike a sauna, which promotes physical well-being and healing. It allows the body to rid itself of toxins through sweating and the spirit is renewed through the ritual. It takes place in a dome-shaped structure made of stone or mud; the size varies and can accommodate from two to twenty people. We were required to strip, wrap ourselves in towels and sit in the temazcal. At the centre was a fire, which was periodically doused with water to create steam while the curandero recited various chants intended to expel the evil spirits. Ian, Janette and I felt cleansed after about twenty minutes as it was boiling hot. Rosemary stuck it out for the full hour.

Following our stay in Guadalajara, we headed about an hour south to Ajijic which is a little town on the shores of Lake Chapala.

Compared to the USA the dollar goes a lot further in Mexico and as a result there is a large American/Canadian retirement community. Between them they have organised lots of social clubs and activities which include a three-hundred-seat theatre run by an Englishman.

He asked if any of us would like to perform as they were about to have a local talent night. Rosemary, who does cooking demos, didn't have enough kitchen equipment with her, and the Krankies didn't have their props and costumes and weren't keen to do a sub-standard performance of their act. However, Nick our director was keen to film something, so Ian said he'd write a sketch for us to perform. He wrote a little routine about an Englishman and a Scotsman trying to enter the USA and being interrogated by a U.S. immigration official.

We asked one of the locals to play the immigration officer. Ian wore a tam-o'-shanter for the Scotsman and I wore a bowler hat as the posh Englishman. We learnt and rehearsed it very quickly with a local actor. There were many acts on the bill and the theatre was full. Suddenly we were on and we had great fun doing it…

COMEDY SKETCH
Ian, Paul & one other

U.S. Immigration officer standing on stage.
Enter Ian and Paul as two Brits trying to enter America.

Immig. Officer: Hey, where do you think you two are going?
Both: We are going to America.
Immig. Officer: You can't come in without passing 'The Test' created by President Trump. First question goes to you, sir.
Paul (posh Englishman): Yes I'm ready!
Immig. Officer: Where was the Declaration of Independence signed?
Paul: At the bottom of the page!
Immig. Officer: Second question goes to you, little fat Scotsman.

Ian (Scotsman): Yes.

Immig. Officer: There are lots of different nationalities
    that live here. Can you tell me the difference
    between people who are from Dubai and people from
    Abu Dhabi?

Ian: People who come from Dubai don't like the Flintstones
    but people from Abu Dhabi, Dabba, Dabba Doo!

Immig. Officer: Next question is to you posh Englishman.
    It's about currency. If you had fifty dollars in one
    pocket and fifty dollars in your other pocket and
    fifty dollars in your back pocket. What would you
    have?

Paul: Somebody else's trousers on!

Immig. Officer: What's a hospice?

Both: Oh! About five litres.

Immig. Officer: What do you call a Greek baby?

Ian: A kebaby.

Immig. Officer: What do you call a Greek baby that is
    crying?

Ian: A shish-kebaby.

Immig. Officer: And a girl baby is...

Ian: A donna kebaby.

Immig. Officer: Religion is very important in our
    country. What were the first words Adam said to Eve
    in the Garden of Eden?

Ian and Paul: Oh, that's a hard one...

The audience, mostly American expats, laughed and Ian and I came off stage feeling like we'd just cracked it in Mexico. I kept ribbing Ian that he didn't need Janette any more and we should form a double act. We really enjoyed ourselves even though we were only on for three minutes. When we saw Janette and Rosemary we expected bouquets, congratulations and applause. However, they didn't seem as impressed with our comedy routine as we were. As it turns out they were right because when the episode aired, it had been cut. Well that's showbiz.

The wonderful thing about doing the *Marigold* shows, other than the trips themselves, was being invited to take part in them. Most performers in their late sixties and seventies don't expect to be asked to appear in a primetime network show that appeals to all ages. It's true what they say in this business: 'You never know what's around the corner.' The problem is they don't tell which corner and you end up freezing your arse off. Luckily for me when *Marigold* came along I was on the right corner at the right time and as a result I travelled to some great places, met some lovely people and had a fun and enriching experience.

With television and film you can edit out the bits that don't work. You can't always do that with entertainment, especially with live theatre – it's a risk every time you go on stage.

Still, whether you're singing, dancing, acting or doing all three at once, you have to jump in and take your chances and hope the odds are with you.

They certainly have been for me. To paraphrase a song written in 1927 by Herbert Farjeon, 'I've danced with a girl, who's danced with the Prince of Wales.' Well, I danced with Cyd Charisse who'd danced with Gene Kelly and Fred Astaire and they were certainly show-business royalty.

My lifetime challenge was trying to tip the odds in my favour, certainly where theatre and film are concerned. It's always a question of knowing your strengths and trying to exceed them. I suppose it comes down to having the courage to challenge oneself. Will I succeed as Claude in my first West End show, *Hair*? Can I reach the high notes as Jesus in *Jesus Christ Superstar*? How nasty should I be as Gavin Sullivan in *EastEnders*? Will I succeed in producing *Grease* and *Saturday Night Fever* in the West End and on Broadway?

How did I land the part of Vince in *Just Good Friends*? Was *Singin' in the Rain*, directed by Tommy Steele, a lifetime ambition? Could I learn to wire-walk and juggle as P. T. Barnum? Will I ever have a hit record? What the devil was I doing as Father Merrin in *The Exorcist*?

Performing means having a lot of fun, most of the time; but it's more than that. Performing for me is a great release, a way to exorcise the demons. No matter what is going on around you there is always a character you can escape into. It always has been that way for me even when

I was starting out. Even as a child. There's a real world and there's a fantasy world and I found my world somewhere between the two. It's been lively, fun and quite a journey. I've made mistakes, errors of judgement, sometimes got tangled up every which way but I learned and I survived, sometimes only just.

Let me tell you all about it.

CHAPTER TWO

Let the Sun Shine In

'… Darlin', give me a head with hair, long beautiful hair
Shining, gleaming, streaming, flaxen, waxen
Give me down to there hair, shoulder length or longer'
   – *Hair*, Shaftesbury Theatre, 1968

EARLY IN 1968 I read in the *Daily Express* about an outrageous show playing on Broadway that was about to come to London. The show was headline controversial. There had never been anything like it. It had four-letter words and, even more alarming, nudity. It's hard to imagine looking back how shock-horror were the mainstream reactions to words and displays of human flesh which on television today don't make most people blink. Yet this show was as raunchy and wild as it got in 1968. Which was the year of the worldwide student revolution.

The show was called *Hair* and Robert Stigwood was one of the producers.

Robert had bought Associated London Scripts (ALS) which involved him in the management of so many household names such as the incorrigible Frankie Howerd, Rita Tushingham and Lionel Jeffries. It also included Tony Hancock's writers Ray Galton and Alan Simpson who created the very popular television series *Steptoe and Son*. He also had the talents of Johnny Speight which meant Alf Garnett too. Robert had a lot to do: in the works were film versions of Speight's *Till Death Us Do Part* and Frankie Howerd's sitcom *Up Pompeii*. Nevertheless, there was always time for new enterprises and *Hair* was one of them.

I had not been in contact with Robert Stigwood for more than a year. Robert had been my manager when I was trying to be a pop singer the first time around. I hadn't succeeded and now, at twenty-three, that was behind me and I was going nowhere. I decided to call him and he happily arranged for me to audition for *Hair*. It was to be an open call, or what is known as a 'cattle call', which is a general sort of en masse audition.

On the appointed day I arrived at the stage door of the Shaftesbury Theatre. A nervy young man in glasses was running around taking our names and organising things. It was his job to organise the audition and introduce the actors to the creative team. He was very diligent and very enthusiastic. His name was Cameron Mackintosh. Cameron went on to become one of the all-time great theatre producers with hit shows like *Cats, Les Misérables, Phantom of the Opera, Miss Saigon* and *Hamilton*. Today he was an assistant stage manager.

Suddenly Cameron called my name – Paul Beuselinck. No more Oscar (the stage name under which I'd recorded a few pop records) but not as yet Paul Nicholas. I walked on to the stage, crossed to the audition pianist and gave him my music. I had sung 'I Who Have Nothing', the 1963 Shirley Bassey hit, many times but this was my first ever audition and I hoped it would show off my 'big voice'. The pianist played the intro and I started to sing.

I'd been doing the song as a comedy routine with the group 'The Soul Savages'. We used to dress in animal skins, like cavemen; at the dramatic high point of this particular song I'd raise my leopard skin and show a little bit of leg, much to the amusement of the audience. Now, without the leopard skin, I sang it straight.

It must have sounded all right because I was given a couple of scenes to read. They weren't long scenes and, although I'd never read dialogue on a stage before, the character was my age and the dialogue was very 'street'. I'd been watching American films all my life and so the American accent came pretty naturally.

I was asked to wait while others auditioned and then we were recalled to the front of the stage in a line. There were about thirty of us. The director, Tom O'Horgan, asked us each to give our names and then sing a short version of a song without music so he could be reminded of our voices. I wanted to be remembered and, being a bit of a smart-arse, when it came to my turn I gave my name and sang 'God Save the Queen'. Definitely a smart-arse. There were a couple of mild chuckles and then it was decision time.

It was like a scene from *A Chorus Line*. A voice from the stalls shouted, 'Okay, working from right to left… You go. You stay. You go. You stay. You stay. You… go.' They got to me – 'You stay.' There were about twenty-three of us left standing across the front of the stage. Then a voice called out to us from the gloom: 'Thank you, we will be in touch. Leave your name and your agent's details with stage management.'

I didn't have an agent so I left my own name and address. I was excited. Maybe as well as singing I would get a speaking part. It could be a whole new direction and they would pay me to do it. Could it get any better?

It did.

A few days later the script arrived. They'd offered me the part of Claude. I remembered the name as it was the character I'd read at the audition. I read the script and not only did Claude have at least five featured songs including the title song 'Hair' – he was essentially the lead part.

The writers, Gerome Ragni and James Rado, were a couple of out-of-work actors, who got together with the composer Galt MacDermot, who'd already won a Grammy for his composition 'African Waltz' in 1960. Simply, they wanted to create a musical celebrating the hippie culture. Thousands of young Americans were disenchanted with the conservative values of their parents and America's continued involvement in the Vietnam War.

The character of Claude was pivotal to the musical. The main protagonist, Claude cannot make up his mind whether to protest the war – 'Hell no. We won't go' – or to leave the hippie 'tribe' and fight for his country. In the very last scene, he makes the choice. We see him dressed in an army uniform with short hair. He goes to war and is killed. It was the breakthrough for me – the first job that made me realise that maybe this was something that I could do and earn regular money… if it ran. I had a family to support.

Although I hadn't done any acting, I'd certainly done quite a lot of singing; and the show was about young people living on the street which I understood. I was lucky the producers weren't looking for trained actors, dancers or singers – performers who looked like they'd spent years learning to tap or could spout Shakespeare beautifully. The only require-ments were that you looked like a hippie and you could sing. I fitted the bill perfectly (although, when I opened in the show, my hair wasn't very long so I had to wear a wig until it grew). If it had been any show other than *Hair*, I wouldn't have passed the audition. They were looking for realism, for people who looked authentic… even though I was married with children and lived in a four-bedroom house in Hertfordshire.

We started rehearsals, six days a week for six weeks. It was a fantastic learning experience and I took to it like a duck to water. I'd always loved American musicals and here I was working with Americans. I loved the looseness, the ease of the American musical performers. I enjoyed the discipline of the rehearsals, and we had a good director in Tom O'Horgan who had directed the original *Hair*. Tom, who founded the La Mama Company in New York, took the off-Broadway production and reworked it, and the American tribal love rock musical *Hair* opened at the Biltmore Theatre in New York on 29th April 1968. For Broadway, it was a new form of musical theatre: a rock musical that had something to say. It seemed appropriate in 1968. The year of revolution.

Gerome Ragni and James Rado – by now 'Gerry and Jim' to me – came over to the UK to oversee our production and to make sure that it was going to remain the hit it had become in America just a few months earlier. There was one aspect of the West End production that was making them a bit nervous: not the quality of the show or the actors, but the possibility of censorship.

In Britain, the Establishment were still running things; and part of that Establishment was the Lord Chamberlain's Office, whose role then included theatre censorship. Nudity was one issue for the censor, but there were also a few four-letter words in the show. There was no way the Lord Chamberlain was going to let that happen on the London stage. Such scenes were banned under the 1737 Licensing Act, which made it illegal to stage a play without the permission of the Lord Chamberlain.

For the writers the nudity was purely an honest expression of truth. For the producers it was also an honest expression of box office. They had taken a gamble by buying the rights to *Hair* prior to the abolition of the Lord Chamberlain's role as censor, which was due on 26th September 1968. If the show opened before then, it was inevitable that the strong language and infamous nude scenes would be cut. So along with the rest of the cast I was put on a retainer for three months while we waited for censorship to be abolished.

I was terribly excited about performing again, especially in the theatre which was nearer to my heart than I had realised. I had always been drawn to acting and half fancied myself as an actor but lacked the confidence to do anything about it. Events had pushed me, given me the shove I needed.

When I began rehearsals in July 1968, I knew for the first time in my life what I wanted to do. I had found a home. It was luck and timing. *Hair* was a freewheeling show and my lack of experience didn't matter. If I had been cast in *Oklahoma!* I would have found it difficult because I lacked the stagecraft and would never have had the chance to learn. It was a complete saviour for me to stumble into a show where the main requirement was to be young, look the part, be reasonably attractive and able to sing. I qualified on all counts. I was ahead of the game. I was not a total off-the-street and I had a big enough voice within the context of the show. The soft-rock theatrical songs in the show were perfect for me. I sang them in the same keys that they were written in. They were rock-based but weren't true rock 'n' roll, although it was marketed as the first rock musical.

It was a whole new world, a new beginning. I never found out until some years later that the rights for Robert Stigwood to bring *Hair* to London had been negotiated by my father, Oscar, who was a famously flamboyant lawyer specialising in the world of media and entertainment.

When he did the deal, he knew nothing of my interest in the show but he did know about the content, the drug references, the language and the nudity. When I got involved he did not want the family name associated with that, so he encouraged me to take a stage name. The sex, nudity and drugs didn't personally worry him at all. It was a matter of business. He was then at the height of his fame as a lawyer, representing MGM, the Beatles and rising stars like John Thaw, and he was concerned about his professional reputation which he had spent a lifetime building up. Plus, if I was crap he'd have been embarrassed.

As far as Oscar was concerned, *Hair* was my first venture into high-profile, serious show business. He said he didn't think Beuselinck was a good name with which to launch oneself into the British theatre. He also said, 'I've sued a lot of people and I don't want anyone saying to you, you're the son of that bastard lawyer – I'm not giving you a job.'

It was heavy-duty stuff and I could see his point. So I changed my name, from Paul Oscar Beuselinck to Paul Nicholas.

I had met a number of Oscar's high-profile clients and I was especially impressed with John Thaw. It was many years before *Morse*. He had been in the television series *Redcap* for four years but had just made *The Bofors Gun* with Nicol Williamson when I met him. They were buddies and real, legitimate actors. John Thaw was a nice bloke. He and I talked a lot about acting and it was interesting for me. Everywhere I turned I was learning about the theatrical world, and also learning to play the game. I was Paul Nicholas now and ever after.

It was as Paul Nicholas that I was introduced to the interesting bunch of people in *Hair*. I was Claude and the other leading character, Berger, was played by Oliver Tobias. Tim Curry – before *The Rocky Horror Show* – was one of the 'tribe', as were Elaine Paige and Murray Head who would go on to be the original Judas in *Jesus Christ Superstar*. There was also a girl called Marsha Hunt. She was one of the most exotic people I had ever met. She had an enormous Afro which matched her outsized personality. *Hair* was a show of its time: peace, love and the world of protest. By the time it opened in London in 1968, it may have been a little after its time. However, it was a celebration of cultural and ethnic identity. It was a time when people were very heavily into their roots.

The popular variety show *The Black and White Minstrel Show* (you get funny looks just mentioning it today) was then playing at the Victoria Palace in London. One of the cast members of *Hair* was a forty-year-old black American woman called Gloria Stuart, who took great exception to *The Black and White Minstrel Show*, which depicted white males in blackface and curly black wigs representing Negro minstrels. Their appearance was deeply offensive to black people, so Gloria decided to audition for the show. When she arrived back later that day, she was fuming. The producers had told her she was not quite the right colour. Apparently, she wasn't dark enough.

Undaunted, Gloria returned to the Victoria Palace, this time armed with a placard protesting the show. Despite her efforts and those of countless others, it would be another ten years before the much-applauded demise of *The Black and White Minstrel Show* from British television prime-time Saturday night viewing.

As for me, I was one of the stars of a West End musical. A rock musical. No one had ever seen that kind of show before. I could hardly believe it. My life was changing. *Hair* was opening my eyes to all kinds of things. There had been a rigorous rehearsal period which I found very avant-garde. It involved getting 'in touch' with yourself. It also required a lot of touching each other. Looking back, I can see how good it was for me as it helped me learn to open up. It was touchy-feely, very un-British. We had to explore each other and ourselves. Break down all our inhibitions and fears and learn to trust each other. We were called 'the tribe' and that's what they were trying to create between the actors. A oneness. A commune.

We all knew about the nude scene that came at the end of Act One. It was an expression of innocence, a natural beautiful expression of who we were as human beings. You didn't have to do the nude scene. It was left up to the individual cast member and how they felt on any given night. Some nights everybody did it, other nights only a few. It remained honest. There were no financial incentives. It was 1968. The time of 'Peace, Love Freedom, Happiness'.

During the seven weeks' rehearsal, I felt truly happy. It was where I wanted to be. Up until then I wasn't sure of my destination and I didn't know the route. The combination of music and drama suited me. I felt I belonged in this world.

Hair was the key. It unlocked a world of musical theatre that, without knowing it, I had been looking for. I was twenty-three. Most of the cast were in their late teens. I was married with children. Getting in touch with myself was very good for me – but as it turned out not for my marriage.

The first night was looming and because it was quite a physical show the producers thought it'd be a good idea to give us all vitamin B shots. We wanted to do the best for the show that we could – for many of us it was our first show – so we said, yeah, okay, what does it do? It just gives you a little lift, we were told; so they brought over this doctor from America, a real 'Doctor Feelgood'. After the final dress rehearsal, we all popped up to a dressing room and got our shots; and boy did they give you a lift. I don't know if the vitamin B had been laced with any other ingredients but we had enough energy to do three shows on the trot that night.

Hair finally opened at the Shaftesbury Theatre on 27th September 1968, the day after the Lord Chamberlain's role was abolished and theatre censorship ended in Britain. Along with Oliver Tobias, Annabelle Leventon, Elaine Paige, Peter Straker and Marsha Hunt and the rest of the cast, I took to the stage for the first time to perform the most controversial production to have opened in London for two hundred years. If *Hair* had opened a few days before, I and all the other actors could have been arrested because of the show's scenes of nudity and explicit language.

The *Daily Telegraph*'s esteemed theatre critic of the time, W. A. Darlington, was not impressed with *Hair*. He had 'tried hard' with the show but found it 'a complete bore'. He was seventy-eight years old and this was to be the last musical he reviewed before he retired. *The Times* kindly warned readers: 'There is plenty of blasphemy, perversion and other material taboo until yesterday, to alarm unwary customers.' (*Hair* closed on Tuesday 19th July 1973 after a run of nearly two thousand performances.)

At the beginning of the show, the audience would enter the auditorium and be welcomed by the 'tribe' offering flowers and greetings of 'peace' and 'love'. A strong smell of incense hung in the air. It was a different experience for theatregoers, as they were being invited to participate in not just a show but a 'happening'.

The music began gradually with the house lights still on. The mystical sound of guitars and bells wafted through the theatre. In slow motion, the tribe began to move down the aisles and over the seats and heads of the audience towards the stage, where I sat wrapped in a blanket like an American Indian chief.

'*When the moon is in the seventh house, and Jupiter aligns with Mars; then peace will guide the planets, and love will steer the stars. This is the dawning of the Age of Aquarius...*'

'Aquarius', 'Hair', 'I've Got Life', 'Ain't Got No', 'Good Morning Starshine' and 'Let the Sunshine In' all became hit songs. Their enduring quality is evident from the fact that they have since been recorded many times by different artists.

The first outrageous moment in the show was a song called 'Sodomy'. It was a send-up of all the sexual prejudices and hypocrisy of church and establishment. It involved the cast adopting sexual poses in a religious context to demonstrate the lyric of the song.

'*Sodomy, fellatio, cunnilingus, pederasty,*
Father why do these words sound so nasty?
Masturbation can be fun,
Join the holy orgy everyone...'

Many of the audience got up and walked out. The rest of them didn't know what the hell we were singing about. I certainly didn't!

The first half finished with the famous nude scene. There was never an empty seat, for no one quite knew what to expect. The curiosity factor was a huge marketing tool. It was a beautiful scene and very tastefully done. The song, aptly titled 'Where Do I Go?', reflects Claude's dilemma. Should he stay with the hippie commune or join the army? It was four minutes long. Towards the end of the song, the cast would disappear under a huge white silk sheet like a parachute which covered the entire stage and removed their clothes. At the climax of the song and the word 'freedom', the cast would reappear from beneath the sheet and present themselves to the audience naked. It was meant to convey that 'we are all one and naked in the eyes of God'. The lighting was such that the actors felt comfortable doing it. However, as the years went by and people got more used to nudity, the lighting got somewhat brighter!

I was the guy in the middle of all this, singing the song. It's funny but no one ever remembers me in that particular scene. I wonder why? However, I was quite relieved. I wouldn't have been comfortable taking my clothes off in public. I would have found it embarrassing, especially when I saw the competition from some of the other lads who were standing there.

The highlight of Act Two involved a take-off of vocal group The Supremes who were famous for wearing shiny, sequinned blue dresses. Marsha and two other black girls – Ethel and Joanne – sang a song called 'White Boys', extolling their virtues. It was a direct counterpoint to a number in the first half sung by three white girls called 'Black Boys' with the same message. Marsha and the girls were revealed on a moving platform that was trucked down to the front of the stage. It appeared to the audience as if they were wearing three tight-fitting blue sequinned dresses à la the Supremes. At a crucial moment in the song, the girls parted to reveal that they were in fact wearing one large blue sequinned dress. The audience found it hilarious and it was a real show-stopper.

Nudity was one of the contentious elements the Lord Chamberlain would have censored; the other came in the second act when Claude is awakened from his bad trip by Berger. Halfway through the scene, without warning, the F-bombs began to land on the unsuspecting audience:

Berger: I hate the fucking world, don't you?
Claude: I hate the fucking world. I hate the fucking winter and I
    hate these fucking streets.
Berger: I wish it would fucking snow at least.
Claude: I wish it was the biggest fucking snowstorm. Blizzards
    come down in sheets. Mountains, rivers, oceans, forests, rabbits,
    cover everything in beautiful white holy snow and I could hide
    out a hermit and hang on a cross and eat cornflakes. Fuck!
Berger: Fuck!
Claude: Fuckity Fuck Fuck!

At which point the audience would collapse with laughter and the intro to 'Good Morning Starshine' plays.

At the end of the song Claude is isolated in a spotlight as snow begins to fall. The tribe enter from all directions. They are wrapped in blankets and banging cans, flutes, garbage cans, sticks, in protest at the Vietnam war. The scene continues with the tribe calling out for 'Claude, Claude'. Claude appears dressed in an army uniform with his hair cut. Visually it was a powerful image for the audience. Claude sings:

'*We starve, look at one another, short of breath*
Walking proudly in our winter coats
Wearing smells from laboratories
Facing a dying nation of moving paper fantasy
Listening for the new told lies
With supreme visions of lonely tunes.'

The song continues and builds in rhythm and intensity and finally the company sing the chorus of 'Let the Sunshine In' which builds and builds into a fantastic finale to the show.

The band didn't have a set number of bars for the final chorus as it depended on the feeling in the theatre on any given night. It was truly a theatrical experience that totally consumed the audience. One night the audience was so swept up in the moment that they stood and climbed onto the stage and joined the cast singing and dancing. It was not planned. They just did it spontaneously. Thereafter it happened every night. It didn't happen in New York; it started with the London show, which is surprising as British audiences were considered rather conservative.

We were a big hit. I remember John Lennon and Yoko Ono sitting in a box watching. One night, I turned around in the finale and there was Princess Anne dancing next to me. *Hair* by Royal Appointment. She knew Rowan McCulloch who was one of the girls in the show. Rowan was the daughter of 'Uncle Mac', Derek McCulloch, who had presented *Children's Hour* on BBC Radio which I listened to as a child. Princess Anne saw *Hair* three times and always danced on the stage at the end. She loved it.

I received a fan letter from the film star David Niven: 'What a wonderful show. Keep up the good work.' We were visited by famous actors like Katharine Hepburn, Gregory Peck, Sidney Poitier, Nina Simone and many big stars from the entertainment world.

My most treasured memory of all was meeting Judy Garland. The 2019 movie with Renée Zellweger as Judy is based on the last weeks she spent in London. She was a slight woman, like a little sparrow. She was tiny, fragile, warm and friendly. She took the trouble to visit everybody in the cast. Judy Garland, imagine that? Sadly Judy died not long after, in June 1969, in London. She was a remarkable talent as well as being a wonderful singer and actress. She was also very funny. I particularly loved her performance with the great Fred Astaire doing 'A Couple of Swells' in the 1948 film *Easter Parade*, which I saw as a child. It's on YouTube; Judy is still the one you look at.

Hair was the hit show everyone was talking about. The Vietnam war was still raging and the American youth, the so called 'hippie culture', had had enough. Reflecting on it half a century on, the show's anti-war message is loud and clear and still very relevant.

The other important ingredient that every musical needs for it to be a success is music, or more specifically good songs. The show's composer, Galt MacDermot, would at that time have been in his early forties. He was a quiet, rather understated gentleman compared with the restless unstoppable energy of Jim Rado and Gerry Ragni. Gerry died in 1991 aged fifty-five. In 2017 I met Jim and Galt again at the London revival of *Hair*; Galt died in December 2018 aged ninety. The songs were of course a huge part of the show's phenomenal worldwide success as you never leave a show humming the scenery. Great music makes for a great musical. It doesn't matter how interesting the story is, if you don't have the music and songs you might as well forget it. *Hair* had songs that became standalone hits. We were young and we could hear that these songs were good and that gave us the confidence to perform at our best. The songs and the anti-war message allowed us to create an emotional connection with the audience, and as a result they became caught up in it. Every great performance has to have the ability to touch an audience and make them feel that they are a part of what is happening on stage. That's exactly what happened with *Hair*.

I was centre stage, and for the next fifty years I was rarely off stage.

CHAPTER THREE

I Got You, Babe

'We haven't got any glue, Pauly'
   – actor Paul Barber, 1971

I 'D FOUND WHAT I NEEDED, a combination of acting and singing. It was something I could do and hopefully keep on doing. I was being paid once a week, every week. Back then it was good money. Yet, the money wasn't the big attraction. I was on cloud nine as a performer.

In 1969, at the age of twenty-four, being in *Hair* got me a part in a movie and I was on my way to Paris. I was given time off from the show to co-star with Jane Birkin and Serge Gainsbourg who were the continental equivalent of Sonny and Cher. She was the English rose chanteuse and actress and Serge was a famous musician, composer, painter, director and actor. We were about to appear in a film called *Cannabis* as a couple of drug dealers.

Serge couldn't have been more French. He was all Gauloises and designer stubble. That, at least, was the image. They had a big success with the record 'Je t'Aime Moi Non Plus', and Serge's body of work over the years has placed him as one of the most important French artists of all time. It was an intriguing experience. It was a French production and also known as *Les Chemins de Katmandu*. I played Serge's American drug-dealing sidekick.

Before filming began I went to meet Serge and Jane. Previously Jane had been married to the James Bond composer John Barry. I went to their flat in Paris which was completely decorated in black. Everything was black. I thought it was weird, and that was before we had ventured out to have dinner.

Serge could barely speak English and I couldn't speak French. They took me out to eat at a very expensive and fashionable restaurant, and all they served at this restaurant were flowers. I am a north London boy and I hadn't acquired a taste for nouvelle cuisine so when the meal arrived, I looked at my plate and I wasn't sure what to do. It was a plate full of rose petals and other assorted flowery delicacies. I looked at the plate and looked at the waiter and said, 'Can I have a few chips with that?' I passed on the rose petals but the chips were good.

Serge was tremendously charming and always had a mischievous look in his eye. He was funny. I really liked him. Jane was also twenty-four. She was beautiful, terribly English and spoke perfect French. They were a very nice, kind couple. They took me out and introduced me to the actor Alain Delon. They also took me to the very fashionable Chez Régine in the Latin Quarter where we had a drink with Régine who was the proprietor.

The film's scenes were not easy. I was briefed to learn my French dialogue phonetically but I got in a terrible mess. Ultimately I was dubbed in French and Serge was dubbed in English. This meant that when we did scenes together Serge would speak in French with a bit of broken English and I would speak in English with a bit of broken French. The result was hilarious as neither of us knew when to speak. We laughed a lot. I never did see the film. During the sixties Serge and Jane were huge stars in France and while working with them, I learnt a lot about filming.

After completion of *Cannabis*, I was offered another film but this time with a British company called Amicus Productions, based at Shepperton Studios. Amicus was founded by the American producers and screen-writers Milton Subotsky and Max Rosenberg. Their company specialised in horror movies, not unlike Hammer Film Productions, and they had worked a lot with the actors Peter Cushing and Christopher Lee who were both big stars in horror films. Amicus differed from Hammer as their horror films weren't gothic period pieces but set in the present day.

The film I was offered was no exception. It was entitled *What Became of Jack and Jill?* and was based on a book called *The Ruthless Ones* by Laurence Moody. I played a young man called Johnny who, along with his girlfriend, tries to scare his rich grandmother to death by convincing her that the young were plotting to exterminate the elderly. It was directed by a very nice man called Bill Bain.

This was really my first proper acting job as there was no singing involved. I was very nervous and there were only really three of us in it. The first thing that surprised me was that my 'grandmother', played by Mona Washborne, was very posh and well-spoken. I hadn't anticipated that as I thought she'd be a little more downmarket. This meant I had to upgrade Johnny's accent.

The other problem was my girlfriend, played by Vanessa Howard. We didn't connect on or off camera. I could never work out why there was such a distance between us. We were a similar age but rarely laughed or spoke to each other throughout the filming. Vanessa was the star. She had already filmed the 1969 horror-comedy *Mumsy, Nanny, Sonny and Girly* which is now a cult movie. Vanessa, who died in California in 2010, and I were supposed to be quite lustful. We had love scenes that were always very awkward and uncomfortable so we never actually kissed. I tried but I could never actually land one which would have made it so much easier.

We had one scene where we had to make love which was supposed to be drenched in passion. Once again it was physically awkward and felt like a wrestling match. I was trying to kiss her and she clearly didn't want to. It was embarrassing so in the end I settled for holding and hugging. Something seemed to be troubling her; maybe it was me. I never did find out why there was such a distance between us. Perhaps she was just staying in character. The film had a limited release in the UK and America. I never saw it until a couple of years ago when I found it on YouTube. Vanessa and Mona are both excellent in the film, and I'm sort of okay considering it's my first proper acting job. I'm definitely a bit too posh.

I returned to *Hair* which was still the toast of the town. The genie was already out of the bottle. The boundaries of taste were changing by the day. It was the time of women's lib, Grosvenor Square demos, smoking pot, Andy Warhol, the Beatles and the Stones.

The Lord Chamberlain having been vanquished brought about a tremendous change in theatre, both in straight drama and musicals. Of course, the commercial success of *Hair* led to a series of similar shows. Robert Stigwood, never one to miss an opportunity, produced *The Dirtiest Show in Town* which had even more nudity. The most famous of these shows was *Oh! Calcutta!* which Michael White co-produced with Kenneth Tynan, the renowned doyen of theatre critics. Tynan convinced John Lennon, Samuel Beckett and Sam Shepherd to contribute material. There was lots of nudity and outrageous sketches; one of the lines was, 'This show makes *Hair* look like *Mary Poppins*.' In another scene Arlene Phillips, years before her renowned choreography and her time as a judge on *Strictly Come Dancing*, performed a nude ballet. *Oh! Calcutta!* prided itself on being the most outrageous show in the West End, so much so that at the end of each performance the cast would stand on stage completely naked and tell the audience how daring and dangerous the show was, which was somewhat labouring the point.

On its first night at the Royalty Theatre, having transferred from the Roundhouse, I was sitting in a box with Ken Tynan's wife Kathleen and the producer Michael White when a man in the stalls shouted to the naked cast on stage: 'A pound for the first one who farts!' Everyone looked embarrassed. I thought it was tremendous. I'm sure Ken Tynan – the first man to say 'fuck' on British television – would have loved it. The man had got the biggest laugh of the night.

Although there were still elements of a puritanical Mary Whitehouse world, times were a-changing radically, and it was also a pivotal time in my own life. *Hair* had given me the opportunity to test myself and learn more about theatre as well as acting. I became the production's artistic director which meant I went in and watched the show, rehearsed the cast and auditioned new artistes when cast members left.

I gave the lovely Patti Boulaye her first job, a good decade before she won the *New Faces* talent show in 1978. Her victory in what was the *X*

Factor of its day made her a star but it was happenstance that began it all. She was sixteen when she went on a visit to Madame Tussaud's Wax Museum in Marylebone with a group of friends. She joined what she thought was the queue to get in, but the line was for the *Hair* auditions at the Shaftesbury Theatre, so she thought, why not? She came in and sang, of all things, 'The Sound of Music'. She was good as she was used to singing back home in Nigeria. But unlike Marsha she was not into Afros. She was more conservative with plaits and a silk dress. She could sing but she said she did not want to take her clothes off. I gave her the job. She didn't do the nude scene, and she never ate the hash cake the cast baked for her on her seventeenth birthday. She is a very beautiful and talented lady.

I found myself doing more and more behind-the-scenes work as well as appearing in the show. The producers asked me to play Claude on a national tour doing long runs in Manchester and Liverpool. They wanted an experienced lead that could also help them audition a touring cast.

At one audition I saw one of the most beautiful girls that I have ever seen in my life. She was of mixed race. She was completely gorgeous and I instantly became attracted to her. I found out some facts about her. Her name was Linzi Jennings.

Before joining *Hair* she had been a PA in the government but, luckily for me, had decided on a career change. I acquired all this information from one of the other girls in the show. I was too shy to talk to her myself. The girls that you really like are the ones you can't talk to. I could talk to all the other girls but around Linzi I would get very tongue-tied.

In any case, there was a problem. I was married with kids, and just not on her radar. To her I was just another scruff in the show. She had recently returned from a German production of *Hair*, where she had played the part of Chrissy as well as one of the trio of black girls who sang 'White Boys'. I was one white boy she was clearly not remotely interested in.

We went on tour and in Manchester I was sharing digs with the actor Paul Barber, who was an eighteen-year-old kid then. Everyone would know him later as Denzil, a regular on *Only Fools and Horses*, and as one of the stars of *The Full Monty*. I had found out that Linzi was staying with two other girls from the show in the Lincoln Service Flats in Manchester so I managed to wangle a flat above Linzi's.

I knew I was beginning to fall in love with Linzi, but she seemed so unobtainable. There was nothing show-business or pretentious about her. She was very down to earth. I had fallen for her from the moment I first saw her, and I was with her night after night during the show. Sometimes on our nights off the girls would come up to our flat to watch television. So close, yet so far.

Ten weeks went by. The only thing in my favour was that she later realised I was not a dirty hippie. I was clean. In fact I bathed every day. Cleanliness was to be my saviour. Not my self-promoting witty repartee watching television.

One night the girls had once again been up to our flat, and around eleven o'clock Linzi had decided to go to her flat so that she could hear the end of a programme we had been watching. I had been talking through-out the programme, trying to get her attention. Later at about one a.m. Paul and I were fooling around and broke a lamp. We needed to stick it together but Paul said: 'We've not got any glue, Pauly.'

Quick as a flash I said, 'Maybe they've got some glue downstairs? I'll just pop down and see.'

I knocked on Linzi's door and she answered. I tried to look my most vulnerable.

'Have you got any glue?' I said, and that's how a lifetime of love began.

CHAPTER FOUR

Jesus Christ Superstar

'Over 'ere Jesus'

– Photographer, *Superstar* press launch, 1972

'God! That's fantastic.' The words were out of my mouth before I quite knew what I was saying. I was still enjoying being in *Hair*, and Murray Head who had joined the cast had just played me his recording of the song 'Jesus Christ Superstar'.

The Bible is packed with good stories but this song reflected the most potent one of all: the last seven days of Christ's life. Murray had recorded an album with Ian Gillan, the lead singer of Deep Purple; Murray sang the role of Judas and Ian was Jesus. It had been written by two guys I had never heard of, Tim Rice and Andrew Lloyd Webber. It was a cracking song and brilliantly sung by Murray but it also had an intriguing title, 'Jesus Christ Superstar'.

In 1971 to call Jesus Christ a Superstar was almost sacrilegious. Tim Rice and Andrew Lloyd Webber had started working together as teenagers in 1965. They had used the Bible as a source for *Joseph and the Amazing Technicolor Dreamcoat* which was originally written as a school concert piece – a pop cantata. It was good enough to get them involved with David Land, who until then had received most of his income from managing the Dagenham Girl Pipers. Land had a partner, property developer Sefton Myers, and together they were a company called New Talent Ventures.

Andrew Lloyd Webber and Tim Rice were certainly talented and new, but I don't think anyone could have imagined what heights their work and fame would reach. What Murray had played for me was the promotional single from their soon-to-be-released concept album of *Jesus Christ Superstar*. It was controversial. It was also of the moment, and timing is important.

It was an early lesson for me in the genesis of a powerful and successful project. The rock opera *Tommy* by The Who – a ninety-minute recording released in May 1969 – was selling incredibly well. Tim Rice said their influence was *Hair*, not *Tommy*, but it was the record sales that gave them a commercial edge when it came to promoting *Jesus Christ Superstar* the rock opera.

Murray Head had worked with the distinctive and gritty-voiced Joe Cocker on his celebrated cover version of the Beatles' 'With a Little Help from My Friends'. Tim Rice had known Murray from his days at EMI Records, and MCA Records did a double album of *Superstar* in October 1970.

David Land was looking for a company to produce it as a theatrical extravaganza. His friend Leslie Grade had warned him about the subject matter, suggesting it would offend Christian and Jewish communities. Harold Fielding, who was famous for producing shows like *The Music Man*, was regarded as the theatre's musical mastermind and Land took the project to him. Harold, a lovely man who produced shows for Tommy Steele and Michael Crawford in their early days (and whom I was to work for later), was enthusiastic and a deal was almost done. The contracts were called up but not signed.

When Murray Head played me his version of 'Superstar' I thought it sounded like a hit so I took the record to Robert Stigwood and played it to him. Robert has a fantastic ear for a hit and when he went for it, like all great entrepreneurs, he went for it. Within twenty-four hours he was on the hunt. Robert sought out Andrew Lloyd Webber and Tim Rice and his enthusiasm was so overwhelming they were convinced he was the one to produce *Jesus Christ Superstar* on stage. They talked David Land, who was managing them at the time, into going with Robert and the package abruptly changed gear. It would be a very different production from the more formal opera presentation envisaged by Harold Fielding.

The album, which featured Mike D'Abo as Herod and Paul Raven (before he renamed himself Gary Glitter) as the Priest, was very successful in America, and Murray's recording of the title song got into the Top Fifty. The album sold more than two million copies in less than a year. There was a demand, an expectant audience for a live stage version – so much so that pirate versions were being staged before Robert intervened with his plans for a Broadway production. Tom O'Horgan, who had directed *Hair* and continued to surprise and often shock audiences with *Lenny*, his theatrical interpretation of the life of American comic and drug advocate Lenny Bruce, would direct. The show opened with Jeff Fenholt as Jesus and Ben Vereen (a future Broadway star and 'Chicken George' in *Roots* in 1977) as Judas Iscariot, and it was huge – a sensation – primarily because of the concept of Christ as a Superstar. Jeff Fenholt was featured in costume on the cover of America's *Time* magazine, a great accolade then from a publication whose cover image gloried in what was considered important and newsworthy.

It was a brand new world of musical theatre. No one realised the renaissance being created. It was an artistic revolution and a hit. I went to see it in America where it was breathtaking. The cast performed with hand-held microphones – there were no discreetly concealed radio mikes. It became a massive hit.

From editorial pages and pulpits there were strong reactions on the merits or lack of them of *Superstar*. It was, of course, all good for business at the box office of the Mark Hellinger Theatre in New York. Religious groups demonstrated on West 51st Street but no one really knew who was under fire or being attacked. Was it blasphemy? Was it anti-Semitic?

I believe it was and is simply a brilliant piece of musical theatre when staged correctly. Some critics thought that Tom O'Horgan's production in New York was too elaborate, too fussy. Frank Rich, who had the title 'the Butcher of Broadway', had a go and so did the *New York Times* which wrote that the set was 'like the Christmas decorations on a chic Fifth Avenue shop'.

Andrew Lloyd Webber and Tim Rice were not happy with what they saw as the over-the-top nature of the Broadway show. They demanded something much simpler for London, and Robert brought in Australian Jim Sharman as director. He had guided *Hair* in Sydney where he was also famous for a production of *Don Giovanni*. His reputation as a director was much trumpeted. He, on the other hand, was the opposite: pleasantly low-key, a shy man.

In 1972 they began to cast *Superstar* for a London production, at the Palace Theatre in the West End. I wanted to be seen for the part of Jesus. I listened to the album over and over. The issue for me was the vocal range required for the role. It had been written with Ian Gillan as Jesus. Ian was a great rock singer with the vocal range of a tenor and I am a baritone. I was twenty-six, still quite young, and my top note at that time even with a strong wind behind me was F above middle C. That meant that I was at least possibly four to five notes short of what is required for the role of Jesus.

The music was far more demanding to sing than *Hair*. This was a 'rock opera' that had the underbelly of a rock band plus a classical feel. There was no dialogue, it was all sung. Andrew Lloyd Webber, like a lot of composers, wants the songs to be omnipresent. Andrew writes music with vocal lines that resonant to the ear and have presence. Most rock songs, other than maybe a few by artists like Neil Diamond, are written for singers with a strong upper register. Great rock singers have a high vocal range: think of Ian Gillan, Robert Plant, Paul McCartney, Elton John, Steven Tyler, Jon Bon Jovi, Roger Daltrey... the list really is endless, and the role of Jesus required that vocal ability. I had a problem.

My only saving grace was that although Ian Gillan could easily have sung the role using the upper register of his voice, because the part in many ways requires a torturous element to the vocal performance he elected to use his falsetto, thereby increasing the drama and agony that Jesus was enduring. Luckily for me, I too could reach the really high notes using my falsetto and thereby create the dramatic vocal effect the character required. The audition was imminent. I practised a lot in our room in Muswell Hill; I think the neighbours must have thought I was strangling the cat. After much practice, I managed to make 'Gethsemane', Jesus's big finish at the end of Act One, sound effective.

I certainly hoped I had when I went for the audition at the Palace Theatre. The original meetings had been at the Shaftesbury Theatre where *Hair* had played for three years, but the roof had fallen in and *Hair* later had to transfer to another theatre. *Hair* had survived 1,997 performances. There was talk of knocking the Shaftesbury down, so I had the idea of staging a rally to try and stop the demolition. I went to Equity, the actors' union, and with their help and a group called 'Save London Theatres' the *Hair* cast held a rally outside the theatre in protest to draw attention to the proposed scheme and raise money to save the Shaftesbury. It was our 'thank you' to a theatre that had been good to us for the past few years. The Shaftesbury Theatre had survived.

Now, I needed a miracle at the Palace Theatre.

I was introduced to a rather quiet, shy, young man. He had a nervous energy, a restlessness about him, and he turned out to be Andrew Lloyd Weber. He was a dandy, dressed to the nines in a velvet suit and a cravat. With him was a tall, witty and easy-going man who was Tim Rice. What was refreshing about Tim and Andrew was that they were so English, so very English. They were managed by David Land who, when things didn't go well, was often heard to exclaim, 'Who pissed on the chips?' They were a remarkable team. A creative force unto themselves. We were so used to American musicals dominating the West End but it was soon about to change.

It was the beginning of something special for all involved. I sensed that during my six auditions. They hadn't been happy with the New York show even though it was doing well. They wanted to make sure that the show and their leading man were spot on. However, they couldn't make up their minds. Robert Stigwood told me he had fought for me – in fact, for the rest of his life he told me he fought for me. Knowing Robert and his tenacity he probably did fight for me, although with the amount of money involved he wouldn't have put my career ahead of the show. He knew I could sing it and he had seen my acting performance in *Hair* so he must have been convinced.

It was a time of enormous change in musical theatre. This was to be a different concept: a new kind of musical that had no dialogue. The story – like an opera – was told with continuous music. We now accept 'sung through' productions as musical theatre; in 1972 this was a brand new concept for a modern musical. *Jesus Christ Superstar* was the first of its kind. Tim Rice and Andrew Lloyd Webber would write many more, but this was the first.

There was a lot of media expectation about who was going to play the title role. It was reported that over three thousand people applied to audition for Jim Sharman, Tim and Andrew. The hunt for who would play Jesus was on. It was like a forerunner to *The X Factor* and a great marketing tool for the show. The press were on to it. Where is Jesus? At the time he was living in a bedsit in Muswell Hill.

I had been the lead in *Hair*, the first rock musical, and now I was up for the starring role in another ground-breaking show – the first rock opera. The hardest part always is getting the job. I was and am adaptable and was completely aware of the potential singing problem when I went along to audition. I also knew that I was coming off the back of a big success, *Hair*, which didn't hurt. People like to associate themselves with success. My determination came from having a family to support and really wanting the job.

The thing I did have in my favour was that I looked pretty good because I was quite slim and had the traditional Jesus look – beard and long hair. I looked right physically, gentle but steely. I had spent an awful amount of time sitting in our one-room bedsit in Muswell Hill practising with Linzi's help.

Back in 1971/72, unlike today, the standard of rock/pop singing was such that there weren't so many singers doing musical theatre. Gary Bond, who did Tim and Andrew's *Joseph and the Amazing Technicolor Dreamcoat*; myself; David Essex who was already playing Jesus in *Godspell*, and a few others. At that time the attraction of musical theatre for young performers hadn't really kicked in. Young male singers in the late sixties and seventies were mostly trying to be rock stars. There wasn't the same amount of competition or talent for musical theatre among young performers as there is today.

Students today leave stage schools as 'triple threats'; they all sing, dance and act. I didn't go to a stage or drama school, though I had been singing since I was fifteen and now, at twenty-seven, I knew I could sing in tune. With three years performing on the West End stage as well as the national tour of *Hair*, plus a couple of film roles, I felt I had learnt quite a lot and stood a chance even though this would be only my second musical audition.

There is one elusive quality that cannot be trained, and some performers have 'it' and others don't. Call it presence, energy, charm, or star quality. You watch some performers on stage more than others. You are drawn to them. They just have 'it'. They are born with 'it' and 'it' remains something mysterious in all art forms. Well, perhaps I had a touch of 'it' that day when I auditioned for the part of Jesus in *Jesus Christ Superstar*. There were probably better singers, but they saw something in me. However, whatever 'it' was that they saw in me, 'it' took six more auditions before 'it' was finally offered to me.

In June 1972, I was about to be revealed to the assembled media as Jesus in *Jesus Christ Superstar* in the bar of the Palace Theatre. I was also a little naive. I had been cast in the most iconic role there is and when I turned up for the press call, I wasn't prepared for what was to come.

They introduced me to the press and I felt like a lamb to the slaughter. The bar was packed and suddenly I was devoured by the scrum of photographers and reporters waiting to see me. They elbowed each other out of the way to get their photographs and fired questions at me so fast that I felt overwhelmed. I wasn't expecting the mayhem and I was a little freaked by it.

The photographers shouted: 'Over 'ere Jesus!' … 'Look this way' … 'What are your religious beliefs?' I managed to blurt out that I was not very religious and I didn't go to church and had been brought up in the Church of England and yes I had gone to Sunday school. I didn't say it was so I could play snooker in the church hall. I wasn't *that* naive.

It was all a bit daunting. I hadn't been prepared for the overwhelming press interest in me. It was my first brush with fame and I wasn't sure that I liked the attention. As with *Hair*, I had no billing outside the Palace

Theatre. *Jesus Christ Superstar* the show was the star. The costume designer had billing out front and when they later sacked her, her billing remained. Which always amused me as I wasn't aware of the importance of billing then. I was just happy to have secured the part. I wasn't a star and was unsure of how to deal positively or carefully with the press.

Following numerous questions in the bar, the photographers asked me to go outside for more photographs in natural light. So we all trooped out and headed for a bit of green space in Soho Square. I was almost knocked down by a van as I was crossing the road. The PR lady went white. A couple more feet and there might have been a need for an instant resurrection.

Someone suggested that we do a photograph of me having a celebratory drink having won the role of Jesus. A good idea, I thought, as by that time I needed one. So the pack and I did a deal. Yes, they could take my photograph drinking a pint of beer, if they left after it. The next day the newspapers carried the pictures. One clever snapper had managed to take a few shots of me once the main pack had gone. There was a big picture of me with a pint of beer in my hand and the headline 'Jesus has a pint'. To cap it and unbeknownst to me, he even managed to catch a nun standing behind me in the background of the photograph.

It had been my first day as Jesus in *Jesus Christ Superstar*. Now it was time to start focusing on the show. The New York production was up and running; the London production was to be completely new with a different director, set and costume designer.

The first major change was the set. In America Jesus appeared from within a huge artichoke effect and his followers emerged climbing over a large rotating wall. It was quite spectacular. In London the idea for the set design was based on the painting of 'The Last Supper' by Salvador Dali. The stage had illuminated squares which were raised and lowered as blocks of lights depending on whatever the scene dictated. It was simple and modern and very different from the more traditional, though spectacular, New York production. The set designer, Brian Thompson, went on to design many shows including *The Rocky Horror Show*.

Jesus Christ Superstar was novel in both form and execution. It had rawness to the music, an explosion of energy that didn't compromise either musically or lyrically. It had a dangerous title. It was a daring piece. It was Jesus as seen through Judas's eyes, with Judas's lyrics suggesting that it was all about Jesus's self-glorification.

The music was powerful and, besides the title song, the other song that became a standalone hit was 'I Don't Know How to Love Him' which Mary Magdalene sings to Jesus. It became a hit for Yvonne Elliman who played the part on Broadway. Overall the score is a combination of a driving rock band complemented by lyrical melodies and exciting recitative. It was the first time a rock opera had been performed on the West End stage. Like *Hair*, it was an event. It was a milestone and a beginning of something new that was going to permeate throughout the West End for decades to come.

Until that moment we had always played second fiddle to America. Broadway came to us, our musicals rarely went there. Lionel Bart's *Oliver!* was one of the rare exceptions to the rule. It was the birth of the British musical invasion and I was a very small part of it. It was my second job and we were all learning how to do it.

Tim Rice once told me I was the best Jesus he had ever seen. I said, 'I bet you say that to all the Jesuses.' There have been many. Although there's always special warmth for the original cast. Paul Jabara, an American performer who had also been in *Hair*, was cast as Herod. He had problems getting a work permit so he chained himself to the railings of Number 10 Downing Street with a placard that read 'I must have this job'. It worked – he made himself such a nuisance they gave him a permit. Like Richard Burton's great mate Victor Spinetti who also played Herod, Paul arrived on stage in a giant, inflatable bed, surrounded by beautiful women. It was a wonderful scene and gave the show the moment of comedy it needed.

I'd originally suggested Richard O'Brien for Herod but Richard only played the role up to the previews of the show as it was felt he wasn't quite right for it. It was a breakthrough nevertheless, even fate, because he met our director Jim Sharman. Together they went on to have a fabulous success when Jim directed the show and the film of *The Rocky Horror Show*, which began its initial run in a small space upstairs at the Royal Court Theatre. I went to see it with both Richard playing Riff Raff and Tim Curry playing Frank N. Furter. I'd worked with them both in

Hair where coincidentally they had both played the same character, Margaret Mead. It was a small beginning for *Rocky Horror* but all the songs that Richard had played me on tour were in there and they worked perfectly. Tim and Richard were great and the show just worked... but I digress.

Stephen Tate, a brilliant actor, was cast as Judas and he played him as a student rebel that was very much of the times. The 1968 riots and demonstrations were still a vivid memory for many people.

A couple of weeks before we were due to open in previews, Sylvia McNeill, who sang beautifully, had been cast as Mary Magdalene. She had won the role over more than five hundred other contenders but suddenly one day she wasn't there. We were told she'd left the show. We never knew why, other than she said it was a family matter. So Dana Gillespie was brought in to play Mary Magdalene. She was an extraordinary woman. She had been the British water ski champion for four years up to 1967. Dana was great fun, she loved to laugh and I enjoyed her company. She could certainly sing 'I Don't Know How to Love Him'.

Andrew Lloyd Webber and Tim Rice are perfectionists. Although they had written *Joseph*, it had not been produced in the West End. This was their first West End show and they were quite rightly very nervous. We were all in the spotlight. On the first night we had a host of protesters singing hymns and waving placards with 'Jesus Is Not A Superstar' and 'Jesus Christ Super Sham'. It did not help my first-night nerves.

Although I'm not religious, the defining moment for me was dealing with the first time we rehearsed the crucifixion. I cried. I was completely overcome. I am not a religious person. It just hit me, the sadness of the moment captured perfectly by the theme of 'Gethsemane' played by the orchestra string section. As I hung there as Jesus I felt so very vulnerable and alone. I understood for the first time how much Jesus meant to so many people.

Thirty years later I saw a West End production at the Lyceum Theatre. Steve Balsamo played the role of Jesus. Steve sang the part brilliantly. Vocally his performance ranks within the top two or three of all time. The only disappointment I felt watching the show was with the crucifixion. We saw Jesus drag the cross around the stage on his back. Then the cross was laid on the stage and Jesus is put on it and the nails hammered in. Finally the cross is lifted. It was no doubt pretty authentic but the powerful image of Jesus hanging on the cross was diluted because the audience could see what was coming.

What was wonderful about Jim Sharman's production was that I was taken away to be crucified. I went below the stage where I was attached to a thin cross-shaped frame. I adopted the crucifix pose and in doing so masked the thin frame. Then slowly I rose up through the centre of the stage. There was smoke and wailing music. I was revealed to the audience, looking to them as if I was hanging in mid-air. It was a wonderful theatrical moment. I could feel the audience hold their breath. It was a wonderful visual effect. It blew them away. Jesus says: 'My God! My God! Why have you forgotten me?' before being stabbed with a spear. Simultaneously the choir and orchestra crescendo and as Jesus is dying, the sound dies with him to a last breath. Jesus says, 'Father, into your hands, I commend my spirit.' Jesus dies and the theme of 'Gethsemane' plays. It is a beautiful theme, played at a slow tempo on cellos and violins. It is incredibly moving. The audience were transfixed and the only other sound I could hear was that of people weeping.

Of course, as with all shows, after two months and eight shows a week it became a little more routine. Sneezing was a hazard the crucifixion presented. It only happened once and I think I managed to disguise it as a 'death agony'.

Technically, I have always believed that other than 'Gethsemane', Judas is a great vocal part and has the title song, but Jesus is the title role and he does have the crucifixion. A great moment in theatre. It was beautifully staged and encapsulated everything that was good about that particular production. It was simple, honest and that's what made it work. The American production was fussy and extravagant. It didn't allow the music to breathe. The cornerstone of the show is the brilliance of the music and lyrics and, of course, the story.

Of course you cannot please everybody playing Jesus. Whether people are religious or not, everyone has an image of what their Jesus looks like. It's most probably not you. When I came out of the stage door, there were always people waiting for me. I had fans in *Hair* but this was different. It felt as though they looked at me differently and wanted more than just an autograph. It may have been my imagination but they seemed to look at me in a more intense way. Anyway as soon as I lit a cigarette and headed for the pub, any expectations of my divinity were quickly dispelled.

The worst thing about playing Jesus was that there weren't any laughs. I had to curb my natural inclination to be a little bit naughty. The only time I gave in during my ten-month run was when, at the beginning of the second act, I took my position in the blackout at the front of the stage. A chap in the front row sneezed. I couldn't resist: I whispered, 'God bless you my son.' Only a few front seats heard me. There was a little chuckle from the man who sneezed. It was very naughty but the devil had clearly got to me.

Some of the media attention came from unexpected quarters, such as when Dana and I were asked to appear in the 1972 Christmas special of Johnny Speight's hit BBC sitcom *Till Death Us Do Part* starring Warren Mitchell as the bigoted Alf Garnett. Alf has been dragged along to see the show and, after the performance, spots Dana and me having a drink in the pub. Suddenly very excited, he starts pointing at me and loudly exclaiming, 'It's him! It's him! It's Jesus! Alf rushes over, grabs my hands in amazement and starts examining them for evidence of stigmata. However, it doesn't take very long for him to notice Dana's low-cut dress and very soon he becomes far more interested in examining significant parts of *her* anatomy. It was great fun to do and just one of the many fringe benefits of being in a hit West End show.

Jesus Christ Superstar was to be the making of Rice and Lloyd Webber and it was a great beginning for me. The show had mixed reviews. Benedict Nightingale gave me a terrible notice in *The Times*. I was going to write to him and I said to Oscar, 'This guy has given me an unfair review. I want to respond to him.'

Oscar dismissed this nonsense with, 'Don't be ridiculous – that's part of the game. You have to be able to take it.' I did.

Many people used to make fun of Andrew Lloyd Webber. They'd say, 'Oh, Andrew nicks tunes.' It's of course nonsense. Andrew, Tim, Cameron Mackintosh and Robert Stigwood have done so much for

British musical theatre. They have elevated the reputation of the British musical around the world. The theatre industry makes a great deal of money for the UK and generates more than television or film. As just one example, take the Broadway smash hit *Hamilton* which Cameron brought to the UK in 2017. Many months later, in 2020, people still have difficulty in getting a ticket.

In 1973 Tim and Andrew's *Jesus Christ Superstar* made them multi-millionaires. They were honoured by the government for export earnings of £13 million and that was just the beginning of their success. *Jesus Christ Superstar* ran and ran. Bernard Delfont called it 'the musical *Mousetrap*' and when the show finally closed in 1980 after 3,358 performances, the curtain was only down for a moment. The show was immediately resurrected and went on a provincial tour of the UK. It has been revived ever since by many producers including myself. Norman Jewison directed it as a movie in 1973 with Ted Neely as Jesus. The film did not detract from the interest in theatrical productions, which is always a fear for producers and writers. *Evita* was the next Rice/Lloyd Webber show to be made into a film and that took until 1997 when Alan Parker cast Madonna as Eva Peròn.

Jesus Christ Superstar has been translated into twenty-two languages and earned more than £100 million. It changed the world view of theatre and it began the explosion which made London the epicentre of musical theatre.

Shows were being created to run not for months as in the past, but for years. When it closed in the West End after eight years *Superstar* had overtaken *Oliver!*, *The Sound of Music*, *My Fair Lady*, *The Boy Friend*, *Fiddler on the Roof* and *Me and My Girl* as the longest-running musical in British theatre history. I was lucky to have been a small part of it all, for it was indeed the beginning of a revolution. A time of change in British musical theatre. It would no longer be just a wall of Rodgers and Hammerstein and Lerner and Loewe musicals. There was a new team in town and they were British – Tim Rice and Andrew Lloyd Webber. Between them they would dominate musical theatre for the next fifty years.

I had been playing the leading part in a brand new musical that was the talk of the town. I was earning good money. Being in a hit show provided tremendous financial security for me and was the backbone of my existence for many years. It's why I believe in the theatre so much. More than sixty per cent of actors are out of work at any given time. For me, to be in a show that might run a year meant financial security and, with a family to support, being in a long-running show is about as secure as it gets for an actor.

Much can be attributed to karma, to providence, but you still have to create the right circumstances and try and make the right career moves. It's difficult because as an unknown actor you have very little control over your professional life. Most performers dream of stardom when they start out. Unfortunately for most actors it's not that easy. There can be long periods of unemployment, times when you think you'll never work again. It is very easy to feel discouraged but it's a magical business and anything can happen when you least expect it. One moment you're in the depths of despair, the next you're on a plane jetting to LA to appear in a movie. It's never predictable and so the dream never dies. You just need to stick with it. There are very few actors who make it overnight, but your time may not be now; it may come later in life. It may never come, but one thing's for sure – it's better than working for a living.

When you're starting out as an actor nothing is wasted. That is one good lesson I learned while playing a pair of boots in 1971. That's it. Boots! As in cowboy boots, to be precise. The film was a vehicle for Mia Farrow who became a star on television with *Peyton Place* and on film with *Rosemary's Baby*. She was trying a different movie genre. In *See No Evil* (released in the UK as *Blind Terror*) she played a blind girl who was hunted by a psychopath at a country estate. It was an edge-of-the seat thriller directed by a great Hollywood veteran, Richard Fleischer. He had worked with John Wayne, Orson Welles and many names stretching back to the *Hopalong Cassidy* Westerns of Howard Hughes' RKO Studios.

My place in this roll of honour was 'the boots' aka 'Jacko the Psycho'. Jacko was very pissed off because his shiny cowboy boots got splashed when Mia's family car went through a puddle. Jacko, who is obviously a fashion victim, decides to murder the whole family. A little harsh I thought. After murdering the husband, wife and daughter, he spends the rest of the film trying to throttle Mia Farrow, who is now better known as the mother of Ronan Farrow – a hero of the 'Me Too' movement with his 2019 bestselling book on the Harvey Weinstein case, *Catch and Kill*.

In the film all the audience see of me are my boots. I wasn't called on to the set with a respectful 'Mr Nicholas, you're needed on set now please.' It was 'Boots! Come here.' It was a little bit degrading but I learned how to hit my mark and a lot about filming. The irony was I had a very good agent called Joy Jameson who arranged a stand-in for me. A stand-in is someone who stands in for the star while the director of photography lights the shot. It can take a long time and the star mustn't be tired and sweaty when it comes to doing the scene. When it came to my scenes, a chap in exactly the same pair of boots as mine stood in for me. Then when the scene was lit, I stepped back in and my boots were filmed.

Jacko the Psycho was a stable lad and I had one line in the film. Other than my big scene when I try to drown Mia in the bath, this was the only time you see my face in the film. I knew this was my one and only chance to demonstrate my acting prowess to the world. I practised the line at home until I thought I had it off perfectly.

The scene is set, the horses are playing up and Jacko the Psycho knocks on the door and delivers the line to the hero. I prepared myself. Richard Fleischer, the director, shouted 'Action!'

I knocked on the door. 'Come in,' said the hero. I opened the door, leant in and said my line.

'It's the mare, Mr Redding.'

'Cut!'

Silence. Nobody said anything.

'Okay! Take two. Action!'

I knocked on the door. 'Come in.'

I opened the door and leant in. 'It's the mare, Mr Redding.'

'Cut!'

Richard Fleischer whispers to the first assistant who comes over to me with the script. 'I just want to check the line.' He points to it in the script.

'Yes,' I say. 'That's it.'

He walks back to the director and they nod at each other. First assistant shouts, 'Okay! Let's go again.'

'Take three. Action!'

I said the line again.

'Cut!' Richard Fleischer has clearly had enough. He walks over to me. 'I can't understand what you're saying. What's the line?'

I said, 'It's the mare, Mr Redding.'

'Ah,' he said. 'Yes, that's what I thought. Okay, let's do it again,' and so we did.

'Cut!' Fleischer was beginning to get testy. He said, 'I still can't understand what you're saying.'

'Oh,' I said. In my effort to obtain at the very least an Oscar nomination, I had given Jacko the Psycho a West Country accent. It must have been pretty authentic because no one could understand what the hell I was saying.

We went again and this time I modified it and we completed the scene. About a month later I got a call from my agent. She had heard from the film company that they wanted me to go in and dub my line, so I did and Jacko the Psycho ended up sounding like he'd been to Eton.

After *Hair, Jesus Christ Superstar* and a couple of films, I felt I didn't know enough about acting. I was on the lookout for opportunities all the time. I went to see shows, movies, revues. Anything that would help me learn.

Important lessons were arriving wrapped up in nostalgia and the tight angora sweaters of 1950s college America. *Grease* was a big Broadway hit and a young Richard Gere – who was replaced in New York by John Travolta – was about to be brought to London to star in the show. It was to be produced at the recently built New London Theatre in Drury Lane. It was perfect for me, but it was one of the most popular opportunities in town.

I hadn't bothered to arrange an audition for myself but my friend Andy Foray from *Hair* thought he stood a good chance being American. He asked me to play piano for him so I went along with him and played for Andy's audition. While I was there I thought I would have a shot at auditioning myself so I asked and they said okay. I was pleased that I had but a little embarrassed. They offered me the second lead, Kenickie, to Richard Gere's Danny. Poor Andy didn't get offered anything. He phoned me the next day and said, 'Next time, I'll play the piano.'

As it turned out I wasn't interested in playing Kenickie. I wanted the lead, Danny, so I turned it down. When Richard Gere left, they asked me to take over with Elaine Paige as Sandy and together we joined the show.

Jim Jacobs and Warren Casey wrote the lyrics and the music. The show was based on Jim's experience at the William Taft High School in Chicago. It first played in the city but changed shape and songbook when it opened off-Broadway at the Eden Theatre in downtown New York on 14th February 1972. Though *Grease* opened officially off-Broadway, it did so under first-class Broadway contracts and was eligible for and received seven Tony Award nominations. Many familiar names of those days – John Travolta, Patrick Swayze, Treat Williams, Jeff Conway, Adrienne Barbeau and Marilu Henner – appeared during the show's run.

I'd seen the original New York cast with Barry Bostwick as Danny and Carole Demas as Sandy and loved the production. It was a terrific hit, outrunning *Fiddler on the Roof*; at one point it was Broadway's longest-running musical theatre success. It was huge. The love story of Sandy Dumbrowski and Danny Zuko was centred on Jim Jacobs's sentimental schoolday memories. There's a lot of acne and angst until Sandy and Danny get together.

Grease never dates. It's about teenage years and growing up and most of us know what it's like to feel soppy over a teenage romance. All that coupled with a funny script and a strong score means that *Grease* will always work as a show.

It was my third big show. A hat trick – each show the leading man and another valuable learning experience about musical theatre. Danny is tough, vulnerable and funny and he has to sing and dance. He's a real character. This was a real comedy role and I began to enjoy that aspect of it more than any other. I learned about timing a laugh and just what a delicate thing comedy is. It still fascinates me that no matter how good a joke or a funny situation is, the audience will not respond if the timing is off. Even a slight move by a fellow performer or a cough in the audience can kill a laugh stone dead. I enjoyed learning that skill; some performers are lucky enough to have instinctive timing, others don't. I discovered that I did have a pretty good natural inclination for comedy, something that was to be useful on and off stage.

The potential difficulty for Elaine and me was joining an established cast as the 'new' Danny and Sandy. The original cast had already established a special bond as the original company. New cast members often find it difficult to blend in. Having just left *Jesus Christ Superstar* where I was crucified eight times a week, I was more than ready to have some fun. *Grease* was an eye-opener.

Elaine was a wonderful Sandy, Eva Peròn, Edith Piaf and Norma Desmond in *Sunset Boulevard* which were to follow and it wouldn't be Sunday now without her on Radio 2. As Sandy, she really kicked her heels. She and I were very similar in that we both tended to be apprehensive about our ability to play a part. That said, I've never seen a performance from Elaine where she didn't deliver. We both learned to have more faith in ourselves over the years. She was marvellous as Sandy; I hadn't realised what a great voice she had until I heard her sing 'Raining on Prom Night'.

Grease was a terrific show but it was never deemed a hit in that first London run. The New London Theatre was newly built and it was felt at the time that the public weren't familiar with its location. It could also have been the mood of the times. *Superstar* was still the big show along with *Godspell* starring David Essex as Christ at Wyndham's Theatre. *Godspell* had opened before us at the Roundhouse in Chalk Farm on 17th November 1971 and was running in the West End at the same time as *Superstar*. Starring with David Essex were Julie Covington, Marti Webb and a gentleman who had a really fine speaking voice who was the Narrator. It was clear and arresting and I thought to myself, 'Oh yes! A proper actor.' Indeed, Jeremy Irons became a proper star.

Most of the shows going into the West End were from America. With *Grease* we didn't have that power of high-school nostalgia that existed in America. Britain was more interested in *Oh! Calcutta!* and *Let My People Come*. We were looking forward rather than looking back. Nevertheless, we ran for nine months, but did not achieve the success the production deserved. In 1974 it was the right show at the wrong time. It left me out of a job and I had got used to regular money coming in.

How do you follow three major West End productions? A couple of old acquaintances helped out. One was Pete Townshend; the other was a director who enjoyed breaking the casting rules.

Chapter Five

To Be, or Not To Be

'Still looking for that blue jean, baby queen
Prettiest girl I ever seen
See her shake on the movie screen, Jimmy Dean'
    – David Essex, 'Rock On', 1973

BRITISH CINEMA, IF NOT the theatre, was thankfully keen on nostalgia. In 1973, David – later Lord – Puttnam had produced a film titled *That'll Be the Day*. It was written by the journalist Ray Connolly, and Keith Moon was involved as musical director as well as being in the film. It looked back at 1958 when things began brightening up following the blues of the post-war years.

David Essex played Jim MacLaine in what was essentially a coming-of-age drama. There was quite a bit of realism in it, with the added attraction of some novelty casting in the shape of Ringo Starr and Billy Fury. The story had restless youth Jim leaving his family and drifting around in an attempt to be a pop star. It was a fun film, especially for people like me who grew up in that world and who so wanted to be part of it.

A year later much of the same team made a sequel called *Stardust*, in which David's Jim MacLaine finds and loses fame. This time I was in the cast along with Adam Faith, Marty Wilde and Larry Hagman who would later become J. R. Ewing in *Dallas*.

I played Johnny who is the leader of the 'Stray Cats' group until David Essex takes over and Adam Faith kicks me out. One night during filming we returned to the hotel and David picked up a message from his manager Derek Bowman to say that his single 'Rock On', which he had also written, was number one in America. Keith Moon with great excitement said, 'That's bloody marvellous – The Who have never been number one in the U.S.!', and promptly ordered a bottle of champagne to celebrate.

Off screen Keith – who was reprising his role of J. D. Clover – wasn't happy. He thought the script didn't feature him enough which was a bit cheeky. Keith felt snubbed. Ray Connolly, the writer, was always around during the filming and I could see there was tension between Keith and Ray. It all came to a head on a night shoot in Manchester. We were filming at the Belle Vue Ballroom; Jimmy Savile had been the resident DJ there. It was very late, around two a.m., and Keith and Ray started sniping at each other. Their voices got louder, they began to lose their tempers and suddenly it kicked off. Keith leapt at Ray who wasn't about to capitulate without a fight. Suddenly they were both rolling around on the floor. My one abiding memory is of watching the make-up man who jumped on a chair and screamed at Ray, 'Don't hit his face! Don't hit his face!' He was worried about continuity. Of course no one was hurt and thereafter Keith and Ray were fine with each other... and the make-up man didn't need to worry.

For me, it was a terrific experience. I enjoyed working with such familiar names and watching them, always learning. Larry Hagman was a larger-than-life character even then. He was playing a brash American manager and you knew when he was around, on and off screen. He was way over the top but fun, zany and loveable with it. He brightened up everyone's day. I needed brightening up.

I've always been a worrier, and although everything was going well in the theatre and with the added bonus of occasional film roles, I felt things weren't quite right. I felt I wasn't properly established in a particular area of entertainment. I still did not feel like a real actor. I was approaching my thirtieth birthday so maybe I was at that dangerous age.

*

Frank Dunlop gave me more to worry about. Frank – who was ninety-four in February 2021 – was a legitimate theatre director with immense theatrical experience. He ran the Edinburgh Festival for eight years and didn't have an ounce of snobbery about him. His taste was eclectic. In 1996 he directed Cliff Richard in *Heathcliff* which was horribly criticised. I don't think it was the fault of the direction, or Cliff; I went to see it and Cliff's voice sounded superb. Ultimately, the piece was not quite good enough but Cliff proved his popularity by selling thousands of seats. I went backstage after to see Cliff and congratulated him. He'd been to see me play King Arthur in *Camelot* directed by Frank. Cliff wanted to make sure that he liked Frank's direction prior to *Heathcliff*.

I'm sure Frank saw *Heathcliff* as something new for his wonderful imagination to take on. He's like that. He'd founded the Young Vic in 1969 and was very open-minded about who he cast in his productions. One of his 'finds' was Jim Dale who had enjoyed a wide-ranging career. In the 1950s he had four pop record successes, in 1967 he won an Oscar for writing the theme song to the Lynn Redgrave and Charlotte Rampling movie *Georgy Girl*, and he was a regular in the *Carry On* films. At first glance, not a candidate for the National Theatre or the Young Vic; but that is not the way Frank Dunlop works. He cast Jim as the title character in *Scapino* and his acrobatic performance was wonderful. It took him to New York and on to international acclaim as a musical artist.

Now Frank wanted me for the part of the impulsive Claudio in *Much Ado About Nothing*. For me it was a lot of to-do. I had never read a Shakespeare play, much less acted in one, so I bought a paperback copy of *Much Ado* and I went to meet Frank Dunlop.

He was very matter of fact. 'Would you like to be Claudio?'

I replied, 'I don't know if I can do it.'

'Of course you can.'

'Err...'

'Rehearsals start in three weeks.'

And they did.

I started studying the text. I had seen *Hamlet* when I was about nine at the Old Vic. I was confused and did not understand a word of it. My reaction was much the same when I began reading *Much Ado About Nothing*. The Shakespearean text was difficult and it took me about three weeks before I knew what I was talking about.

When I went for the first read-through everyone was very nice, very chummy. It was not the hippie world of *Hair* or the rock 'n' roll of *Grease*. This was the legitimate theatre. A brave new world. A luvvie world. They were a totally different breed of performer. I was surrounded by 'proper' actors and had to read a play that I barely understood. The worst thing was having to read in front of them. It was intimidating but I got through it and it didn't sound too bad.

Frank seemed pleased. He was very jolly and did not give a toss about anybody and always loved a bit of aggravation. He liked to send the fighter planes in. I was flying one. He was very kind to me because I wasn't an experienced actor. I was still learning, so to be invited to join the Young Vic company was a huge honour.

The snobbishness that pervades so called 'legitimate' theatre was instantly apparent. The musical performer in those days was regarded by some theatre actors as inferior. For the most part, that is nonsense. It takes as much skill to perform in a musical show as it does to play Shakespeare. Also, comedy is as difficult to do as drama. You are either funny or you're not. In drama you're convincing or you're not.

I played Count Claudio, a rather prissy character who falls in love with Hero, but is then tricked into humiliating her during their wedding ceremony. I worked with two different young actresses, both of whom had famous fathers: Tamara Ustinov, daughter of Peter, and Zoë Wanamaker, daughter of Sam. I toured Europe with the Young Vic and it was interesting to be involved with an acting company. I'm sure there's much to be said for Shakespeare's plays but *Much Ado* was long. I swear by the third act I could see an early morning mist beginning to rise over the audience.

There was one particular actor in *Much Ado* who was very resentful of what I was. He was very snooty. We were friends in the play but off-stage it got so bad one night that we both snapped and ended up having a little dust-up. The actors on stage were waiting for us to make our entrance while we were in the wings being very stupid. Finally we were thrown on stage and became the instant great friends our parts required. What skill! I truly was an 'actor'.

And a very lucky lad, for Pete Townshend had called offering a meeting with Ken Russell who was being touted in the newspapers as 'the world's most successful director'. It was for a role in Russell's film adaptation of The Who's rock opera *Tommy*. Roger Daltrey had the title role and the other talents involved were Ann-Margret, who was Hollywood royalty, Oliver Reed, Eric Clapton, Elton John, Tina Turner and Robert Powell who had played my mate in my very first BBC play many years before. It was called *Season of the Witch*. Robert and I played a couple of hippies who were after the same girl played by Julie Driscoll. She'd had a big hit with 'Wheels on Fire'. Robert and I both ended up playing the role of Jesus: me on stage and Robert in Zeffirelli's film *Jesus of Nazareth*.

I met Ken Russell and Pete Townshend at the Ramport Studios in Battersea, London. Ken was full of energy and very enthusiastic. I'd learnt the song and they played me the track. Over the next hour I recorded the track. We did several takes and both Ken and Pete directed my performance until they were happy. I left the studio not knowing if they were going to hire me or not. The following day I got a call telling me that Ken Russell wanted me to play the nasty, 'orrible Cousin Kevin who terrorises poor, blind Tommy. I was thrilled. It was one song and, although not a big part, it made quite an impact. I was dragging Tommy around by his hair, spraying him with a fire hose and really putting him though the mill.

The late, great characters Oliver Reed and Keith Moon were in the picture and I heard that there was a lot of hell-raising rivalry between them. If there were any larger-than-life antics, they happened away from the set.

Tommy was an amazing movie with a soundtrack to match. At the premiere, I was a bit embarrassed because when the credits came up there were so many big names, then suddenly my name and people wondering: which one was he?

It was an important film for me to be associated with and preparation for my own singing career; yet it was anger that made me a pop star and a little bit famous. I was enjoying my success in the theatre and work in the movies. However, as always, I wanted to do more.

There is a need in most performers to be taken seriously. It's why Tony Hancock wanted to play Hamlet. Tommy Cooper did it for laughs on television but comics, like most entertainers, have thespian dreams. I would gladly have played Hamlet. I nearly did. I was to be cast as the Dane in New York in a Broadway musical production.

In London, I had joined the Prospect Theatre Company which was a very worthy outfit run by Toby Robertson. They were involved in a musical version of *The Pilgrim's Progress* entitled *Pilgrim*. Toby's wife, Jane McCulloch, was the librettist/lyricist. The former Manfred Mann singer Paul Jones was Christian, whom composer Carl Davis had written as confronting demons and temptations. Ben Cross, who co-starred in that 1981 Oscar bonanza *Chariots of Fire*, played Faithful. Peter Straker was a flaming Apollyon and Giant Despair. I had five parts including Mrs Giant Despair but the most fun was a character called Mr Worldly Wiseman. I wore a bowler hat, red lip gloss and a jacket without a shirt. The costume would come in handy a little later down the line. It was a strong cast and the music worked, but there was a lack of oomph about the production.

We were on tour with *Pilgrim* in Liverpool when my agent phoned me. 'I've just had a call from America from a director called Gower Champion,' he said. 'They've seen you in *Tommy* playing Cousin Kevin. They want to fly you to New York to audition for a new musical called *Rockabye Hamlet*. They want you for the part of Hamlet. Will you audition?'

'Which way is it to Heathrow?' I replied.

I was given time off from *Pilgrim* to fly to New York to meet Gower Champion. He was an American dancer/choreographer who had appeared with his sister Marge in fifties movie musicals like *Mr Music* and *Show Boat* and was now a director. All they had seen me do was drag poor Roger Daltrey around by his hair in *Tommy*. I was not going to argue. I auditioned and Gower said, 'We want you to play Hamlet. We want you to come back to America. We open in twelve weeks.'

I was released from *Pilgrim* so that I could begin rehearsals. There was just one snag. 'No, we don't have a work permit for you at this point but we don't see it as a problem.'

Then as now, producers had to justify to the acting union – American Equity – that you were a name of such standing that you justified the part over an American actor. I had to organise my portfolio of credits and send it to the Department of Immigration who issued the work permits. Off I went to America.

I was on a tourist visa and living in a hotel room. I rehearsed with Gower every day and learned the music to his version of *Hamlet*. Every day they said the permit was in the post. The opening night deadline was fast approaching. The full cast had to rehearse and they still hadn't cleared their Hamlet with the U.S. Government.

I joined up with my old friend Paul Jabara in New York. He was very much into the gay scene. He loved Bette Midler and would regularly watch her sing at the baths in New York. She was a friend of his and we visited her apartment and had tea with her. Paul and I went to a bar called Reno Sweeney's to see her piano player/musical director whose name was Barry Manilow. He was playing the piano with a guitar player and singing and wasn't a name in his own right then. I didn't know who he was but I couldn't believe how good his songs were. I thought they were classy. So much so that we had a drink with Barry afterwards and I told him I made records and that I would like to record a couple of his songs. He gave me some demos and later I recorded one of them entitled 'I Am Your Child'. I still have the demos.

I met him again years later when I was performing panto in Manchester. I was playing Buttons in *Cinderella* and Barry Manilow came to see the show. I used to get the kids up on the stage to tell a joke. The audience knew Barry was in the theatre that night and one of the kids came up to tell his joke and it went like this. The kid said, 'What time did Barry Manilow arrive at the theatre tonight?'

'I don't know. What time did Barry Manilow arrive at the theatre tonight?' I replied.

All the audience were laughing because a lot of them could see Barry in the theatre.

The kid said, 'Ten minutes after his nose.'

The audience roared. I'm sure Barry did as well. He came backstage after the show and I reminded him about our first meeting with Paul Jabara at Reno Sweeney's years before. He looked like he was trying to remember, or forget. I think my being dressed as Buttons in *Cinderella* in Manchester didn't help. I didn't mention the kid's joke.

The kid had more success with his joke than I did on my trip to New York. This was to be my big break on Broadway: to play the role of Hamlet in *Rockabye Hamlet*. Unfortunately I didn't get the permit and someone else played Hamlet, and the show opened at the Minskoff Theatre on 17th February 1976... and closed on 22nd February 1976 after six performances. I got no satisfaction from that.

I was disillusioned when I arrived back in London. I wasn't famous enough or exceptionally talented enough to qualify over an American actor for a work permit, so I decided to try and change that. I had to become famous. I was determined. The theatre did not reach enough people and with shows like *Hair* there was no individual billing. I had only done a little television and a few films. Music was the answer. I would make records. Hit records. Fame was the game. It wouldn't be easy to achieve but I was driven.

At thirty-one, I decided to try and find a song to record and with which to have a hit. Now, all this will sound simple stuff but it's not so easy to achieve. To have a hit record, you need a good song; and to find a good song, you need good writers. I had written a couple of songs with Chris Neil who had been my understudy in *Superstar*. Chris would produce the records with me. He has a great pair of 'ears' and his background was similar to mine. Chris's other strength was his harmonies. He had a fantastic, natural talent that gave the couple of songs we'd recorded a very commercial, individual sound. What we didn't have was a hit song. We had recorded some songs for the RSO (Robert Stigwood Organisation) label, one of which was called 'Shuffling Shoes'. It did not become a hit but it got enough radio plays for RSO to allow me to make another record. I realised my own songs weren't good enough for the Top Twenty and I needed to look elsewhere for the hit I needed.

An old friend from *Hair*, Jonathan Bergman, told me about two song-writers called Dominic Bugatti and Frank Musker. They lived in two rooms on Prince Albert Road in north west London so I went to see them. They played me a lot of their songs but none of them sounded like a hit. As I was going out of the door I looked back and pleaded, 'Have you not got anything else?' They reluctantly put on a song called 'Reggae Like it Used to Be'. I think they were embarrassed to play it as I think they felt it was a little too bubblegum. I listened and after about thirty seconds I thought, 'That's it. That's the one!' I knew instantly. I had no doubt. It sang hit to me.

I took their backing track and played it to Chris Neil. He liked it too. So we went into a studio. I put my voice on the track and we added a saxophone and some violins. The writers sang harmony along with Chris. I took it to RSO Records and they released it.

What I didn't have was an image but I remembered the Mr Worldly Wiseman costume from *Pilgrim* and opted for a bowler hat and open jacket with no shirt.

RSO got me onto a television show. I was booked on an afternoon pop show for kids. I was to sing 'Reggae Like it Used to Be' on the first day of the record's release. Unfortunately for me, the then Prime Minister, Harold Wilson, decided it was time to call it a day. 'Wilson Resigned!' They cancelled the show. I was not pleased. Mrs Wilson was.

Luckily, a week is a long time in politics. Politicians go but television keeps on broadcasting.

It was 1976. I found a great record plugger called Brian O'Donoghue who became my manager and 'Reggae Like it Used to Be' made number eighteen in the Top Twenty.

It was one of the most thrilling moments of my life to have a record in the charts. I had fooled around with bands for most of my early career, always dreaming of having a hit record, and now in 1976 at the age of thirty-one, I had found my hit. I became a pop star.

Brian did his stuff. I was finally on *Top of the Pops* and achieving what I set out to do. I was marginally famous. DJs were playing a Paul Nicholas song and it was wonderful. Even more wonderful was that people were buying my records. I had a record in the charts and I loved it! I wanted another song from Bugatti and Musker, who were also performers. They wrote 'Dancing with the Captain', gave me a version to do and also did their own. As performers we were competing against each other; as song-writers they were competing against themselves which was a bit odd.

To make a pop record you have to pay attention to detail. These were catchy tunes, but even with bubblegum music there has to be something to chew. The trick is to make the song live for two minutes and forty-eight seconds. It's not always easy, particularly with an out-and-out pop record. They were not written to be interpreted as hip, deep and mean-ingful... although the term 'dancing with the captain' does have a bit of 'street cred', as can be seen if you look it up in the Urban Dictionary. Far too saucy to be described in this genteel tome, but it's hilarious – who knew! I must look up 'Grandma's Party'. I bet that's really filthy!

Choosing the right song was key. We were aiming for the early teen market so the records needed personality and a youthful vibe. They had to be energetic and fun. I have a pretty good ear and I chose the songs. If it didn't grab me in the first thirty seconds it was invariably rejected. I had to instantly like it. For years I'd listened to record producers and that had never worked.

'Dancing with the Captain' got into the Top Ten and earned me a silver disc. Hey, I wasn't a one-hit wonder – I was a pop star and I began to try and live like one. I was starting to hang around with music busi-ness people in Morton's in Berkeley Square. I am not good at drinking but I tried. I used to exaggerate my capacity in the odd newspaper story to boost my 'wild' image, which was ridiculous as I was selling a sweet wholesome chap in a bowler hat. The truth was and is a pint of shandy and I'm merry!

I got my comeuppance. Chris Neil is a terrific record producer and he said to me one day: 'You've done two really good pop songs. You should do a ballad. I have this great idea for an arrangement of "If You Were the Only Girl in the World".' The song was a ballad from way back. I agreed. He produced a great version not unlike 10cc's 'I'm Not in Love'. There were lots of Chris overlays of voices singing harmonies and technically it was brilliantly made, but the public didn't go for it. No one was remotely interested. What Chris had tried to do was give me more credibility with a classier record but unfortunately no one wanted to buy it. It was released, got a few plays and then it died. We had tried to change my direction after only two hits. There's nothing wrong with that except that the song that we chose wasn't strong enough.

Britain loves Christmas songs. There are always a handful of artists vying for the top spot. Mine was 'Grandma's Party' and there was no question in my mind that it would be a hit. It was lightweight but it was very catchy. It was well produced by Chris and waltzed into the Top Ten. Everyone, for a very short time, wanted to be at 'Grandma's Party' and it gave me another silver disc.

I was in limbo, lost. I had three hit records in the UK and I was all over the fan magazines. The writers wanted to do stronger, classier material but the music I was selling was on personality, on affability, songs to sing along with, not heavy rock. I was never a heavy rock singer. Still, I was thirty-two years old and had done okay. Professionally, my profile was rising higher and higher. Granada Television had given me my own TV show called *Paul*. It was a successful afternoon pop show for kids. It had guest stars every week and I sang three or four songs.

I was digging myself into the pop-music world more and more, but it was not as fulfilling as I expected. I enjoyed the television appearances and European trips to do television shows, but ultimately it was not that satisfying. It would have been when I was seventeen but not at thirty two. The interesting part for me was picking the right song and Chris and me producing the track in the studio.

I didn't like just being a singer. It had given me a much higher profile but it was a dead-end street if you didn't write the songs. Sooner or later the songs would dry up. Yes, it was a lot tougher being a composer – as I soon found out when my old friend from *Tommy* called.

Ken Russell was the 'enfant terrible' of the cinema with movies like *Women in Love* (1969) with the late Oliver Reed and Alan Bates, as well as *The Devils* (1971) with Reed and Vanessa Redgrave; and, more importantly for me at that point, his *The Music Lovers* (1970) with

Glenda Jackson and Richard Chamberlain as a somewhat troubled Tchaikovsky. Before *Tommy* he had made a film of *Mahler* with Robert Powell and now it was the turn of Wagner and Liszt with *Lisztomania*. This was Ken's interpretation of the life of the brilliant Hungarian pianist and composer Franz Liszt. Born in 1811, Liszt was a child prodigy who went on to compose *Les Préludes*, *Orpheus*, *Hamlet* and *Liebesträume* – and these are just some of his hits.

Roger Daltrey had been cast as Liszt, a pop star of his time. 'Lisztomania' was a term coined to describe the enthusiasm at Liszt's virtuosic piano performances. Audiences of screaming women were often limited to standing room only. Ken asked me to be Richard Wagner who was born in 1813 and German. He wrote *The Flying Dutchman*, *The Ring* and *Parsifal*. He was Hitler's favourite composer (what an endorsement, and something not missed by Ken and reflected in his film). After Wagner's first wife died he married Liszt's daughter Cosima.

The film was Ken's usual mix of sketchy biographical detail and mad surrealism. In one scene Wagner turns into Dracula and sinks his teeth in Liszt's neck, suggesting that Wagner is sucking musical inspiration from Liszt's lifeblood. In another, I was made up as Frankenstein's monster dressed as Hitler. I looked ridiculous.

Ken Russell's body of work was intriguing. He had started as a stills photographer and framing the shot was his strength. He hired good actors who knew their craft. It allowed him the freedom to indulge the imagery and texture of the film. Ken had such a terrific imagination, and was always more interested in the visual aspect of the film rather than the narrative. He didn't write *Women in Love*, one of his best films; most of his successful films were not written by him. If he wrote the script, it tended to be overwhelmed by the imagery. Ken had a touch of genius, and for six weeks on *Lisztomania* I was swept along by it.

The climax of the film is when Liszt – who has taken minor orders in the Roman Catholic Church – sets about exorcising (later, a speciality of mine) the Devil from Wagner. It was a complicated shot. I had to fly around the set on a wire while debris was propelled in the air by a wind machine. It took a lot of time to set up which meant we weren't going to get many attempts at filming it. Suddenly I was flying around the room, seven feet off the ground, when without warning the wire snapped. I crashed to the ground and landed heavily. I thought I'd broken my ankle... I had. Under the circumstances it was a good result. I did not make too much of a fuss and Ken was attentive. He said, 'Thank you. That was very good but we did not quite get it. Would you mind doing it again?'

Being young and keen and ignoring the excruciating pain in my right ankle I said, 'Of course Ken.' I did it again with a broken ankle. If you ever see *Lisztomania* you'll notice that in the second half of the movie I'm walking around with a very large right foot. That's because they had to draw a huge mock shoe over the plaster cast to allow me to finish the filming. It disguised nothing. Once, with my foot in plaster, I had to pretend to kick Ken's dog as part of the scene but just toppled over myself. I think Ken wanted his dog in the film.

Looking back, I realise how lucky I was to work with such a talent as Ken. He was a very creative man who made each day's filming exciting. Sometimes difficult, but exciting. Some of the producers whose money he was spending, and spending very freely, were not quite as excited about working with Ken as I was. After we'd completed two thirds of the filming, Ken disappeared. I don't know why but we pretty much finished it ourselves. Rick Wakeman scored the film and ended up playing a character called Thor who is created by Wagner à la Frankenstein's monster. Thor comes to life, rises, walks to a blazing log fire and pees on it. Wagner crosses to Thor and screams, 'Put it away! Put it away!' You had to be there. It was my one and only contribution to the film's script. Yes, even I'd started writing bits of dialogue. Ken eventually returned but it seemed that his heart wasn't in it.

I was still a pop star that acted and I was in a void. What I did have were contacts and friends from *Hair* and *Superstar*. They were my alma mater.

During the first *Hair* tour I worked with an actor called Richard O'Brien. Some people thought he was a little strange but I put him down as funny and friendly. I saw great potential in him. He had a quick, creative mind. What fascinated me was that while others would take off for dinner or the pub, Richard would go off and work on his musical. He played a couple of the numbers he had created and I was impressed. The songs were for a show he was writing called *The Rocky Horror Show*.

I said, 'Richard, the songs are great and I'd like to record a couple of them;' so we used the *Hair* band and went into a studio in Manchester and recorded two of his songs. It was 1971, a year before *Jesus Christ Superstar*. That was the first professional recording of 'The Sword of Damocles' ('That Ain't No Crime') which Richard would go on to use in the then yet to be produced *Rocky Horror Show*. The 'B' side was a song that introduced the characters of Brad, Janet and Dr Scott with Richard doing all the voices.

A few years ago I sent Richard a copy of the songs we'd recorded in 1971. I suggested that *Rocky Horror* fans might like to hear the early recordings we'd made in Manchester, and listen to his take on Brad and Janet and Dr Scott. Richard wrote back that he didn't think so. So they are still sitting in the original tape box from 1971.

As I mentioned earlier, the legend of *Rocky Horror* and its star Tim Curry began in the small Theatre Upstairs at the Royal Court in 1973. *The Rocky Horror Show* remains one of the great, camp takes on over-the-top Hollywood horror movies.

My enthusiasm for Richard's ideas and music resurfaced when three years later he wrote *T. Zee*. This time, because of the success of *Rocky Horror*, he was given the main stage of the Royal Court to mount his show.

The play's theme was that two explorers, played by Richard and Belinda Sinclair, enter into a fantastic Hollywood underworld of sexual shenanigans. I played the 'Bully of the Boulevard'. The late Warren Clarke – who had a great presence and would later become popular as the first half of the *Dalziel and Pascoe* detective duo and countless other television and film roles – was a hilarious Tarzan who roamed around the audience looking for his Jane. Diane Langton was 'Princess La' and her motivation was that she couldn't get enough sex. The show ran its course at the Royal Court but it never achieved the cult status of *Rocky Horror*.

Chapter Six

Music Man

'I was a star... well, a pop star'

P OP MUSIC WAS getting into a rut and professionally I felt the same. The punk movement shook it up with Johnny Rotten as the flip side of pop music. The safety pins and torn T-shirts were an antidote to songs like 'Dancing with the Captain'.

But the world – and most of all America – still enjoyed an occasional cuddle with their records, and there was never a cuddlier song than 'Heaven on the Seventh Floor'. When it was released in the States I was sent there to promote it.

In 1978 the talk shows dominated afternoon and late-night television. In America Johnny Carson was God, and several others were popular, and I was perfect for their TV shows: this harmless, cute, blonde-haired British singer with this unthreatening pop song. American television producers had pushed the pause button on punk. I performed on *The Dinah Shore Show* (her boyfriend was Burt Reynolds, then the biggest movie star in the world), *The Mike Douglas Show* and *The Merv Griffin Show*.

With the help of that nationwide exposure, 'Heaven on the Seventh Floor' was steaming up the U.S. charts, and suddenly the record was

Number Five on the Billboard Top Hundred and I was awarded a gold disc for sales of over a million records. It also made number one in New Zealand. It was about a guy who gets stuck in a lift with a beautiful girl and they fall in love. I was a star… well a pop star.

At the same time, my friend Paul Jabara from *Superstar* was enjoying a huge songwriting career. He had written a song for a movie called *Thank God it's Friday* which was all about the problems at a Hollywood discotheque. Paul's song 'Last Dance' became a disco anthem sung by Donna Summer, whom I'd met years before when she came to see the London production of *Hair* having just finished the German tour of the show.

That connection – and they are so important – led him to write 'No More Tears (Enough is Enough)' which became a number one hit in America for what was a dream team, Barbra Streisand and Donna Summer. He wrote it for Streisand's movie *The Main Event* at her invitation. He told me: 'On the way over to Streisand's house to talk about the film I was a wreck. I couldn't believe I was writing a song for her. The only thing wrong with the song was that there was not a singing part for me.'

It was a joy to be with Paul and see the success he had achieved. He was a wonderful, funny man and a good friend. He'd appeared in John Schlesinger's *Midnight Cowboy* (1969) as a hippie handing out pills, and in Schlesinger's *The Day of the Locust* (1975) where he sang a cover of the Marlene Dietrich song 'Hot Voo-Doo' in drag.

Paul was overtly gay and loved muscle men. He was also very proud of his appendage which he referred to as 'Orca'. He wrote 'It's Raining Men' which was a big hit for The Weather Girls in 1982.

In Los Angeles it was the beginning of what people were then calling a 'virulent cancer' but later became the 'curse of Aids'. Living in Los Angeles I became aware of it as early as 1980. Paul said to me, 'There's this cancer that's killing all the queens.' Paul Jabara was forty-four when he died in Los Angeles on 29th September 1992, of complications from Aids.

During our time together in *Jesus Christ Superstar*, Paul and I had worked together on his musical *Rachael Lily Rosenbloom (and Don't You Ever Forget It)*. We did demo recordings in London. One of my favourite numbers from the show was 'Ochos Rios' and Paul regularly performed it in people's living rooms when trying to find someone to back the show. He eventually convinced Robert Stigwood and Ahmet Ertegun to produce it on Broadway. Paul had written it with Bette Midler in mind but she passed so Ellen Greene took the title role.

In November 1973, after a few previews, it was clear that it would never work and so it closed before it even opened. Frank Rich, the theatre critic of the *New York Times*, noted the musical had a small hardcore group of fans who had followed its evolution from the beginning and had already seen it several times. He wrote: 'In scattered pockets throughout the otherwise shell-shocked house were claques of theatregoers who sang along with the musical numbers and gave mini-standing ovations at the end of most of them.'

Paul was devastated that the show he had been trying to get off the ground for so long was a flop; so he moved to LA, stuck at it and still dared to dream. Paul ended up writing many hit songs including the aforementioned 'Last Dance' which won him an Oscar, a Grammy and a Golden Globe, as well as winning Donna Summer a Grammy for Best R&B Female Vocal Performance. Not bad eh Paulie?

Later, when Paul was a success, he was able to make a video of 'Ochos Rios' with him playing Rachael Lily Rosenbloom. You can watch it on YouTube and enjoy what I saw many times in many front rooms around the world... without of course the production values.

Paul and I had both enjoyed success in the American music charts when I returned to Britain. I came back a pop star and went back almost by return to Hollywood for a movie. It was not *Gone With the Wind* but it was a lavish Tinseltown production of *Sgt. Pepper's Lonely Hearts Club Band* which was produced by Universal Studios and Robert Stigwood's organisation. A loose storyline had been created around the Beatles' classic, best-known album. Peter Frampton was a big music star at the time having had a hit single 'Show Me the Way' and sold eight million copies of his album *Frampton Comes Alive*. Peter starred as Billy Shears and I was his brother Dougie Shears, the manager of Sgt. Pepper's Lonely Hearts Club Band who were the Bee Gees – Barry, Maurice and Robin

Gibb. The late, lovely Frankie Howerd was the villain, Mean Mr Mustard, a character who appeared in the Beatles Abbey Road album.

Frankie and I had gone to Hollywood at the same time for the movie which had an astonishingly diverse cast. There was the almost unknown Steve Martin; the great character star turn Donald Pleasence (I'd been at school with his daughter, Angela); and topping it off were Alice Cooper, Earth, Wind and Fire and a very fresh-faced Aerosmith.

The tremendous bonus for me was working with George Burns who even then was getting on. He was eighty-two and wryly amusing. I used to visit George in his Winnebago and we'd chat. Bing Crosby had just died and the obituaries in the *Los Angeles Times* and the *Los Angeles Herald Examiner* both reported Crosby's age as seventy-three. George looked up from the paper: 'Bing always lied about his age. He was seventy-seven. I watch these things – got to keep an eye over your shoulder in this business.'

Another thrill for me was recording the film soundtrack of the Beatles' songs with the legendary George Martin who produced all their hits as well as the original *Sgt. Pepper* album. The Beatles graduated from writing catchy pop songs to the more surreal music they played on *Sgt. Pepper*. George Martin was great to work with. I had four songs to record: the opening to 'Sgt. Pepper's Lonely Hearts Club Band', 'I Want You', 'Good Morning' with Frampton and the Bee Gees, and a duet with Diane Steinberg of 'You Never Give Me Your Money'.

I was in Hollywood for four months. It was a big production but a slow process. It was great to do a Hollywood movie and to work with Peter Frampton and the Bee Gees who were at their peak and selling millions of records.

Sgt. Pepper was premiered in Los Angeles and the following day the cast were flown to New York for a reception hosted by the then Mayor, Ed Koch. The premier was held at Radio City Music Hall, the home of the Rockettes. Despite the razzamatazz the press didn't go for it. Michael Shultz, the director, had done his best but the script by Henry Edwards wasn't weird or interesting enough for such a cult album. The film was like a pantomime and although musically it was excellent the concept and script were weak.

I returned to Britain and, having been a pop star, acting-wise that's what I was being offered. I wanted to work so there I was rolling around in the back of a Rolls-Royce with the original Hollywood *Baby Doll*, Carroll Baker. She had followed that censorship-breaking classic by working with James Dean in *Giant* and Alan Ladd in *The Carpetbaggers*; and now here I was, lusting with her in the back of a Roller.

The film was *The World is Full of Married Men* and was based on Jackie Collins' first novel which she'd written eleven years earlier. On publication the book was condemned as in bad taste. It was banned in Australia and South Africa but became a runaway bestseller in the UK and America.

The film version was something of a Jackie Collins morality tale but with all the sexy sequences intact; *Variety* called it a 'sexploitation melo-drama'. Tony Franciosa was Carroll's philandering husband and she was taking revenge by having sex with willing lads like me. I paid the price as I got shot at the end of the film. Deservedly so as my character was called 'Gem Gemini'… they should have shot me in the beginning.

It did not stop me being enchanted by Jackie Collins. Jackie was gorgeous, she laughed and had a lovely voice. She was great mates with Ian McShane and in his pre-*Lovejoy* days wrote a film for him titled *Yesterday's Hero* in which he played a footballer not unlike the great George Best. The love interest was the American actress Suzanne Somers who was a big TV star in the States in *Three's Company* which was the Hollywood version of *Man About the House*. Adam Faith played the team manager and I played an Elton John character: a pop star who owned a football club, with the marginally more acceptable name of Clint Simon.

I was certainly being pigeonholed as a pop star who acted. I had tried to find fame via pop records. It brought success and name recognition but it harmed my credibility. It had worked in name recognition but now I was known as a lightweight pop singer – which is what I'd become. If you present yourself that way it's not unreasonable for people to think that's who you are. Actors, by the very nature of what they do, should be able to play many roles. I knew I was playing a character, a fun youthful chap wearing a bowler hat; but if you're a casting director casting a part in a serious drama, you're not going to think, 'Hey, what about that guy in the bowler hat who sings "Dancing with the Captain".' No matter, I'm glad I did it because to have a hit record was always a very big dream of mine. Still, for the moment I was seen very much as that persona, and was playing third leads in those kinds of films; but no matter how frustrating it was, I had a chance of being employed in Hollywood.

My contacts were limited to Paul Jabara and Marsha Hunt, whom I stayed with for a little time. I had rented a room from her until I found my own place. It took me three months to get a Hollywood agent, for there are plenty of actors in Hollywood. Everyone is an actor, be they a waiter or petrol-pump attendant. Everyone is 'resting between acting jobs' so getting an American agent was something of a mini-triumph. I got a guest spot on the Californian Highway Patrol series *CHiPs* with Erik Estrada.

Then – irony of irony – I was cast as a pop singer, an English punk, which I was not. I had the right haircut and spoke with a London accent so I was a punk, a Johnny Rotten-type, as far as the Hollywood casting agents were concerned. It is similar to when they put English characters in U.S. sitcoms like *Friends* or *Frasier*. They cast what they think it should be, not the reality. Yet it was important for me; a small part in a big movie. It was a remake of *The Jazz Singer* and the star was Neil Diamond, making his acting debut. The other big name was Laurence Olivier who certainly had more acting experience than I did.

It was a troubled production and Richard Fleischer, who had directed Mia Farrow and my feet in *See No Evil*, was brought in to take over filming. Richard told the story of Olivier wandering around the Goldwyn Studios looking for the set of *The Jazz Singer* when a production girl encountered him and handed him a page and a half of new dialogue. Olivier read it and his remark became part of Hollywood legend. 'You know this piss is shit?'

Luckily, my role in the movie did not involve too much angst on that level. I had to sing a number titled 'Love on the Rocks'. The scene in-volved Neil coming into the recording studio and nicely telling me, the punk singer, that I was ruining his song. 'No, it should be sung like this.' He then does his marvellous version of 'Love on the Rocks' which would become a big hit for him when the movie was released. He finishes and

I clap my hands in mock appreciation and mirthlessly tell him to 'piss off'. Which is close to Olivier's take on the film.

I'd heard many Olivier stories from Victor Spinetti. Victor (who died aged eighty-two in 2012) was a wonderful actor and an amazing raconteur, and was great friends with Olivier. They both lived in Brighton and Victor would often go round to see him. Victor would arrive and Olivier would greet him: 'Come in, dear boy. Come in. Take me, my wife, whatever you want...'

Victor also told me how Olivier would stand naked in his dressing room staring at himself in front of a full-length mirror and ask: 'How can such a great actor have such a small dick?'

I once shared a dressing room with Olivier, which I will tell you more about in Chapter Eight. If nothing else I can claim to have worked with no fewer than four ennobled knights of the theatre: Olivier, Gielgud, Richardson and McKellen – five if you include the Lord Sutch Who Doth Scream.

While living in Los Angeles, I was invited to take part in a music festival in Tokyo. On 8th November 1979, I was in Japan representing America at the Yamaha Music Festival. Eric Carmen was the special guest artist and somehow I became involved with Eric's management and they wangled it that I would take part in this song competition. It was a televised show in the most enormous hall but the stage was the size of a tennis court. I was told to perform in a six-foot circle.

The song I was singing was a ballad; to give it some dramatic interpretation I emoted, and in doing so strayed outside the six-foot circle. When I finished, a couple of Japanese chaps rushed towards me pointing and screaming. I braced myself expecting a 'kekomi' (thrust kick) to my nether region.

'You left the circle! You will be disqualified!'

They were going mad. I apologised and, because Eric was the star guest, I was put through to the final, which was the following day.

That night I roamed around Tokyo feeling very fed up and lonely. Later that evening I received a message that my son Alexander had been born. I really didn't want to be at the Yamaha Music Festival as I was homesick, but I couldn't return to England until four months had elapsed. I'm in Tokyo, representing America with a song I don't like and with people I barely know. My newborn son and family are three thousand miles away. To cap it all, I'm losing my voice but I resolved to appear no matter what. I'd come a long way from LA to Japan to represent the USA and by golly that's what I was going to do.

By the following day, I had completely lost my voice. All that remained was a passable impression of Lee Marvin murdering 'I Was Born Under a Wandering Star'. I thought, I can't sing so I will speak the whole song à la Telly Savalas doing 'If'. So that's what I did.

I'm afraid America didn't win the best song at the 1979 Yamaha Music Festival. In fact I think the Japanese audience were very underwhelmed with the American entry, as was another American lady singer who told me, 'God did that to you 'cos you didn't stay in the circle.' I thanked her for her support. Although on reflection I had without knowing created an early form of rap.

Before leaving Tokyo I was presented with a gift so I would always remember my time representing America at the Yamaha Music Festival Tokyo November 1979. It was a Seiko watch which, although presented in a small beautifully wrapped gift box, didn't work. I deserved nothing more. I still have the watch and it still doesn't work.

My career might have been over had the 1980s not found me as a star of Britain's favourite television situation comedy and what, as of 2021, is far and away the most successful piece of musical theatre of all time.

I was like the cat that got the cream.

CHAPTER SEVEN

Nine Lives

'There is no limit to what cats can do with their bodies'
   – *Cats* choreographer Dame Gillian Lynne, 1980

THERE WAS NO BAND PLAYING, red carpet or any job offers when I first returned to Britain from California. 'Out of sight, out of mind.' Or so I thought.

My year in America had provided the money for a lovely house but there wasn't a lot left over after living away from home for a year. I needed to work. I looked around but I didn't want to be drawn back into the pop business. I had done that for four years and that is a long time in pop. I had done it to make a name for myself. That was very important to me. The one thing you want to be if you are a performer is famous.

Warren Clarke, who died suddenly in November 2014, once told me how he got into the back of a cab and the driver said, 'What do you do?'

Warren said, 'I'm an actor.'

Warren had always had a small wart on the end of his nose. The driver looked closely at him and said, 'You won't get very far with that thing on the end of your conk.'

Warren proved him wrong.

Yet you are only as good as your last appearance. Mine was seven thousand miles away. The horrible thing about fame is that, if you have done many different things as I have, people get confused. Are you a pop singer? Are you a musical performer, are you a sitcom actor or do you have the potential to do slightly more serious work? We all want to be big Hollywood stars and do high-quality work but sometimes you have to take what you can get. My motto along with many others has always been that this business is a marathon, not a sprint; some artists get a break early on and others don't. Much like life. It is the luck of the draw. You only have to do one decent movie and you can live off it for the next ten years.

It's 1980 and I am back home. I was lucky enough to get a Yorkshire Television play titled *A Little Rococo* with Judy Cornwell in which I played an antique dealer. It was a romantic comedy about a young man falling in love with an older woman. Of all the millions of people who watched it, one proved to be very important: John Sullivan, the creator and writer of the sitcom *Just Good Friends*. Of course, I didn't know at that time that John had seen me in it. Or what it might mean for me a little further down the road.

After I'd finished the television play I spent a lot of time twiddling my thumbs waiting for something to happen.

Then, out of nowhere, I got a call from Andrew Lloyd Webber.

'Hello Paul. How are you?' he asked.

'I'm fine,' I said.

'Have you ever read *Old Possum's Book of Practical Cats* by T. S. Eliot?' I replied 'Er...?'

He said, 'Well, I'm doing it and I'd like you to be in it.'

That's how I first became involved with *Cats* and creating the role of 'Rum Tum Tugger'.

Such is the enormity of the theatrical success of *Cats* that it was only in 2019 that they turned it into a movie. In September that year, I found myself reminiscing about the original production, back in 1982, on BBC Radio 4's *The Reunion* with director Sir Trevor Nunn, set and costume designer John Napier and some of the rest of the original cast – Elaine

Paige, Bonnie Langford and Wayne Sleep. Who would have thought? Certainly not me!

Back in 1980 I told Andrew that I hadn't read *Old Possum's Book of Practical Cats* but I would and I did. It's a series of poems in celebration of cats, which had now been set to music by Andrew.

Andrew has a church in his back garden at Sydmonton Court in *Watership Down* country. He said he would be doing a workshop of *Cats* and would like me to take part, along with Gemma Craven and Gary Bond, for the music festival he has at Sydmonton every summer. Before he put the telephone down, he said, 'I will send you a tape.' The tape duly arrived of Andrew playing the piano and singing the original score of *Cats*. I have saved it for posterity and to possibly auction should I fall on hard times.

I went to meet Andrew at his house in Eaton Square in London. He played me some more of the show and I was quite taken with it, but I thought: hang on – there's no story. This is a collection of poems, whimsical cat tales, and Andrew has put some nice tunes to them but I have not heard a hit. On further consideration, I thought as Andrew is the one with the church in his back garden, a large house in Eaton Square and several hit shows – who am I to judge?

I took off for Sydmonton Court to rehearse with the director Hugh Wooldridge, Gary and Gemma. We spent the weekend working. We rehearsed on the Friday and performed the workshop of *Cats* the following evening. The show was a presentation of the songs; there was no dance. We had no idea this was the genesis of a show that would go global, be translated into ten languages and keep going round again and again. It was the first British musical to play in Moscow. It has been seen by tens of millions of people. That evening, in Andrew's back garden, the performance of T. S. Eliot's poems to Andrew's music was much appreciated by the small audience of two hundred and especially by Valerie Eliot, the widow and former secretary of T. S. Eliot. (In 2020 the royalty payment from *Cats* to the Eliot estate totalled around $130 million.)

Andrew knew he had something and from that small workshop, he formed the idea of staging *Cats* as a full-scale musical. Andrew and Tim Rice's partnership had broken up and Andrew had not renewed his contract with Robert Stigwood. (The contract Stigwood had bought out from David Land and Sefton Myers)

Andrew now had control of his financial as well as his artistic freedom but he still had to find around £400,000 to stage *Cats*. No one seemed especially interested in a show about cats, but what they didn't understand was that Andrew was creating an entertainment – a dance show with wonderful music – that would travel. There were no boundaries, no borders and no dialogue, just music and dance. It would play as well in Tokyo as Torquay. This was still the beginning of the modern musical, the international production with the world's theatres waiting.

The day of the big-budget musical entertainment had begun and Cameron Mackintosh – the man whom *Cats* would catapult on to become the 'Tsar' of such shows, with incredible productions like *Les Misérables* and *Miss Saigon* – is trying to tempt a few quid out of me. Andrew and Cameron had teamed up with each other and the Royal Shakespeare Company (RSC). The RSC's artistic director Trevor Nunn, designer John Napier and choreographer Gillian Lynne were going to put on this extravaganza at the New London Theatre. You'll recall I had played in *Grease* there; by now, the theatre had been going for eight years and up until then the only time it had had any success was when Bruce Forsyth did a one-man show for a couple of weeks. There were not many 'angels' clearing their bank accounts to invest.

As I said, Cameron was so desperate for money that he came and asked me if I would like to invest in the show. Now, I had saved a bit but not enough that I wanted to blow it on a show about cats, in a theatre that nobody liked, on a bunch of songs that didn't sound like hits. I said, 'No thank you Cameron.' It is one of the worst investment decisions that I have ever made in my entire life because that show must have recouped a thousand per cent and more for the investors.

Still, I have no professional regrets as *Cats* put a lot of cream back into my career. The concept of the show was that all cats are invited to the 'Jellicle Ball' where one cat gets another chance at life. That cat was to be Grizabella, who has lived most of her nine lives; Judi Dench was cast in the role, having proved herself musically in *Cabaret* and *The Good Companions*. Big Brian Blessed, whom everyone knew from *Z Cars* and *I*,

Claudius was Old Deuteronomy, and Wayne Sleep was Mr Mistoffelees. Stephen Tate, who had been Judas to my Jesus, was the aged Gus, the theatre cat; and Finola Hughes, whom I would later work with in a Jackie and Joan Collins film called *Nutcracker*, was the 'white cat' featured at the beginning of the show.

I was asked to play the Rum Tum Tugger – who else? He was, as someone described him, 'the pop star puss'. The show's Elvis. I might not have wanted to risk my money, but I needed a job and it was a great opportunity to work with Trevor Nunn and Gillian Lynne.

Also in the cast was a dancer who'd worked with the all-girl dance group Pan's People. Her name was Sarah Brightman. I used to give Sarah a lift to Euston Station where she caught the train home to Hemel Hempstead. Sarah was a laugh. She had a good sense of humour. She had been in Hot Gossip who were run by Arlene Phillips, and had a hit with a song called 'I Lost My Heart to a Starship Trooper'. I'd always thought of Sarah as a dancer and a pop singer. She sang a section at the end of 'Memory', which I was quite taken with, but thought no more of.

One day she made me think again. She had recorded a disco version of 'The Sound of Music' and she played it to me. Suddenly, I heard this wonderful soprano voice and it was clear that this was more than just a parody of Julie Andrews. We were quite good friends in the show. Sarah told me she had a fascination for piano players. That was her thing. She liked musicians, particularly piano players. She told me about this bloke she was seeing. She wouldn't tell me his name, only that he was a piano player and that she was very taken with him. The piano player turned out to be Andrew Lloyd Webber whom she later married.

I recorded a single for Andrew of 'Magical Mr Mistoffelees', as much as a promotion for the show as anything else. It went out in November 1980 and did well on the radio but didn't make the charts. I sang it on Michael Parkinson's chat show and other television shows to promote *Cats*. Andrew would do the interview and I would sing the song.

What concerned me more was me. Could I hack it? I enjoyed dancing but I was not classically trained. Gillian Lynne was a former ballerina with the Royal Ballet and much of the dance in *Cats* would be balletic. I had to start six weeks prior to the rest of the cast to get myself to a standard that would be acceptable as a genuine member of the cast. I wanted to be in the show so no matter how much my muscles ached, I kept at it.

When we started the main rehearsals in Chiswick, Judi Dench and I quickly developed a bond. Judi is of course a fabulous actress who went on to win an Oscar for *Shakespeare in Love* and amongst many parts has played 'M' in the James Bond movies; but, like me, she is not a trained dancer so we found ourselves drawn together.

On the first day, the cast formally met the director Trevor Nunn, Andrew and Gillian. We talked about the general ingredients of the show and how they were going to be achieved. During a tea break Andrew made an announcement. 'I have written a new song for the show which will be sung by Grizabella.' It was all very melodramatic and he added, 'I would like to play it to you.'

Andrew had thought 'Magical Mr Mistoffelees' would be a good song to promote the upcoming production, but clearly he had decided he needed something stronger. He put the tape on and the tune of 'Memory' started to play. I had never heard it before. I had heard all the other songs but this was new. I could feel a tingle run down my back and I thought: that's it. That is the hit song we need for this show. At that point the song only had half a lyric – just the tune and some semblance of words – but that didn't matter, it had captured me.

'Memory' was not directly from a T. S. Eliot poem. It was bits from Eliot's work, magically woven around an almost new tune of Andrew's. I qualify 'almost' because there are so many tunes playing in his head. It is only when they drop into place that a light bulb goes on and then they are polished for their proper setting. This was to be Dame Judi's song as Grizabella – the glamour cat's big song. Tim Rice and Don Black each wrote versions of the lyric, but the final version was created by Trevor Nunn who used fragments of Eliot's existing poems and moulded them together. In deference to Eliot, I think that was the best solution.

We were rehearsing every day. We would begin each morning with an hour's warm-up. We had to be able to touch our toes and stretch our hamstrings plus tone up our muscles. I was thirty-four and quite fit but not dancer fit. I couldn't put my legs behind my head or twist my body like a piece of spaghetti and I knew Judi couldn't either. Judi and I were generally hiding at the back of the class, hopefully just out of Gillie's eyeline, while Wayne Sleep and the rest of the cast were leaping all over the place.

Gillian Lynne was a complete perfectionist. She was in her early fifties but she had the energy of a teenager. Excitement was building. This was a big chance for Gillian and she was determined not to let it slip by. Her energy never ever faltered; I worked with her again more than thirty years later on the Jerry Herman show *Dear World* when she was eighty-seven. Even then she took a warm-up class in the morning; she was as agile as ever and it nearly killed me.

Trevor Nunn seemed to be nipping in and out, making points here and there; but when it came to staging the dance, he was clever enough to leave that to Gillian. What Trevor bought to the production was structure – and, with John Napier's wonderful set, an environment for the cats to live in. Trevor gave every cat a character and one word that identified that particular cat and gave the dancer a clear sense of who they were. As the Rum Tum Tugger, my word was 'capricious'. Once I'd looked it up I thought, that makes sense.

Judi and I were still at the back during rehearsals. We weren't touching the stars with our toes but we were getting better. Then one afternoon Judi was walking across the rehearsal room – not even dancing, just a normal walk – when suddenly she had a terrible pain in the back of her leg and collapsed on the floor. We all rushed over but there was nothing we could do. She could not walk. She was in agony. Her face was contorted in pain. There was no screaming but I could see how much she was suffering. She'd snapped the hamstring in her leg walking across the floor. Whether the exercise had contributed to it I don't know, but she'd snapped a hamstring and we were two weeks away from opening.

The first plan was to wait until she'd recovered but that was never going to be possible. It was clear that Judi couldn't continue with the show, so the call went out for Elaine Paige. Elaine had gone from the chorus of *Hair* and *Superstar* to playing Sandy opposite me in *Grease* and also Rita in the musical *Billy*. *Evita* had made her a name and it was that name that jumped into Andrew's mind after Judi injured herself.

The one thing the show needed – and it is amazing how these things work out – was someone who could really sing 'Memory'; give it the power and emotion it needed.

Judi is a wonderful actress and has had great reviews in musicals, and she would have done a great version of that song. I imagine it would have been an actor's performance but perhaps without the big theatrical finish the song became famous for. What it needed was a 'big voice' and Elaine Paige has one. With Elaine performing the showcase number, *Cats* had its big finish. Barbara Streisand had a hit with 'Memory'. Elaine recorded it along with six hundred people and performed it many times on television which helped to promote the show.

Still, it was an edge-of-the-seat production. It wasn't until the evening of the first preview that Cameron had gathered together the last £10,000 of the budget and even then Andrew had personally guaranteed a giant chunk of the money.

Opening night at the rubbish dump arrived. I was still wondering how the audience were going to receive *Cats*. The feline creatures were everywhere, leaping out of dustbins, scooting and crawling around John Napier's set which was built to cat's scale, about three and a half times normal size. I knew audiences would be intrigued by the set. The New London Theatre had been a dud up to this point. However, what it did provide was a revolving stage. The best seats were reserved for those seated on the revolving stage and, as the overture began, the audience found themselves slowly moving as the stage began to revolve. Cats' eyes flashed from every corner of the theatre. The audience were completely disorientated. What a great opening.

No one cared about the plot. This was all about production. Which is where the magic of Trevor Nunn and Andrew and Cameron came in. The concept, the perception and the vision. That is what tilted *Cats* into such an enormous hit. It was as if Gillian Lynne had squeezed every ounce of energy into every dancer's leotard. Now it was bursting onto the stage of the New London Theatre.

When Elaine sang 'Memory' for the first time live in public, it tore the place apart. This was Grizabella the glamour cat at full throttle. It was sheer musical theatre and what you strive for – a showstopper!

87

As the Rum Tum Tugger I was like that landmark Esso advert – 'A tiger in the tank'. I could not be tied down. He was a strutting, capricious cat who seemed to jump here, there and everywhere. I said to Trevor, 'What the Tugger needs is a big entrance. Why don't we have him smash open the cyc at the back of the set and enter that way?' Trevor thought it was a good idea so that's how I entered.

My opening number had a big dance break in the middle and I thought, there's no way I can stay on stage and cut this, dancing with all these fantastic dancing cats. I have to think of something else. My plan was to spray the audience with a large tin of deodorant because to cats humans smell bad. I put this to Trevor Nunn but he thought Health and Safety might not take too kindly to me spraying the audience. We agreed I could run around the audience and fool around, sit on people's laps, stroke their hair and behave like a cat. A very cool cat, of course.

When Prince Charles came to see the show, I found the famous bald spot and ruffled the hair around it. When Princess Grace of Monaco came, I sat on her lap. It gave the audience a little humour and a chance to laugh and it was totally in character for the Rum Tum Tugger.

The first act finishes with the big set-piece 'The Jellicle Ball' and again my dancing was probably not strong enough so I thought it best to leave. On my way off stage I would come across the nasty master criminal cat Macavity whom I would nut (headbutt) and continue to walk off. It always got a few laughs, usually from a handful of geezers who'd been dragged along against their will to watch a lot of poncey dancing. I'm sure that moment isn't still in!

A bomb scare didn't take the sparkle off the opening night. The audience loved us but we could not take our bows. Brian Blessed had to go on stage and ask people to leave the theatre, telling them, 'This is serious.' A man with an Irish accent had called saying there were three bombs in the stage revolve. Nothing was ever found. As it turned out, it was a new form of musical theatre that had exploded.

In 2019, almost forty years on from the original London production, the film of *Cats* was released. I have yet to see the *Cats* movie but I will. It would seem that it was pretty much condemned before it was released. I'm not sure what the moviegoing public were expecting but I read reports that the cats weren't to scale and were out of proportion with the set and props. I suspect that many moviegoers were expecting a more cuddly Disney cartoon film which *Cats* isn't.

There's not much I can say other than the bits I've seen from the trailer seemed pretty representative of the show. I'm sure Andrew would have kept a close eye on the film so perhaps it just doesn't transfer so well from theatre to film. Hugh Jackman as *The Greatest Showman* worked as an original film musical, *Grease* worked from stage to film, and both have strong storylines as does *Les Misérables*. *Cats* doesn't have a strong underlying narrative and is very much a musical ballet. Unless you love to watch dance and enjoy the music there isn't a great deal of story or characters for an audience to get involved with. In the theatre you feed off the performers and are swept along by their energy and physicality. Once that's removed and without a strong narrative it makes it doubly difficult to touch the audience.

CHAPTER EIGHT

Just Good Friends

Penny: 'No Quasimodo jokes! People always make Quasimodo jokes visiting Notre Dame'
Vince: 'Yeah. It's enough to give you the hump'
  – *Just Good Friends*, 1986

T HE BLUE TOUCH PAPER under my career was lit but it was still waiting to really take off. An opportunity appeared. Tim Rice had a bee in his bonnet about Richard the Lionheart and the Crusades. In 1970 Tim and Andrew Lloyd Webber had developed a children's musical around that theme called *Come Back Richard, Your Country Needs You*. Now, Andrew was working on his own material and Tim created *Blondel*, a two-act play with music by Stephen Oliver who had won attention for scoring the Royal Shakespeare Company's *Nicholas Nickleby*.

When Tim conceived the show it was a small-scale satire based around those medieval adventures. By 1983 the ambition was much inflated and it was now to be a big musical about King Richard being rescued from an Austrian prison by Blondel, the wandering minstrel. Stephen Oliver's experience was mostly in opera and the ideas for *Blondel* were operatic. It was a witty musical farce with four singing monks who narrated the story with a cappella harmonies. Cameron Mackintosh asked me to play Blondel as a minstrel pop singer.

Blondel reopened the Old Vic, which had been completely refurbished by its owner, Canadian businessman Ed Mirvish. The gala performance was to be attended by the Queen Mother and Sir Laurence Olivier. Lord Olivier was there to make a speech celebrating the theatre's reopening. He didn't have a dressing room and asked if he could share mine. I said of course. He was very gracious. I could never have imagined when wearing a leopard skin with Screaming Lord Sutch that one day I would be sharing a dressing room with Sir Laurence Olivier.

Following the performance we were presented to Her Royal Highness who was very jolly and personable. Blondel had a backing group called the Blondettes and my big final song was called 'I'm a Monarchist'. One of the newspapers called it a 'polished pantomime' which was about right. The *Daily Telegraph* thought it 'a good-natured romp which nevertheless failed to hit the heights'. Despite some even more disparaging notices, we moved from the Old Vic to the Aldwych Theatre in the West End where we played 278 performances.

I didn't have much time to get depressed about it as the role of my career was just around the corner. Soon everyone would hear about Vince and Penny and the sitcom *Just Good Friends*.

The writer John Sullivan, as I mentioned earlier, just happened to have seen me in a TV play called *A Little Rococo*. I arrived home one evening and there was a script waiting for me. It was the first episode of a new TV sitcom. I read it and thought it was very funny. Gold dust. I was surprised that they wanted to see me as I was doing musical theatre at that time.

It was arranged that I go to the BBC to meet with John, the producer Ray Butt, and Jan Francis, who I vaguely knew from seeing her on television, to talk about the show. I turned up at the BBC Centre and sitting in reception was this very attractive girl – Jan Francis. We introduced ourselves to each other and I said I thought the script was good and she agreed. We were trying to laugh off our nerves, rather than be dreadfully serious about the audition. We made each other laugh and seemed to get on well. A hint of the chemistry to come. This is always a good thing if you are going to audition with someone.

Hoping that perhaps we might get away with just meeting them, we went in to see John Sullivan and Ray Butt. Ray (who sadly died in the summer of 2013) was very 'sarf London', a short man who looked like Kenneth Connor from the *Carry On* films. He kept calling us 'mes enfants' which always made me die. John was very quiet and introverted like a lot of writers, and also from south London.

We told them we liked the script and then they asked us to read. I read the part of Vince Pinner, who was a working-class character from Walthamstow, and Jan read this slightly aristocratic, middle-class girl from Chipping Ongar, Essex. John had had the idea while reading the problem pages in one of his wife's magazines. There was a letter from a woman who, five years after being left at the altar, had once again met the man who jilted her. The woman's problem was that to her surprise – not to say distress – she found there was still something about him that she liked. This was the basis of Vince and Penny's relationship, which rekindled romance into my life and the public's imagination.

What was so clever was that here was a situation comedy that had an ongoing storyline with a constant cliffhanger. Would Vince and Penny get together again? Would they finally make it to the altar a second time around? I thought the writing was excellent.

Jan and I read and they seemed quite happy. Ray said alright and John said yeah. Ray and John seemed to know what they wanted and it wasn't too long until I got the call saying the part was mine. Jan dithered a little as she wasn't sure if she wanted to play Penny. She had a background in straight drama including three series of *Secret Army*, the popular World War Two drama about a group helping Allied airmen escape occupied Europe. She hadn't performed much in front of a 'live' audience since earlier in her career. She'd also just got a good part in a new movie, *Champions*, the story of the jockey Bob Champion. So there was a nervous waiting period before we became a television couple.

Jan wanted to see three episode scripts to help her make a decision. Yes, it made absolute sense to read three episodes to see if the quality of writing was sustained. I really loved the characters and I thought Jan was the perfect Penny. She was gorgeous, refined and vulnerable and I enjoyed working with her. I wanted to get going with the show. It felt so right.

In the meantime, John Sullivan and Ray Butt came to see me in *Cats*. I took them for a drink after the show and they told me they were still waiting for Jan's decision. They were very keen for her to do it. Being a compulsive worrier, I thought they might not go ahead without her. I hadn't a clue we were going to make a little bit of television history, although I did believe we were on to a winning series so I was crossing everything.

Another two scripts arrived and they were equally funny. There was something so special about the writing. This was a sex and class war but there was never anything unkind. I was really pleased with it, so I was relieved when Jan decided she would do the show.

We did some outside filming for the first episode. Then, we did the first show in front of a live audience. We were both very nervous. It was a new experience for us but we had rehearsed and we knew our lines and the audience were laughing. Jan and I just clicked and the studio audience really took to the show; you could just feel it was genuine. They understood the characters and the situation instantly. That coupled with the brilliance of John's writing and Ray's direction made me feel that we had a hit show.

John and Ray were exceptionally pleased; you could tell they were happy with the result and we all felt that we were onto a winner and that the BBC would commission a series with Jan and me playing Vince and Penny. At that point, we were only booked to do the pilot episode which meant that if one of us didn't cut the mustard, they could recast. I had no illusions about that.

John Howard Davies, who was then the BBC Head of Comedy, was not convinced that I was right for the part of Vince. John had been an actor (he played Oliver Twist in the classic 1948 film) and had seen the pilot episode and wasn't sure about me. I think that having been a pop singer a few years before didn't help. He felt that I might not be able to sustain the character over six episodes.

I felt that the writing and the reality of the situation was such that this was not a sitcom to be played in the style of *Hi-de-Hi!* or *'Allo 'Allo!* It was about real people, in real situations, that the audience at home could identify with. It was not a farce. A lot of sitcoms seem a little hysterical. This is usually because a lot of the time the actors are nervous and groping for their lines. Plus they're delivering laugh lines for the first time and are never really sure what the audience's reaction will be.

I thought that the essence of Vince's character was that he wasn't flash, he was naive. You didn't need to overplay him. Vince – like John Sullivan – was always trying to give up smoking and he had this placebo, a plastic cigarette. In the first show Vince tells Penny about a visit to an acupuncturist to try and help him give up smoking. Penny asks Vince, 'Did you feel a prick?'

Vince replies 'Well, I did feel a bit silly.'

The lines were so well written that it was unnecessary to hit the back wall, and that was one of the compliments that John Sullivan paid me. What he liked was that I was letting the lines play themselves. But I think John Howard Davies may have preferred – and to be fair he only had one episode on which to judge – that my performance was a little more 'Jack the Lad'.

Ray Butt decided to do some intensive research. He screened the pilot for three BBC secretaries who gave me the thumbs-up. I am grateful that John Howard Davies was big enough to change his mind and allowed me to do the show.

I had done a sitcom in 1979 called *Two Up, Two Down* with Su Pollard who went from there to become Peggy in *Hi-de-Hi!* We were two revolutionary squatters who took over a terraced house in Manchester, much to the annoyance of the newlyweds who'd just moved in. It was a great learning vehicle for me and meant I was not a novice at the format, but we shot it like a normal TV play – there was no audience.

With *Just Good Friends*, neither Jan nor I knew to begin with what working with a live sitcom audience was like, tackling a first night every week. It's nerve-shredding no matter how experienced you are as everything can and often does go wrong. It's always full on no matter how many times you do it. You can work in front of a live audience. You can work in front of a camera. Put the two together and it becomes a little more difficult.

It was something we both had to learn and, as the show progressed, the critics – as well as the public – agreed we had. Jan and I got on so well as people and I think we were able to communicate this through our characters. The trick is to know your lines as you don't have a lot of time. You see the script for the first time on Tuesday, read it through, block it and rehearse that week with a run-through on Saturday morning for lighting and camera. Then Sunday evening you do the show live in front of an audience. You have to know your lines well enough so that you can say them automatically without thinking, because if you don't, when the red light goes on and the studio audience start laughing, it's quite easy for your memory to go for a walk in the park. I know that sounds like a very obvious thing but there is knowing your lines and *really* knowing your lines. Some episodes were just two-handers and that meant sixty pages of dialogue to be learned in five days. On a movie you might have ten pages a week.

The audience were great; they knew they were there to laugh and they always played their part beautifully. Even if we made a mistake and had to redo a scene they'd laugh again. The audience were very important and their reaction was very helpful because it gave the director a guide on how to edit the show; what the audience found really funny or just funny. The real audience, of course, were sitting at home watching the television.

John Sullivan had started off as a scene shifter at the BBC because he didn't know quite how to get into television even though he'd been writing. He had already done *Citizen Smith* with Robert Lindsay as 'the 'Che Guevara of Tooting' and *Only Fools and Horses* with David Jason as, of course, the perfect Del Boy. He'd had two enormous hits and now Jan and I were in the front line of his attempt at a hat-trick.

Luckily, the producing reins were again in the hands of Ray Butt, who happily complemented John's work. There was nothing luvvie about their relationship or indeed about the show. There was no theatricality about it. Ray did not muck about. He was a really good, workmanlike producer/director who knew what he wanted and I thought he was a terrific help and great influence on John. The pair of them were like a couple of brothers, Ray being the older. John would say, 'We've been around since dinosaurs ruled the world.' Ray was very experienced and knew where the laughs were. He was forever going on about comedy timing: 'The rule of three, mes enfants.' He was a great teacher for me.

John's most famous sitcom is *Only Fools and Horses* which is still repeated on television and is everyone's favourite, and has now become a hit West End musical written by John's son Jim Sullivan and Paul Whitehouse. John was a generous man who died far too early, aged sixty-four, in April 2011, after suffering viral pneumonia for six weeks.

Just Good Friends changed my professional life. It reflected the power of television, especially in the mid-eighties. People didn't have satellite or cable television so when a show took off, the whole nation watched. People have such good memories of the series that in 2020 we were talking about a reunion show. If Gavin and Stacey can do it, why not Vince and Penny? Although it might look a bit pathetic playing Vince at seventy-six... but then again... No, I don't think so.

I was on tour with *Blondel* in Bath prior to the London opening at the Old Vic when the first episode was shown. I didn't watch it because I was on stage, but the next morning I was in Bath city centre and people kept coming up to me and saying, 'I saw the show last night. Great!' That was when I knew it was a hit.

The great thing about the public is you can tell if something works. You don't have to wait for the ratings because you can tell from people's reactions. There is a distinct difference between people being genuine about how they feel about something and people just saying what they think you want to hear. People were very excited about that show. The only thing I was concerned about was whether it would sustain over the coming weeks.

It did and it became a very, very big hit. My instinct, my nose, in reading it for the first time was correct. It went to number three in the ratings the following week. We went on to make three more series and a couple of specials. A Christmas show brought in twenty-two million viewers and is in the Top Ten of the most watched shows of all time. *Just Good Friends* had a regular audience of close to fifteen million and won a BAFTA award for Best Sitcom. I was also nominated for a BAFTA for Best Comedy Performance.

It gave me a lot of clout. Vince was a lovable rogue whom audiences, both men and women, identified with. There was a lot of newspaper/magazine interest in me and I had lots of requests for interviews. Journalists would try and equate me with the character of Vince. You wait all your life as a performer to get your name known. What's important is that you make sure that your character isn't more identifiable than you.

On soaps like *Coronation Street* and *EastEnders* (and I found this out for myself), the character name is usually better known than the performer. I was more interested in using Vince Pinner to promote Paul Nicholas. I wanted to exploit my own name and show how different I was to Vince Pinner. So instead of having the newspapers try and portray me as Vince Pinner, I made sure I had lots of photographs taken with Linzi and the kids to give myself an image that was the complete antithesis of Vince.

The whole fame thing was very interesting. I didn't particularly like it. I'm not someone who enjoys too much attention. People are very nice, they only want your autograph, but it made me a little bit uncomfortable. I was a little embarrassed by it. I was voted the sexiest man on television and had all the attention anyone could want. I was also elected 'Britain's Best-Dressed Man'. I think that was because Vince wore rather nifty suits. My family went into shock as I've always been a bit of a scruff.

Once I'd had that break with *Just Good Friends* my first instinct was to ensure my family's security. When you are in a profession that is extremely fickle and you have responsibilities to your family, you have to provide as well as you can and when you can. I was now fortunate to be able to do that. *Just Good Friends* had helped to make my name and that was good for all of us.

The tricky thing about showbusiness is that you're never sure what your next job is going to be, or who you will be working with. Before the first series of *Just Good Friends,* I got a call from my agent telling me that he'd had an inquiry for me on a film called *Invitation to the Wedding.* I asked who was in it. He said, 'Two nights.'

'Two nights? That's not very long. I was hoping for at least six weeks.'

'No, the two knights – Sir John Gielgud and Sir Ralph Richardson.' Not enough for a round table.

CHAPTER NINE

Jealousy

'Stop laughing, dear boy'
  – Sir John Gielgud to Paul Nicholas, 1984

YOU KNOW THAT SHOW BUSINESS is fickle, but it's also packed by strange coincidences and paths that cross and criss-cross. My friend Paul Jabara – Herod to my Jesus – and I wrote a song in 1974 titled 'When You're a Lord'. It was for a movie called *The Lords of Flatbush* about a Brooklyn street gang. Sylvester Stallone, Perry King and Henry Winkler – who was still to become The Fonz on *Happy Days* – starred as New York gang members.

The producer of the movie was Joseph Brooks. He'd made a fortune writing songs like 'I'd Like to Teach the World to Sing' (the Coca-Cola anthem) and the worldwide hit 'You Light Up my Life' for Debbie Boone, Pat Boone's daughter. He had a lot of money and he wanted to spend it on his wife Susan Brooks, who was an actress. He was very much in love with his wife and wanted to do something special for her. The best thing you can do for any actress is put her in a starring role in a movie. It was titled *Invitation to the Wedding*. Joseph Brooks produced and directed the film and composed the music.

It was to be filmed in Britain and he wanted nothing but the best talent to co-star with his wife. Not only did he get Sir John Gielgud, he also got Sir Ralph Richardson as well as the lighting genius of cinematographer Freddie Young. Freddie was a triple Oscar winner for *Lawrence of Arabia*, *Doctor Zhivago* and *Ryan's Daughter*, and terrific actors like John Standing, Elizabeth Shepherd and Ronald Lacey were also cast. And me.

I had the most difficult job. I was the 'love interest' for Mrs Brooks. The part Joe wanted me for was an American on a visit to the Home Counties, who meets and falls in love with a young girl, played by Joe's wife Susan.

I was on holiday in Cornwall when I got the call; they brought me back to London to do a screen test. Joseph Brooks was besotted with his wife and, as a result, was very particular about who he cast as the leading man. I did the film test and got the part. A week later, I started on the film which had been written by William Fairchild.

It was the story of a girl who was supposed to marry one man but falls in love with another (my character); she ends up leaving her intended at the altar to be with me. It was a little like Dustin Hoffman and Katharine Ross in *The Graduate*. It was all set in and around a typical English village. Sir Ralph Richardson played the local vicar and Sir John Gielgud was an American evangelist.

I was asked if I could ride a horse; I said no. There were a couple of romantic scenes with Susan and myself on horseback. It wasn't really about riding, it was about sitting on the horse and walking, so they weren't too much of a problem. It was doing the love scenes when things became really difficult.

Joe Brooks was very possessive of his young wife. He had the potential to be very jealous. Susan was very beautiful and I suspected that Joe thought that every man on the set, including myself, was after her. Joe would get particularly tense whenever we had to play any romantic moments and I sensed that we might have some problems when it came to our first screen kiss.

Unfortunately, Joe suffered from a terrible stammer and when he became stressed, it would get considerably worse.

The day of our big love scene arrived and poor Joe was getting extremely agitated. He'd worked it all out. He took me to one side and said, 'Remember Paul, this is not *Emmanuelle*. This is a light romantic comedy and the scene should be played as such, okay?'

I said, 'Absolutely Joe.'

'Okay Paul, I want you to take Susan in your arms and hold her – not too tight. I want you to look into her eyes, tell her that you love her and very slowly, very gently kiss her. I will count to three and you will break. Got it?' he asked.

'Got it Joe.' I'm thinking, this guy's lost it.

So the camera was set up and Freddie Young lit the scene beautifully. Susan and I rehearsed the scene but without the kiss. Joe by now was getting a little edgy but was doing his best to control his stammer, which was becoming a little more pronounced by the minute.

'Okay g-g-guys,' he said. 'Are w-w-we set? Speed, c-c-camera...' He whispered the word, '... a-action.'

Susan and I were standing facing each other. I took her into my arms. Not too tight. We looked into each other eyes. I told her that I loved her. Slowly, ever so slowly, our heads moved together for the 'gentle' kiss. It was all going to plan but in that millisecond before our lips touched, I thought, sod it! I gave her the biggest tongue sandwich I could muster.

Joe is in shock. He can barely speak. His stammer is completely out of control. 'O-o-o-o-o-one, t-t-t-t-t-t-t-t-two...' He couldn't get to th-th-th-th-thh. Finally, blue in the face, he screamed, 'C-c-c-c-c-c-c-cuuuut!!!' I looked at Susan, Susan looked at me and we both collapsed in a heap, screaming with laughter.

For me the bonus was working with Sir John Gielgud and Sir Ralph Richardson. Sir Ralph was quite elderly and finding it difficult to remember his lines and he needed help. I always felt sorry for him because here was this great actor who was now having to rely on cue cards because his memory was beginning to fail him quite badly. He was frustrated by that. The wonderful thing about Sir Ralph was that when he did deliver his lines, the marvellous twinkle and great charm was still there. No matter how difficult he found it, the years could not diminish his skill as an actor. He was always superb.

John Gielgud was famous for having a very distinctive voice. He was also famous for not being terribly good with accents. In the film, he was playing an American evangelist who flies in from the southern state of Alabama to officiate at the wedding. I was full of great anticipation. This was to be a moment I would never forget. I was about to play my first scene with one of the world's greatest actors. The scene was set with us all seated at the dinner table waiting for him to appear. On 'action', Sir John was supposed to burst into the room and announce his arrival.

'Speed, camera, action!'

The door flew open and in walks Sir John as the American evangelist, dressed all in white. White cowboy boots, white suit and a large white Stetson. He opens his mouth and delivers his opening line.

'Howdy folks. I've just flown in from Alabama and I'm right pleased to be here and happy to meet ya all.'

There was a stunned silence. It was the worst American accent any of us had ever heard. It sounded like he had just flown in from Reykjavik, not Alabama. Added to this, he looked completely ridiculous in his white cowboy outfit.

Up until that point I had been feeling very reverential about the whole enterprise but as soon as he opened his mouth, I got the giggles. I did my best but I could not contain myself. What began as a stifled giggle grew into hysterical laughter; and to make matters worse, the rest of the cast were acting as if they hadn't noticed and that this was Sir John at his most brilliant which made me laugh even more.

Finally, Sir John walked over and, very nicely, clipped me around the ear and said, 'Stop laughing, dear boy.'

It was difficult but, like Ralph Richardson, he was a very charming man and I could see that he knew why I was laughing.

Apparently a recording exists of a truly dreadful radio production of Gielgud as Sherlock Holmes, with Richardson as Dr Watson, in which he pretends to be a coalman in disguise and utters the memorable line, 'Good morning, matey, would you care for a bag of coal?' in his customary golden tenor tones.

Richardson replies: 'My dear friend Holmes. Your voice, your face are entirely unrecognisable!'

When the film came out *Just Good Friends* had hit the screen and was very popular, so they switched the advertising in favour of me. I am sorry to say the movie never made any great impact. The thrill for me was working with these two icons of British theatre. Something I will always cherish. I've been very lucky in that respect, working with legendary names from the twentieth century, pioneers in the entertainment business.

Still, I was about to be made bankrupt but happily, only on television.

My effort to avoid being solely identified as Vince Pinner had succeeded. I was now Neil Walsh, an altogether different character; thankfully, one that the British viewers liked almost as much as Vince. From the start Neil had the whiff of a man who does dodgy deals with even dodgier people. The audience first saw him in the bankruptcy court over a less than solid cement deal, owing the bank £129,000. The chap in front of him was declared bankrupt for £2 million and Neil shook his head and said: 'That's where I went wrong. Not enough ambition.'

The series, which they called *Bust,* was very successful for ITV as it pulled in more than eleven million viewers on a Friday night. Phyllis Logan (renowned for Mrs Hughes in *Downton Abbey*) co-starred in the first series as my beleaguered wife Sheila. Belinda Lang (Bill Porter in the BBC sitcom *2point4 Children*) took over the part for the second series. Geraldine Alexander was Janet, the bank trustee handling my financial affairs. It was the mid-1980s. The time of Margaret Thatcher, yuppies and mobile phones and it was perfect.

I felt a change of gear from *Just Good Friends* was right for me as the public were so used to me doing comedy and this was drama. It would give me the chance to show I could play something else. Cab drivers liked the show, so it was obviously working. We did two series of *Bust* until Neil got out of bankruptcy.

I seemed to have found the Midas touch for television. I was in great demand for all sorts of work. Celeste Holm, who in 1956 had co-starred with Frank Sinatra, Grace Kelly and Bing Crosby in *High Society*, agreed to appear with me at a Royal Variety Performance for the Queen. I had always loved the film *High Society* so it was a real thrill for me to perform with Celeste. I was twelve when it was released. I saw it four times and so I knew who Celeste Holm was and I certainly knew the song. We did 'Who Wants to be a Millionaire'.

Royal Variety Performances are always a bit chaotic. I met Celeste on the day of the show, we put something simple together and suddenly we were on. I thought our performance worked and we received a great reception.

In all, between 1984 and 1989 I appeared at four Royal Variety shows. For the 1986 one I appeared live from the Victoria Palace Theatre where Cyd Charisse and I were appearing in *Charlie Girl*. Cyd performed a number from the show, and the company and I sang 'Fish and Chips'. While I was standing in the wings, I heard a voice say, 'Hello Paul.' I turned round and there were Paul and Linda McCartney. I was somewhat taken aback that they knew who I was and we started to chat. It turned out that they were both big fans of *Just Good Friends*. I was very flattered.

This was the second time that I had seen Paul McCartney in the flesh. I first saw the Beatles in 1963 when I was eighteen, at the Majestic Ballroom in Finsbury Park. Brian Epstein, their manager, had put together a package tour featuring the Beatles, Gerry and the Pacemakers, Billy J. Kramer and the Dakotas and The Big Three. I remember we were waiting to hear Paul McCartney sing 'Long Tall Sally' because it was rumoured that he sang it in the key of G which is a tone (two notes) higher than Little Richard's version. He sang it that night in G and we were blown away.

I always enjoyed appearing in the Royal Variety Performance as occasionally you got to work with old friends, such as in 1989 when David Essex, Michael Ball and I got together and performed a tribute to Andrew Lloyd Webber's music.

My favourite Royal Variety, though, took me back to the Victoria Palace Theatre where my dad back in the 1950s had taken me as a boy to see the Crazy Gang. It now gave me the opportunity to work with some great old-time comedians: Billy Dainty, Leslie Crowther, Jimmy Cricket and Bernie Winters. I'd watched them all on TV variety shows over the years, and now it felt great to have a connection with these old pros of variety. I felt that I was joining a very exclusive club, albeit for one night only. I became an honorary member.

The orchestra struck up 'Comedy Tonight' from the Stephen Sondheim musical *A Funny Thing Happened on the Way to the Forum*. I started to sing, the company danced and one by one the comedians would come on, crack a gag and I would act as their feed. I made it to the end of the first verse before Bernie Winters entered carrying a bunch of flowers.

'How very sweet. Who are the flowers for Bernie?'

'Well you see Paul, we're celebrating. One of the young ladies in the show is going to have a baby.'

'Really? Which one?'

'I don't know. I haven't made me mind up yet.'

I get four lines into the second verse and Jimmy Cricket enters wearing one glove.

'Excuse me, why are you wearing one glove?'

'I heard the weather forecast today. It said it was going to be sunny, but on the other hand it was going to get cold.'

And so it went on.

Leslie Crowther: 'Down with the Empire! Down with the Empire!'

Me: 'Who are you?'

Leslie: 'The manager of the Odeon.'

A few lines later:

Billy Dainty: 'What's the difference between a buffalo and a bison?'

Me: 'I don't know. What is the difference?'

Billy: 'You can't wash your hands in a buffalo.'

The number then went into 'Be a Clown' and more acts trooped on; and we finished with 'Comedy! Comedy! Comedy! Toooniiiight!'

Quick, energetic and a fun opening for the show. It was great to work with those old pros: they knew what they were doing up there. They had energy. They hit their mark and their timing was impeccable. Sadly only Jimmy Cricket and I are still here and Jimmy's a year younger than me. I'd better get a move on and finish this book!

When everyone – agents, advisers, Linzi and myself – thought I could do no wrong on television, I made a terrible mistake. I started working with animals.

The series was again for ITV. It was titled *Close to Home* and was about a divorced vet bringing up two children and fending off the incursions of his former wife. It was based on an American sitcom called *Starting from Scratch* which Greg Dyke, then programming director for London Weekend Television (LWT), had picked up. The writer-creator of the U.S. version was Brian Cooke who had written shows like *Man about the House* and *Father, Dear Father* in Britain. He had moved to California and got *Starting from Scratch* on the air. He was going to redo the scripts for British TV, along with other writers. The plan was to adopt the American method of 'team' writing. Sadly, Brian Cooke was not around to oversee the team's efforts.

We had a good cast. Angharad Rees, who played Demelza in the original 1970s television adaptation of *Poldark*, was my former wife and the kids were played by Lucy Benjamin and Andrew Read.

It was quite a nice series but it didn't work terribly well. My veterinarian James Shepherd was never going to worry James Herriot of *All Creatures Great and Small*. There were lots of jokes about tarnished goldfish and parrot gags, some sexual innuendo on the mating habits of cats. That sort of thing.

They thought the idea of me and little animals would work. I was looking for a new series and I wanted to work for London Weekend again having had quite a good track record with them. I listened to the wrong people because when I looked at a video of the American version I thought it was okay. It worked in America but was not that good. By the time it had been rewritten for an English cast, it was even less funny. It just didn't work.

I had made a mistake and luckily I was self-aware enough to know that. We did two series and I admire LWT for trying. They did their best but, despite their efforts, it just didn't work. I should have trusted my instinct, and that was a turning point for me.

No one wants to be involved in something that is a miss, particularly when it is as high profile as a prime-time television series. The terrible thing for an artist on television is that if you find yourself in a non-runner, you are the one who suffers. The writers may go on to write something else, the producer could go on and make another programme; but you, the star, are labelled as the failure for the show and have to bear the cross. It does you no favours at all and it is very difficult to recover from. That said, the trade-off is absolutely right: if you are a success you receive the plaudits that go with that. The profession is full of ups and downs, and you must ride it out no matter how turbulent it is.

Since that moment with *Close to Home* I decided that, whatever I do, I would listen to people but if I had any doubts about something or did not believe in something one hundred per cent myself, I wouldn't be swayed. I have been in show business all of my life and I am going to get it wrong sometimes. I resolved never to lose sight of that again.

CHAPTER TEN

Fame

'There's a sucker born every minute'
  – Phineas T. Barnum, 1861

TELEVISION IS A DRUG especially when you are on it. It had given me an overwhelming share of fame but it had also taught me a severe lesson about how to make my own choices. *Just Good Friends* had been very good to me but I knew I had to keep separating myself from the Vince character. I had the pop world, some movies and the theatre, but it was Vince who brought me to the public's attention. He was funny and charming and with a lot of heart. He was also a little bit of a rogue. Britain loves the 'cheeky chappie' image, whether he is a Del Boy or George Cole's naughty and mischievous Arthur Daley in *Minder*. Vince was a man-about-Basildon version of both. He made me very well known.

Some actors can stand at stage doors talking about themselves for hours to people they don't know and are very comfortable with that. They make all kinds of public appearances, such as opening fetes. The only thing I ever opened was 'Truckfest' in Peterborough, the town where I was born. It's a festival that celebrates big trucks. I was driven to a hotel and was flown from there by helicopter to a packed speedway arena to make my big entrance. It was so embarrassing. We landed right in the middle of the arena and our arrival was announced over the loudspeaker to somewhat indifferent applause. People were waiting to see the 'star' arrive and I was put into this open-top car and driven round the speedway arena, waving to people like a performing chimp.

The chap driving asked me, 'Shall we go around again?'

I said, 'No thank you, I think once is enough.'

I spent all day sitting at a table signing autographs. The most common comment I heard was, 'Oh, you look much younger on the television.' I wasn't comfortable dealing with personal appearances. You have to be polite to people and sign autographs. I find people are generally very nice and don't hassle me, but to be presented as 'Paul Nicholas' outside of a performing context I have always found very, very difficult.

With a couple of exceptions – despite the very good money – I never really got into that. What, ironically, television did do for me was lead me back into the theatre. Theatregoers are fascinated by a television 'name' and that attraction makes them turn out to see you in shows. This was another reason I had to keep Vince Pinner and Paul Nicholas separate. Audiences were not going to see Vince Pinner in *The Pirates of Penzance*. They were going to see Paul Nicholas as the Pirate King.

In 1984, we played *Pirates* at the Manchester Opera House. It was a huge success and Michael Ball's first job. It was interesting to watch him as Frederick, for he had a wonderful voice and was clearly a star in waiting. He made his West End debut only a year later playing Marius in the original London production of *Les Misérables*.

That was after he was cruel to me – in a kind way. The show doesn't begin until the Pirate King gets into the boat and stands on the prow. The overture starts and the boat moves onto the stage. I didn't like arriving on stage for the evening performance too early as I didn't want to go off the boil. Most of the cast appear promptly at the five-minute call, which meant that they were usually standing around waiting for me to appear. I used to arrive on stage about thirty seconds before 'curtain up', and the cast were aware of this and decided to exact their revenge, led by Michael Ball.

One night, without me knowing, they recorded the overture on tape. I was in my dressing room having a fag preparing for the show that night. I was just finishing my second cup of tea with my feet up on the dressing-room table, about to light another cigarette, when suddenly over the tannoy I heard the overture begin to play. Panic set in and my dresser and I started to throw on my costume, mike pack and make-up simultaneously. It didn't occur to me that there had been no five-minute call. I headed for the dressing-room door, pulling my thigh-length leather boots on as I went. I flung open the door and to my surprise, Michael and the entire cast were standing there, pointing at me and roaring with laughter. I was never late again.

It's a matter of respect, and I had so much of that for Harold Fielding. Harold, whom Robert Stigwood had outmanoeuvred with *Superstar*, was a powerful theatrical figure throughout his life. He was a great showman and a very experienced producer. He was also a fan of legends. He had staged one at the London Palladium in 1983 – *Singin' in the Rain*. It cashed in on much of the MGM film's screenplay and used seven of the songs including, of course, the title number. Tommy Steele had adapted the movie, and he directed and co-starred with the late Roy Castle. It was a magnificent production and theatrical achievement.

Harold Fielding was a pioneer of modern theatre and a huge influence. His gift was to know what audiences wanted and what they would spend an evening at the theatre for. He didn't talk down and he didn't overplay. Mostly, he got it right and he did that with his own insight and his own money – he didn't take investors. His insurance was getting a legendary name to appear in his productions. He tempted popular stars of the day like Tommy Steele and Joe Brown, who was one of Britain's first rock-'n'-roll stars. Harold was a romantic impresario, a lavish and enthusiastic producer. His wife Maisie (who died in 1985) was the practical business brain in their relationship.

Harold started building his reputation as Britain began building motorways and people from out of London could more easily travel to see a show. In the post-war 1950s the American tourist industry was gearing up. Harold was a very early exploiter of the charabanc trade from the provinces. What was novel about him was that he was delighted if the critics hated his shows. He knew they were hits and mostly they were: *Half a Sixpence, Charlie Girl, Sweet Charity, Mame* and *The Great Waltz* rolled into the West End during the sixties and seventies.

He was a theatre legend; his first-night parties, sometimes held on the Thames riverboats, were memorable. In fact, sometimes they were more memorable than a show's opening night. Harold was loyal to his productions and would keep the money flowing into them until they found the audience he just knew was out there.

In 1969 when Ginger Rogers arrived by ship to play the lead in *Mame*, she was welcomed at Southampton by a full orchestra playing songs from the musical, and when she got to London she was taken to her hotel in a horse-drawn open carriage. That's showmanship.

You could learn so much just by being around Harold, listening to him. For him, it was always the show that mattered and the show had to go on.

When he staged Noël Coward's *Sail Away* (Savoy, 1962) with Elaine Stritch, it survived a threatened strike by musicians when Harold resigned from the Society of West End Managers and reached a private agreement with the Musicians' Union. 'Although I cannot take my hat off to him morally,' Coward wrote, 'I can certainly drop a grateful curtsey to his guts and determination. He was nothing if not smart.'

Harold's biggest hit was *Charlie Girl* (1965) which was disdained by the critics and provoked the *Daily Telegraph*'s Eric Shorter to describe it as 'charmless, vulgar, obvious and almost wilful in its lack of wit'. While I was charging around trying to be a rock star, the show broke house records and ran at the Adelphi Theatre in the West End for five and a half years (with Joe Brown, Anna Neagle and a young Derek Nimmo who was establishing himself on television with series like *All Gas and Gaiters* and *The World of Wooster*). The happy ending of the updated Cinderella story was acknowledged on stage by Anna Neagle with, 'It's marvellous. Flippin' well marvellous.' And it was.

The show's music was written by David Heneker who in 1958 had contributed the music for *Expresso Bongo*, based on the career of Tommy Steele, which starred Cliff Richard and Laurence Harvey. He later wrote *Half a Sixpence* (adapted from H. G. Wells' *Kipps*) in which Tommy starred both in London and on Broadway; it ran for 679 performances before its year on Broadway in 1965 and subsequent film in 1967. Cameron Mackintosh brought the show triumphantly back to the West End in 2017.

The 1960s production of *Charlie Girl* ran for three years with Joe Brown in the leading role of Joe, after which the hugely popular Liverpudlian Gerry Marsden – of Gerry and the Pacemakers – took over. Two decades later, I was cast in the part. My co-stars were Cyd Charisse, Dora Bryan, Nicholas Parsons (who died, a national treasure, aged 96, in January 2020) and lovely Mark Wynter.

It was a year after Harold's wife Maisie died and, being the sweet man he was, he wanted to revive the show as it had been Maisie's favourite, as much for the box-office success as the show itself.

As a small boy I had watched Cyd in those MGM musicals partnering other legends like Gene Kelly in *Singin' in the Rain* (1952) and Fred Astaire in the movie *Silk Stockings* (1957). It was a dream come true. It was very much down to Harold Fielding that I got to work with her. It was a moment, and I was careful not to step on her toes. Harold had insured her legs for a million pounds.

I danced with the woman who had danced with Gene Kelly and Fred Astaire and that's one of the things that makes show business exciting. It's unpredictable. Cyd was every inch a lady and a star but with Dora Bryan and Nicholas Parsons, it was hard for her – and anyone else – to get a word in. They were both wonderful but you couldn't get them off stage. Dora and Cyd had a duet but Dora and Nicholas would often keep ad libbing, trying to top each other. Cyd was deaf in one ear so she was never certain where they were in the scene. The audiences loved her but Cyd used to sit there every night never quite sure when it was her turn to speak. Still, she was gracious and came in every day and did a full dance warm-up. What I hadn't known until then was that she couldn't tap dance. I'd just assumed it from all the movies, but tap wasn't her discipline. She was a modern ballet dancer.

Successful as the production was (and it ran for nine months), it didn't make its money back. That's the big gamble of commercial theatre. You can run and run but if you're only making your running costs every week you never make your initial capitalisation. In this day and age, to produce a West End musical can cost anywhere between three and five million. The money side of the art of theatre is a science.

Harold Fielding's wife Maisie looked after the financial side and with her gone he had no brake on his romantic ambitions. In 1988, three years after Maisie's death, he invested £2.5 million of his own company's money in *Ziegfeld*, a musical biography based on the life of the legendary American showman. He took a five-year lease on the London Palladium and that's 2,295 seats to fill every performance. But Ziegfeld wasn't a sympathetic central character, even when played by the likeable Canadian star Len Cariou who left the show and was replaced by Topol who had starred in the film *Fiddler on the Roof* as Tevye.

I went to see the show at the Palladium. Ziegfeld opens the show and speaks directly to the audience. He explains, 'When I'm wearing the yellow flower, I am the Narrator; and when I'm not wearing one, I am Ziegfeld.' I thought, oh dear! This isn't going to end well. And it didn't.

Harold tried to save this expensive debacle by making extensive revisions. He had brought in Topol to play Ziegfeld and called in Tommy Steele to take over the direction. Still, after seven months it closed at a loss of £3 million. It was one of the three most expensive failures in theatre history. It was a very expensive production and he had sunk all his own money in it; he was a rich man, but he put in everything he had. Being a proud man, Harold continued to support the show for far too long and at the Palladium there were an enormous number of seats that stayed empty.

There are no guarantees no matter how good the material or how big the stars. The thing about doing a *My Fair Lady* is you do know the product and if you present it in a decent way it stands a chance. Whether the audience want to see it again is another matter, but you've got a substantial piece of work and new audiences are growing up all the time. It's an unpredictable and very risky business.

It was 1986 and I was at the height of my popularity. It was the year that I made my first appearance at the London Palladium, the most famous theatre in the world, in a record-breaking season of *Cinderella* with Des

O'Connor and Dame Anna Neagle. Des, who died aged eighty-eight in November 2020, was someone I admired, a true professional who spent sixty-five years in show business. He was a perfect example of an artist with staying power. He had to take a lot of ribbing over the years but was always a star.

Anna Neagle was eighty-plus when I worked with her and again a true pro. She was playing the Fairy Godmother and I think she had a soft spot for me. She would often say to me, 'If only I were fifty years younger.' I was extremely flattered.

With my career going so well, I was looking for an agent. I needed a good one. I found two: Billy Marsh and Jan Kennedy.

Billy was a very experienced agent. He went a long way back and was very well respected in the business. He handled such great acts as Bruce Forsyth, Norman Wisdom and Morecambe and Wise. Billy was a small, softly spoken man who loved to smoke one cigarette after the other. One of the fascinating things about watching Billy smoke was that he did it in such a way that at least an inch and a half of ash would hang precariously at the end of his fag. It was very stressful wondering whether Billy would manage to get the cigarette from his mouth to the ashtray without the ash spilling all over his suit. Most of the time, he didn't make it. Indeed Eric Morecambe used to quip that when he died, he was leaving Billy ten per cent of his ashes, to be thrown over his lapels.

Jan Kennedy was a former artist who had become an agent and Billy was her mentor. You're never quite sure what you're going to get when you change agents. They all make you feel like you are the most important client in the world, until you join them. Thereafter you become one of forty other artists who proceed to drive them nuts. All you can ever hope for with an agent is that they graft. Jan Kennedy was certainly a grafter. She told me she could get me great deals doing touring productions of major musicals. She also told me I was a star and I half believed her. It was the beginning of a long and happy association and I owe a lot to her and Billy.

Jan was as good as her word. She phoned me one day and asked: 'Can you walk a tightrope?'

I said, 'How much?'

I was cast to play Phineas T. Barnum in the first national tour of *Barnum*. He was the ultimate showman – just look at the movie performance of Hugh Jackman playing him in the singalong musical *The Greatest Showman* (2017). More than three decades earlier, Michael Crawford had created the stage version of P. T. Barnum at the Palladium for a twenty-month run in Cy Coleman, Michael Stewart and Mark Bramble's circus musical.

Barnum is rightly considered to be extremely demanding for the actor playing the lead role, arguably the most demanding musical any performer can take on. Other than the usual acting, singing and dancing, there are certain other skills that are necessary in order to play the part: juggling, unicycling, trampolining and, most difficult of all, learning to walk a tightrope from one side of the stage to the other whilst singing at the same time. Jim Dale, the original Barnum on Broadway, said during rehearsals, 'I can actually walk a wire.' That feat was not in the show until Jim Dale performed it. Thereafter, every Barnum who followed had to walk the wire.

This extra dimension led to a certain mystique surrounding the show. I was in my mid-forties and because of this some people felt it might prove too taxing for me. I wasn't a hundred per cent sure myself so I started training. I was sent to 'Circus Circus', a casino in Las Vegas where the punters gamble surrounded by circus performers doing their acts.

The last time I had been in Las Vegas was in the mid-1970s where at the Hilton International I had seen the king himself, Elvis, perform. Elvis had always been one of my heroes and at that time he still had it. It was an afternoon show and in one of those typical Las Vegas lounge environments. Elvis was in great voice. He looked fantastic but seemed a little bored with it all, and at one point threw a glass of water he was handed into his guitarist's face. Elvis thought it was funny. There were a token eight or nine middle-aged women standing at the foot of the stage. Elvis placed white scarves around their necks. It somehow didn't seem worthy for the king. He was the original, both in appearance and music.

I was met at the airport by my trainers for *Barnum*, Terry and Danuta Parsons. Terry was a former clown and was in charge of all the safety aspects connected with the circus skills in the show. Danuta was a

'Getting older is very liberating because you don't give a hoot.' In traditional dress for a Hindu wedding with Bill, Sheila, Miriam and the groom; buying pants with Bill; in Mexico with Janette and Ian (the Krankies) and Rosemary; with Jan, Wayne and Sheila in front of the Eva Perón balcony in Buenos Aries; me as a ladyboy in Bangkok (my wig was bright blue – I desperately wanted to be a blonde!); and enjoying a hot tub with Dennis in Iceland. (Photos: Twofour)

'This is the dawning': with the writers of *Hair*
James Rado and Gerry Ragni, fellow actor
Olivier Tobias and director Tom O'Horgan

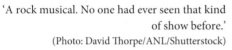

'A rock musical. No one had ever seen that kind
of show before.'
(Photo: David Thorpe/ANL/Shutterstock)

'Serge was tremendously charming
and always had a mischievous look
in his eye': in Paris making the film
Cannabis with Serge Gainsbourg

'My first proper acting job': with
Vanessa Howard in the film
Whatever Happened to Jack and Jill?

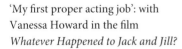

'Have you got any glue?': the beginning of a lifetime of love with Linzi

'I practised a lot in our room in Muswell Hill'

'Over 'ere, Jesus!': being announced to the press as the lead in *Jesus Christ Superstar* (Photo: Getty Images)

'I was lucky to have been a small part of it all': Andrew Lloyd Webber, producer Robert Stigwood, Tim Rice, me and General Manager Bob Swash (Photo: James Gray/ ANL/Shutterstock)

'As I hung there as Jesus I felt so
very vulnerable and alone'
(Photo: John Haynes)

'After checking my hands for stigmata it didn't
take very long for Alf to notice Dana's low-cut
dress': Warren Mitchell as Alf Garnett with me
and Dana Gillespie in the 1972 Christmas
special of *Till Death Us Do Part*

'In the film all the
audience see of me
are my boots': a still
from the 1971 film
See No Evil

'I was more than ready to have some fun': with Elaine Paige as the first British Danny and Sandy in *Grease*
(Photo: Getty Images)

'Ken Russell wanted me to play the nasty, 'orrible Cousin Kevin who terrorises poor, blind Tommy'
(Photo: Shutterstock)

'I was playing a character, a fun youthful chap wearing a bowler hat': my second pop career, in the 1970s

'My friend Paul Jabara was enjoying a huge songwriting career': Paul with Donna Summer who recorded the disco anthem 'Last Dance', which won Paul an Oscar for Best Song

'I was made up as Frankenstein's monster dressed as Hitler. I looked ridiculous': me as Wagner in the Ken Russell film *Lisztomania*

'Suddenly the record was Number Five on the Billboard Top Hundred': receiving a gold disc for sales of over a million copies of 'Heaven on the Seventh Floor' from Al Coury (right), president of RSO Records

'The tremendous bonus of *Sgt. Pepper* for me was working with George Burns'

'The fourth Bee Gee': with Gibb brothers Maurice, Barry and Robin during the making of the *Sgt. Pepper* movie

'The Rum Tum Tugger was, as someone described him, "the pop star puss" – the show's Elvis.' The original production of *Cats*, in 1982

'Stop laughing, dear boy': with Sir John Gielgud in the film *Invitation to the Wedding*

'I always enjoyed appearing in the Royal Variety Performance as occasionally you got to work with old friends, such as in 1989 when David Essex, Michael Ball and I got together and performed a tribute to Andrew Lloyd Webber'

'Jan Francis and I made each other laugh… A hint of the chemistry to come': Vince and Penny in *Just Good Friends*

'*Pirates* at the Manchester Opera House in 1984 was a huge success and Michael Ball's first job. He had a wonderful voice and was clearly a star in waiting'

'I danced with the woman who had danced with Gene Kelly and Fred Astaire': with Cyd Charisse in *Charlie Girl*

'They say you can't teach an old dog new tricks but I'm a living example that you can': the end of Act One of *Barnum* (Photo: Lynn Hilton/ANL/Shutterstock)

'Paul Nicholas, This Is Your Life': surprised by Michael Aspel with the big red book at the *Barnum* curtain call

'I had always said to Linzi, if anybody ever contacts you from *This Is Your Life* the answer is no!': Linzi holds the red book (above right) while I hug my youngest daughter Carmen, and (right) my parents Oscar and Peggy

'The best part of that day was having the award presented by Lionel Bart': receiving the British Academy of Composers & Songwriters Gold Badge for my services to the music industry

'Who pissed on the chips?' – a favourite saying of David Land, seen here celebrating his birthday with his wife Zara, Tim, Andrew and his wife Madeleine, and Linzi and me

'I had always hankered after doing *Singin' in the Rain* because I had been to see it with my mum when I was a little kid': with David Ian, Harold Fielding and Tommy Steele discussing the show over lunch

'Oscar had always wanted to be a lawyer': a drawing of my father presented to him by the satirical magazine *Private Eye* who numbered among his clients

'Oscar was a great guy in many, many ways but he was not the kind of parent who was "hands on"': my father and me aged about two and a half

'As an only child and being the baby, I got a lot of attention and felt secure and loved': me aged about six

'The estate was relatively green and although the house we lived in was rather cramped, I was happy there'

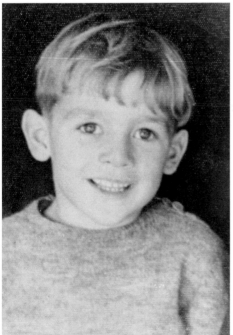

'Most nights of the week, I was a Savage being brutalised by Screaming Lord Sutch'

'My first recording experience was with Sutch and the legendary Joe Meek'

'I was on the British team put together by the Beatles' manager Brian Epstein': the Knokke Festival Song Contest in Belgium with Roger Whittaker, Lois Lane, Gerry Marsden and Dodie West

Adam Garcia in *Saturday Night Fever*
(Photo: Nils Jorgensen/Shutterstock)

On a date night with Linzi

'Robert Stigwood was a remarkable man. I can't think of anybody in show business who has encompassed the breadth of success in so many different areas': Robert with David Ian and me

'Sometimes reviewers differ quite sharply, and *Keeler* is a good example of this': Sarah Armstrong in an iconic pose as Christine Keeler

Singing 'If I Were a Rich Man' as Tevye in *Fiddler on the Roof* and (below right) 'Do You Love Me?' with Sara Weymouth: 'Performing that simple song with her is a moment I will never forget. It was the most genuine I've ever felt on stage with any character I've ever played' (Photos: Robert Workman/UK Productions Ltd)

As the Sewer Man in *Dear World* at the Charing Cross Theatre: 'a small theatre with a lovely cast headed by Betty Buckley' and directed by the legendary Gillian Lynne

'Every time I drive down Drury Lane past the Gillian Lynne Theatre, I see her name up there in lights, where it belongs': Andrew and Cameron with Gillian at the naming ceremony

'Physically at seventy I wasn't unlike Chamberlain, although I could see a little of Harold Macmillan as well': in the film *Masaryk*, a.k.a. *A Prominent Patient*

'Hello, Princess': as Gavin Sullivan in *EastEnders*. They cremated me in March 2021 – I asked them to get rid of the 'syrup' first

'The intensity of the play was something I had never experienced before': as Father Merrin in *The Exorcist*

'My character, Wilfred, is a bit of a dirty old dog and not exactly PC': *Quartet* with Sue Holderness, Jeff Rawle and Wendi Peters

The family.

'I felt very proud to be able to walk our daughter down the aisle': Carmen's wedding to Blake in 2019. I'm the proud father standing on the right

'Come and check me out, Here I'm standing with my crew, yeah': a still from the promotional video for 'Bad Bad Rapper', a track from my new three-CD set *Paul Nicholas: Gold*

trapeze artist who was appearing at Circus Circus and had a wide range of circus skills. They were good teachers.

I began learning on a wire that was only a foot off the ground. After about three days, I progressed to a three-foot wire and finally a wire that was ten feet off the ground. It was a long and at times frustrating process but after six weeks, I was good enough to begin the rehearsals proper with the rest of the cast. All the preparation and learning to walk the wire was now to be put to the test.

The wire walking occurs at the end of Act One. Barnum is going through a personal dilemma: whether to leave his wife Charity for Jenny Lind, the 'Swedish Nightingale'. Barnum had brought her over from Scandinavia to appear in one of his shows. The tightrope walk is there to show the emotional 'tightrope' that Barnum is walking. Jenny Lind stands on a platform on one side of the proscenium arch and Barnum is on the other. The cast affix a wire between the two. In most venues that meant that the wire was approximately forty feet long. Jenny proffers her hand and Barnum begins to walk. That was the most difficult moment. Michael Crawford, being Michael, used to go for a record every time – trying to get across as many times in a run of shows as he could without falling off.

I never worried about that because I knew that audiences like you to fall off; it builds the tension. I didn't want to put myself under unnecessary pressure. If I fell I would look across to Jenny and say: 'You'd better be worth it.'

The only time I felt under pressure was on a press night because I didn't want to give the newspapers ammunition to be negative about the show. I never once fell off on press night.

Thereafter I used to fall off quite a lot. My record was six times in one night. After the sixth time the audience thought they were going to miss their last bus home. You had to complete it because musically it led into the end of the first act. The worst thing about falling off was ripping my trousers and exposing my bottom and having to complete the walk with my derrière in view. The audience loved it and found it very amusing.

I had a difficult trampoline jump at the beginning of the show that resulted in the only accident I had as Barnum. It involved me jumping on a trampoline to where my wife Charity is seated in a theatre box, looking down onto the stage. Having landed on the small platform next to the box, I was to swing round and give her a kiss. This manoeuvre required that after making the jump, I grab the bar that was protruding from the little platform which then secured my landing. I ran, jumped on the trampoline and reached for the bar. It wasn't there. I missed. There was this marvellous *Road Runner* cartoon moment where I hung for a split second in mid-air before crashing onto the trampoline below. For a moment I thought I had broken my back but I was just winded. I felt so embarrassed missing the jump. I immediately went back and redid it to great applause from the audience.

The other complicated moment involved the 'death slide'. At the end of the show Barnum runs to the very top of the auditorium and slides down a rope over the audience's head, onto the stage. It looked very spectacular but it wasn't that dangerous. The hard part was climbing the stairs to the top of the auditorium, changing costume before sliding down the rope. It had to be done in three minutes.

Barnum was a good show. My only disappointment was that I always felt sorry for the children who came to see it. The advertising suggested that this was a real circus show, complete with animals. There were none. Although there were a number of circus skills involved, *Barnum* was quite dark at times.

It was great exercise for me. *Barnum* was physically demanding and eight shows a week kept me in shape. They say you can't teach an old dog new tricks but I'm a living example that you can.

Barnum started off as a man who ran a freak show: a purveyor of bearded ladies and all sorts of so-called curiosities. He introduced the first African Elephant to America and called it 'Jumbo'. When the elephant died, he had it stuffed and continued to exhibit it. He built the 'We American Museum' which he packed with weird attractions. His sole motivation was to get the punters in and make money. He was a showman.

Harold Fielding was, as I explained, also a wonderful showman. Harold knew how to bring people in to the theatre. He was the original producer of *Barnum*. I'd watched Harold and people like him over the years, and detail mattered to them. Harold was very keen to make sure the box-office staff were on the case. Without a good box-office operation, you don't sell tickets. He was excellent at making sure that all the coach firms and party bookers were given good deals and taken care of. He knew the importance of good advertising and, to his detriment with *Ziegfeld*, as I said he was one of the few producers who didn't take investors. He always used his own money. He soldiered on following *Ziegfeld* but never attained the dizzy heights of his original success. He died in 2003 aged eighty-six and left a warm legacy of his incorrigible energy that took him through both triumph and disaster. He was an old-school impresario who was the perfect person to stage *Barnum*. A producer who demanded both artistic and financial autocratic control.

I became a little bit imbued with the spirit of Barnum myself. It began to make me think about what I was doing with my life. How artists, including myself, were slaves to the phone call. I wanted more control. At the end of the 1980s I began to think about getting involved in production.

I was a performer first and wasn't prepared to give up that life and become a businessman. I saw myself as a performer who produces, rather than a producer who performs. I did *Barnum* for a long time and it was very successful. We came in to the West End with *Barnum* and did a fantastic sellout Christmas season at the Dominion Theatre. With several signed performances for the deaf and hard of hearing (Linzi is partially deaf), I had done quite a lot of work, including a TV commercial, for the British Deaf Association and other charitable organisations.

As a result of this work I was presented with a Silver Heart in recognition of my contribution to show-business and children's charities by the Variety Club of Great Britain. They gave a lunch in my honour at the Grosvenor House Hotel. Jim Davidson was the compère and Virginia Bottomley – then Secretary of State for Health – was also present. Sir Tim Rice introduced me and said some lovely things. My family were very proud when I was presented with the Silver Heart. It was a wonderful day, but I had been a little nervous as I am fine when performing a character on stage but not so good at being myself in public.

During the tour of *Barnum*, I was in Bristol one night coming down the 'death slide' at the end of the show. A pulley, not unlike those the army use to transport soldiers across rivers, sagged. I didn't have enough momentum to reach the stage which meant I was left dangling over the orchestra pit. They had told me they were filming a commercial for the show and all I could think of was, this has messed up the TV commercial. It was really embarrassing. It had never happened before. Finally they managed to haul me on stage. It was very ungainly. At that point the audience applauded. I thought they were applauding my heroics. I glanced to my right and on walked Michael Aspel holding the famous red book. He said: 'Paul Nicholas – This Is Your Life.' I had no idea. Then I put two and two together. Of course the cameras were there to film him coming on. It wasn't a commercial. I had been totally conned. Everyone else in the company knew except me. I didn't have a clue.

When I was at the height of my television fame with *Just Good Friends* a few years earlier, I had always said to Linzi, 'If anybody ever contacts you from *This Is Your Life* the answer is no!' I caught them out once on the telephone. It sounded like one of those dodgy calls. They pretended they were from a bookshop and I smelt it immediately. I couldn't think of anything worse than someone trotting out somebody I had not seen for a hundred years and saying, 'Do you remember Malcolm?' I was not remotely interested in being the subject of *This Is Your Life* but now I was backstage about to be whisked away.

They recorded the show in a studio in Bristol rather than on the stage. They'd had a suit brought in for me. My Irish dresser Trish McCauley knew, as did the cast. They'd all managed to keep it secret from me. They gave me time to have a shower and get changed. Then I walked out onto the set in front of an audience. There they were, my family, friends and the rest of the cast. Linzi had known about it since July. She had to keep this secret from the nosiest man in the world and she did. She had explained that I would not be comfortable in meeting blasts from the past, people I had not encountered for years. So it was a very nice surprise to see Jan Francis, Michael Ball, David Essex, Andrew Lloyd Webber, Victor Spinetti, Oliver Tobias, Elaine Paige, Wayne Sleep, Patty Boulaye, Belinda Lang, Dora Bryan, Robert Stigwood and my old employer, Screaming Lord Sutch.

*

This was my life and it was going well. I was also about to take control over my professional life – and all because I decided to become a hired hand again.

I agreed to do another tour of *The Pirates of Penzance*, once again playing the Pirate King. The reason I have toured with *Pirates* so often is simply because it works. It was written in the late 1890s but our version was originally done in Central Park in New York by Joe Papp, with Kevin Kline in the lead as the Pirate King. It was a great success and transferred to Broadway with Kline and Linda Ronstadt (the singer) playing Mabel.

When that production first came to Britain, it had Tim Curry as the Pirate King and Pamela Stephenson, aka Mrs Billy Connolly, as Mabel. George Cole from *Minder* played the Major General. I had seen the Papp production at Drury Lane and it was a fresh and lively version of a show that had been done in the same way for many years. Gilbert and Sullivan's original production had opened in Penzance and New York on the same night. It has fantastic charm; one of the reasons I enjoyed performing in it. It's a great exercise and it allows me to be extremely silly. Above all, when you take it out on a weekly tour around the country, people want to see it. Comparatively, it is not an expensive musical.

The tour began but not with Michael Ball. This time a young actor called David Ian was to play the part of Frederick. David was from Ilford in London and had played Joseph in *The Amazing Technicolor Dreamcoat* and Rocky in *The Rocky Horror Show*. He was an excellent Frederick and sang it as well as Michael Ball.

We hit it off instantly. We shared a similar sense of humour and had a lot of fun on stage together. We had a very good director called Chris Robinson who knew the show inside out having done the West End production. David took his dog, Penny, everywhere which I thought was a nice quality to have. I met his mum Jean and dad Reg and they were a very pleasant family.

I was restless on *Pirates* because I was again working for someone else. David, despite being younger – and I've always hated him for that – had the same frustrations. David turned thirty during the run. When you get to that age as an artist and you aren't quite where you want to be, you start to question what you're doing. You begin to want more control of your life, rather than waiting for the phone to ring or the next audition. It can be a very disheartening business. However, you should never write anybody off. Elaine Paige is a perfect example of that. Elaine was in the chorus of *Hair* and *Superstar*. She played Rita, one of Michael Crawford's girlfriends, in the musical *Billy*. Then, out of nowhere, she got *Evita* because ultimately she had the talent.

If you'd looked at Elaine Paige in *Hair* you wouldn't have believed she could have played such a larger-than-life character as Eva Perón. If you love doing it, you should keep on trying because your opportunity may come when you least expect it... Amen!

It was 1990 and the tour of *Pirates* ended with a run at the London Palladium.

Here's a part review:

5th April 1990

When Joseph Papp first presented his version of *The Pirates of Penzance* in the early sixties, eyebrows were raised. He cast a pop singer as Frederick, an apprentice pirate, and engaged Wilford Leach to create a preppy pro- duction conceived like a new Broadway musical. An international hit at the time, it is being revived with spectacular success at the London Palladium.

The Pirate King is the best I've ever seen: Paul Nicholas returning from TV light comedy to swash his buckle on the musical comedy stage. His zest for comedy and fine romantic singing voice are matched by Bonnie Langford's assured and impressive Mabel. She now possesses an exciting coloratura voice to rival any. David Ian is a fine, manly Frederick. No wonder the General's daughters scream and swoon...

The problem for David was not age; he was unsure of what he wanted to do. He liked the idea, like me, of not having to rely on anybody. To be in charge of your own destiny. One night before the show, he came to me with the idea of doing *Jesus Christ Superstar*.

I said, 'Yes, I'll do it if we produce it together.'

That night we became fifty-fifty partners – theatrical entrepreneurs. It was 1992 and we became Paul Nicholas & David Ian Associates.

CHAPTER ELEVEN

Resurrection

'Fings ain't wot they used t'be'
  – Lionel Bart

I N 1990 I WAS forty-six years old, and playing a youthful leading man was beginning to become a little more difficult. I needed a change; to try something else. I had reached an age when people start reminiscing. I was presented with the British Academy of Composers & Songwriters Gold Badge award for my services to the music industry. It was very nice of them to think of me.

The best part of that day was having the award presented by Lionel Bart. Lionel was born Lionel Begleiter in Stepney in 1930. He didn't think Begleiter was a very commercial-sounding name for a budding songwriter. One day he was riding on a bus that took him past St Bartholomew's Hospital and so he changed his surname to Bart. As well as the shows *Oliver!* and *Fings Ain't Wot They Used T'Be*, he wrote hit songs such as 'Little White Bull' for Tommy Steele, 'Do You Mind' for Anthony Newley and 'Living Doll' for Cliff Richard, as well as the James Bond theme song 'From Russia With Love' for Matt Monro. Bart was also responsible for the discovery of two of Larry Parnes' biggest stars. It was on his recommendation that Parnes went to see singer Tommy Hicks, whom he signed and renamed Tommy Steele; and Bart also suggested that Parnes see singer Reg Smith. Smith went on to score a number of UK hits under his new stage name, Marty Wilde.

Lionel didn't write music; it was all in his head. He would sing it to a lady pianist and she would write it for him. Amazing when you think of the complexity and variety of the music and lyrics he composed. A few years later, once we'd done a little producing, Lionel played us his musical of *The Hunchback of Notre Dame*. Lionel was singing on a little tape recorder that he carried around with him. I think Lionel was troubled at that time with drink and drugs and we didn't pursue his musical.

But Lionel Bart lives on as one of the few legends of musical theatre, and it was an honour for me to receive an award from the great man himself. I have a photograph of us together from that day which hangs proudly in my house.

His work will never be forgotten. And that's never guaranteed.

Tastes change and an older Arnold Schwarzenegger didn't do so well when he returned as the Terminator in 2019's *Dark Fate*; but the gift of musical theatre is that no matter how you reinvent the production, so long as the songs, music and dancing work, you have a fighting chance of success. You can do a show without costumes, without a set as long as the core material works and it's a title you can sell. The most common mistake with theatrical productions is thinking a show with lavish sets and costumes will guarantee a hit.

What I have learnt is that you should always do a workshop. If it doesn't work in a rehearsal room, it isn't *going* to work. The ingredients have to be there from the beginning: strong songs, strong story and if it's a revival, a title that has stood the test of time.

That was why David Ian and I chose *Jesus Christ Superstar* to be our first venture as producers. Having starred in it originally, I would play Jesus, and we'd stage it as a concert with a full orchestra live on stage.

Becoming a real life P. T. Barnum – a producer – in the theatre of the 1990s was not like an old-time Hollywood movie where you simply shout 'let's put on a show', although there were elements of that. David and I were both very hands-on so it was all down to us. We needed a licence to stage a one-off concert of *Superstar* and luckily I knew David Land who had controlled them for Andrew Lloyd Webber and Tim Rice for many years. I told him that we had an idea to do a concert version of *Jesus Christ Superstar* at the Opera House in Blackpool which seats three thousand. David Land granted us a licence for a one-off Sunday concert and from that moment our whole focus was on selling the show.

We booked top-class West End artists to be in it. David, who is a shrewd negotiator, was picking up the phone, talking to and booking the artists. He was fantastic at that. I thought we needed to advertise on radio and I wrote the commercial. We needed a poster, so I designed it. We talked about all aspects of promotion and casting. The beauty of it was that David would then pick up the phone and make it happen. I had at last found somebody who was prepared to do the thing I didn't want to do, which was organise.

As a result of our efforts we sold out the Blackpool Opera House. We made a little bit of money so, of course, we wanted more. We wanted to do another performance. David Land agreed and we took an even bigger venue at the Bournemouth International Centre (BIC) which seats four thousand. Another Sunday concert and two performances and they were both another sell-out. David was working from the bedroom of his house and had made a bit of money as did I. David liked the idea of being a young producer. David has great charm as well as being extremely bright and practical. I could see that he had all the qualities needed to become one of the great theatre producers; and thirty years later, my instinct proved right.

We decided to form a company, and we called it Paul Nicholas & David Ian Associates. We started producing shows and took a little office on a trading estate in Ilford in Essex. We did a little show in Bournemouth called *The Greatest Shows in Town* which was a compilation of songs from hit musicals. It starred Rosemarie Ford and Graham Bickley from the sitcom *Bread*. We devised it, put it together and it worked very well and did a record-breaking season.

We decided that we would try to do a five-week nationwide concert tour of *Jesus Christ Superstar* with myself in the title role. It was twenty years since I first played *Superstar* so, naturally, we called it *The Twentieth Anniversary Concert Tour*. I did not pay myself any money on the tour as we were building a business. We sold out places like the Glasgow Concert Hall, the BIC, Bristol Colston Hall and London's Fairfield Hall. They were big concert venues. We were doing very well and we were beginning to enjoy it. David was also growing in confidence. He had a T-shirt made which said 'He may be Jesus but I am God'. Which is pretty much how it turned out. Everything was divided down the middle between David and me. We never did get round to signing an agreement.

We will always be grateful to David Land for giving us such a terrific start. Sadly, he died just before Christmas in 1995. He was a wonderfully warm and funny man and helped launch Tim and Andrew on the road to great success.

We wanted to move on as a company and considered doing *Tommy* as I'd been in the movie. They were about to put it on in the West End so we had to let that one go. I came up with the not particularly original idea of doing *Pirates*. David pointed out that it was a show, not a concert. I said that there was hardly any set, very little dialogue and that it was basically a light operetta. It would work very well in concert venues. I must have been at my persuasive best.

No one had ever toured a West End show on a nightly basis in Britain. It was for five weeks and again I didn't pay myself anything but I enjoyed myself and in the long term it paid off. The tour did very well and strangely enough *Pirates of Penzance* did better financially than *Jesus Christ Superstar*. I thought it would be the other way around.

David too was enjoying himself, and the company was growing. Of course, we were not in the Cameron Mackintosh league, but we were developing and learning. Holding the financial and creative reins was a winning combination and with David's expertise on the day-to-day production we were going places.

All the high-power business manuals tell you that the best strategic business planning has to be with the future. It is always a good question. What will you do next? We were still learning about production and we'd had success in Bournemouth BIC in the small theatre. We needed a show that wasn't too expensive to produce. *The Rocky Horror Show* came to mind. David had played Rocky and we had a chance of getting the rights because of my friendship with Richard O'Brien. It worked! We got the rights and I would direct. The show was choreographed by Stacey Haynes who knew the show backwards and it starred Peter Blake. Peter had been in *Hair* with me and was well known via his TV character Kirk St Moritz in the John Sullivan sitcom *Dear John*.

The show opened to great reviews and had a very successful summer season in Bournemouth. David and I were flying and we wanted to do something bigger; a fully fledged musical with all bells and whistles. We wanted to do a good revival, but also a show that had not been seen on stage for some time. We wanted a SHOW. A big show that we could get the rights to and produce as a tour. It's cheaper to launch a tour rather than produce something for the West End.

I was racking my brains and then it came to me. *Grease*! It was a show I knew and really wanted to do. It had continued to tour over the years in a small way, but I knew from my youngest daughter, Carmen, that it was still incredibly popular. When they had sleepover parties or kids just hung around the house, the video of *Grease* with Travolta and Olivia Newton-John was always on. When they are small, they watch *Mary Poppins*. When they are going through the hormonal stage, it's *Grease*… I just knew a revival of *Grease* was a winner, so we negotiated the rights for a touring production.

There was a snag. The rights to *Grease* didn't include four songs that were written specifically for the movie: 'Sandy', 'You're the One that I Want', 'Hopelessly Devoted' and 'Grease is the Word'. They, of course, were the key hit songs.

We felt that it would be wrong to produce *Grease* without those songs because the audience would expect to hear them. I thought Robert Stigwood – who had produced the film – might have the rights to the songs. I had not seen Robert since the late 1970s. He had yachted off and ended up living in Bermuda and New York. He'd made so much money from the films *Saturday Night Fever* and *Grease*, plus a string of Bee Gees hits, that he was in semi-retirement. I was aware he had moved back to the Isle of Wight and bought a house called Barton Manor but I had not seen or spoken to him for years.

Prior to my meeting with Robert, I called Jim Jacobs, the co-writer of *Grease* with Warren Casey, who had died some years before. Jim knew me from the original London production. I said, 'Hello Jim. We have the touring rights to your show. We would like to include the film songs and we think Robert Stigwood controls those rights. Would you have any objection to having the film's songs in the stage musical?'

Jim was great and fine and said, 'That's okay with me.' So all we needed now was Robert's permission.

I called Robert and went down to the Isle of Wight for lunch. It was great to see him again and catch up. It was more of a social call. At the end of the lunch I casually said, 'Oh, by the way. I've got this little production company with a friend of mine called David Ian and we've done a few bits and pieces. We're doing a touring production of *Grease*.'

Robert's eyes fixed me with a look. He clearly wasn't happy. We had definitely chosen the right show.

'Any chance you can help us with the rights to the film songs? We'd like to use them on the tour.'

He ummed and aahed and was non-committal.

I said, 'It's been lovely seeing you Bob. Take care and if you can help with the songs that would be great. Thanks very much for lunch.'

I didn't hear anything from Robert and we started looking for people to star in the show.

One Sunday evening I got a call. Robert was on the phone. He said: 'I'm at Claridge's. Come over here. I want to talk to you.'

I said, 'What about?'

He said, 'I'm not telling you. Get over here now.'

I know Robert. When he goes, he goes, so I jumped in a cab. We were in his lavish suite at Claridge's in the middle of Mayfair. He got straight to the point and said, 'You've got the touring rights to *Grease* haven't you?'

I said, 'Yeah. We're touring it.'

He said, 'I want to do *Grease*.'

Apparently he had been at Sydmonton with Andrew Lloyd Webber and had met Cameron Mackintosh. Robert hadn't done anything in the UK for years, since *Evita*. He found himself as the new boy back in town. His juices were flowing. He had been speaking to Cameron and later they had talked about doing *Grease* together. They researched it a little bit and found that Paul Nicholas and David Ian had the rights, which was going to mess them up and stop them doing it. We were in the way, so Robert had to deal with me. Here I was, an artist, not an entrepreneur – as far as Robert was concerned, somebody without any credibility as a producer – but we had the touring rights which meant he couldn't do anything until our tour ended.

He reiterated, 'I want to do *Grease* in the West End.'

I thought for a second and said: 'There's no problem Bob, we'll do it fifty-fifty, straight down the middle, all guns blazing.'

We shook hands on it there and then at Claridge's. David and I would stand down our plans for a tour and become fifty-fifty partners with Robert on a London production which would include all the film songs. We celebrated with champagne. Robert did not stint on that sort of thing. When he travelled from the Isle of Wight, he didn't come by train or car. He came by helicopter. David showed me the cost – £3,000 one way. He was 'Mr Producer'.

David and I were thrilled; we thought it would be great to be involved with Robert who would elevate the revival from a provincial tour to a full-blown West End show. We'd also have the four film songs. It had all suddenly gone up a level. I knew that when Robert did anything, he did it full on and properly and it would be a wonderful association for our new business.

We did the deal and talked about the theatre for the show. I said, 'The Dominion would be great for it.' The Dominion was always considered a bit of a dead duck. Nothing had ever really worked there but it was a good-sized theatre with two thousand seats. It was run by Apollo Leisure, a company I knew through playing in *Barnum* there. Mr Apollo Leisure was Paul Gregg, a straightforward, terrific businessman who had built Apollo Leisure from nothing into one of the largest theatre groups in the country. He had been very good to me in *Barnum*. I thought he was somebody Robert could do business with.

We showed Robert the Dominion and he agreed it was a good venue. The choice of director was a little bit more difficult. The next question was who would play Danny and Sandy. I had played Danny with Elaine

Paige at the New London Theatre. I knew the part and I felt the best person for it was someone that we had been thinking of prior to Bob's involvement: an actor called Craig McLachlan.

I had seen Craig in *Neighbours* in the Jason Donovan/Kylie Minogue era. I had watched him on the series and I thought he was very good-looking, had a naughty charm and a sense of comedy that the part of Danny required. He could also sing. I didn't think Danny would prove too difficult. The essence for me was that he was good-looking and funny. I showed Robert some videos of him and we all thought that Craig would be the man for the job. We flew him from Australia to London and we all met at the Dorchester. Lunch was laid on for Craig and his agent and the deal was agreed that Craig would star. We booked Craig without hearing him sing or audition. He was so charming at that lunch. He was irresistible and obviously had the star quality needed. We still had not found a Sandy, director or a designer.

A designer was key because the look of the show was extremely important. Robert and I have very similar taste and we both thought the show should look very summery. Very much like the movie, in fact, so not all that clever on reflection. The problem with designers is that you book them on the basis of their reputation, without necessarily seeing their designs, so you don't know for sure what they are going to come up with. I knew a designer called Terry Parsons. I'd worked with him before on *Singin' in the Rain* and *Charlie Girl*. We interviewed him along with other top West End designers. Terry was the only one prepared to do a model of the design. Everyone was very sold on Terry's model and he got the job. The look of *Grease* had to be right, just perfect, for the show to work.

We still had no director. We decided to try and get Stephen Pimlott who directed *Joseph*. He was flavour of the month at that time because *Joseph* had been a big success. He didn't work out; he saw the production as being in the semi-round which would have been very expensive and not necessary. So we brought in David Gilmore, who was a very nice amenable man and we all liked him and he got the job. It was decided that (pre *Strictly*) Arlene Phillips, whom Robert didn't know but I knew, was the right choreographer particularly for a show like *Grease*.

We had everything in place but we still didn't have a girl. The most difficult part of the show for Sandy is that she has to sing 'Hopelessly Devoted to You'. For a lot of girl singers there's a point in the song where they have to break from their normal chest voice into a head voice and it's technically quite a difficult moment in the song.

We saw a number of very good West End singers, some top-class girls for that part, and a great many of them couldn't make the change from chest to head successfully, without it breaking or sounding weak. Ideally, we wanted someone who could sing the whole song in chest voice. There were other requirements. They also had to be pretty, demure and be able to act. All of those qualities aren't easy to find. We were only two weeks from the first day of rehearsal and had cast everyone but we still hadn't found a Sandy.

We heard on the grapevine that there was a singer called Debbie Gibson coming over to Britain to do some TV. Debbie was then a very big pop singer in America and remains a popular entertainer in the States to this day. We managed to contact her manager (who also happens to be her mother) and we managed to get her in to audition. She sang brilliantly. She had a lovely warm quality, was extremely professional, hard working, and she sang to die for. She was offered the part and she took it. We were then completely cast.

The first day that we put tickets on sale, we did £100,000 of business. The great thing about it was that the business kept growing. We opened to one of the largest advances ever – £4 million plus. The thing that Robert brought to the show – for which I am indebted – is that you don't do things by half. Great producers do things properly. When you get involved with a producer like Robert, you learn about quality, about style and about not being cheap. Robert was a tough businessman and could be very hard to deal with but what he would never do is skimp on the show and his own reputation. It might not even work but it would be properly produced and you can't say that of every producer.

Grease was capitalised at £2.5 million to put on; and, although we opened with a £4 million advance, it didn't mean we would get our money back immediately. You have running costs which at that time, on a show like *Grease* at the Dominion, were £130,000 every week. You have to pay rent to the theatre plus royalties to the creative team and the authors. There is a terrible misconception that all artists have – which I believed until I started producing – that producers take all the money. The last person who gets paid is the producer.

On *Grease* we had insurance. We were strong. We knew we had fantastic leads. We knew we had a terrific cast. We knew we had a great set. We knew we had a talented choreographer, director and musicians and a great venue. We had the capacity to take over two thousand people every night.

My personal dilemma was how much to risk of my own money. There is a producers' share and an investors' share. I was obviously in on the producers' share, but did I also want to invest? Robert and I could take investors, or we could invest ourselves; so we went for it. Robert liked a flutter. I'm not a gambler but I always remember James Goldsmith's motto, 'Never miss an opportunity.' I decided to take his advice. I was playing for big stakes by my standards.

I had been an artist – quite a successful one – but I had never been involved in a big production on the other side. I thought, this is an opportunity. I have got a piece of it. I want a bit more of this pie but I don't know how the show is going to go. I think it's a hit but I'm not Nostradamus.

It was five months prior to the opening and we had to put our hands in our pockets to fund a £2.5 million production. It is best to be prudent when investing in shows because one out of seven doesn't get its money back. Even if one out of seven runs for six months, it may still never get its money back because it could be breaking even every week but not recoup its capital. *Sunset Boulevard* was one such show and never got all its money back in London. It ran for two years and looked like a big success but it lost money. No one wants to be associated with a miss. It's very expensive.

All this was in my mind as I was considering my financial involvement. We got the rights because we believed in it. I knew from *Carmen* how much kids liked it. In discos when they played 'You're the One that I Want' the boys lined up at one end of the dance floor and the girls lined up at the other and they'd do the number. I decided to have a punt. Oscar had always said to me, 'Never put your own money in a show… any decent producer would always use other people's money.' Yes, all that is true, but I really fancied *Grease*. I invested £500,000 which was a lot for me. I think Robert put in about double that. Oscar told me I was mad. I believed in it and I hoped my hunch was correct – that it would work.

We got Craig to record with Debbie and their 'You're the One that I Want' went into the charts after the show opened. The previews had all gone well except one night when Kenickie's car wouldn't come on at the beginning of 'Greased Lightning'. Other than that it had been standing ovations every night.

We opened and the reviews came out. Robert and I said 'not bad'. They were great and I could tell from the previews that we had a winner. They were going mad. People were standing and dancing. People are not stupid. You begin to smell a hit. You know when applause is enthusiastic and genuine. You can tell. It's a different sound. As soon as the overture started and the audience heard the opening chords to 'Summer Nights' they were clapping along with the music. They wanted it and the show gave it to them. At the end of the evening the audience were screaming for more. They went on and on screaming, a wonderful chorus. It was a magnificent success. A gold-plated certified hit. We were all thrilled with each other. We thought we were the best thing since sliced bread. We were now partners with Robert and were on a winning streak. What next?

Still, I was missing the release of performing. I decided that I would like to do a big show. I had always hankered after doing *Singin' in the Rain* because I had been to see it with my mum when I was a little kid.

Dear Harold Fielding controlled the rights to this, along with some Americans. Harold had produced the show at the Palladium in the mid 1980s and it had been a big success; I knew him through *Charlie Girl* at the Victoria Palace with Cyd Charisse. We spoke to Harold who gave us the rights, but he had sold the set and costumes to Apollo Leisure so we went to see them and asked if we could hire the whole lot for our tour of *Singin' in the Rain*. Apollo Leisure has lots of theatres all over the country. As big provincial theatre owners, they always need a product so they were happy to work with us in staging the show.

Tommy Steele had directed and starred in Harold Fielding's production at the Palladium. I went to see Tommy in a touring show that he was doing at the time called *What a Show*. The show chronicled some of his past hits, and he talked to the audience about his life and family. Tommy knew how to connect with an audience and was completely at ease. It was like we were in his front room. It was wonderful. When I met him after the show he said, 'When people meet me they don't know whether to shake my hand or give me a lump of sugar.' He has a great smile. It adds up to a lot of charisma.

I asked if Tommy would like to direct the show, and happily he said yes. I would play the Gene Kelly part. There was just one slight problem. Like the high wire in *Barnum*, I could not tap dance; I could barely do a time step. But we had the rights and we had a director. It would be a big national tour staying at each venue about four or five weeks. It was a big show to tour particularly with the 'Singin' in the Rain' sequence which was technically difficult to set up. It meant we needed to stay in each venue longer than a week to amortise the cost of the move and it was going to be expensive. It required a lot of trucks to move the show from venue to venue.

The rain scene was a priceless moment. Every show needs something that people look forward to. It is the most famous scene in the film and the audience were fascinated to see how it was done. It was basically a huge shower; a set within a set. The water was pumped up from two water tanks below the stage. It would create the rain effect onto the set and then drain away down to the water tanks below to be recycled. It was important not to upset the crew because it was very easy for them to get their own back. I was always very mindful of the colour of the water.

The only problem was that the set and costumes that we thought we had were non-existent, and so not only did we have to build a new rain set, we had to have new costumes made. It was a costly mistake and one that wasn't built into the budget for the show.

Tommy was very helpful to me in rehearsals and was a marvellous director. Tommy did what most directors don't do: he ran the show every day. What normally happens is that you block the show scene by scene, do a couple of runs and the next thing you know, the curtain is going up. The problem with that is, you take so long to reach the end of the show that you forget what you did at the beginning. Often on the opening night, people are running around and cannot remember where they are and who they are supposed to be with. Tommy's approach worked much better. By running the show every day, and not just the dialogue scenes, we all knew where we were. Even if we only got up to two scenes, he would run it. In that way, everybody knew the order of the show from day one, which I thought was a very useful tip.

Tommy was great to work with because he didn't try and project his performance onto me. My big problem had been learning to tap dance which is one of the most difficult things in the world. It was strenuous, fiddly and hard work. I took two months prior to the rehearsals to learn to tap dance; but instead of learning to tap which would have taken forever, I decided to learn just the routines. The choreographer learned the routines, taught them to one of the dancers and she taught them to me. I wasn't learning to tap dance, I was learning to do the numbers which was a lot easier. And after doing the show for a couple of years I could tap dance my way through the routines quite nimbly. Well, who doesn't want to be Gene Kelly for a moment in their life? We did it. I had a good time and it was a success.

Robert Stigwood wasn't involved with *Singin' in the Rain*, and *Grease* was still going great guns. David and I were thinking about doing another West End Show.

When I finished *Singin' in the Rain* I was asked to play King Arthur in *Camelot*, a wonderful musical and a powerful part. It was a perfect vehicle for me as an older leading man. We did it as part of the Covent Garden Festival, at the Masonic Hall which was the ideal setting for the show.

Based on the King Arthur legend, *Camelot* was written by Alan Jay Lerner and Frederick Loewe, adapted from T. H. White's 1958 novel *The Once and Future King*. It has a beautiful score with a couple of outstanding songs – Lancelot's 'If Ever I Should Leave You' and Arthur's 'How to Handle a Woman'. The original 1960 Broadway production featured Richard Burton as King Arthur, Julie Andrews as Queen Guinevere and Robert Goulet as Sir Lancelot. It went on to win four

Tony awards including best performance in a musical for Richard Burton and Julie Andrews. Not bad for a Broadway show.

Our version had me as King Arthur, Samantha Womack as Guinevere, Robert Meadmore as Lancelot and Jason Donovan as the evil Mordred. It was directed by Frank Dunlop, which was nice, and was a very interesting process. The show's content enables the audience to become very involved in the love story of Arthur, Guinevere and Lancelot. So much so that by the end of the musical – when all three characters go their separate ways – there wasn't a dry eye in the house.

In 1998 I did a concert version with the Scottish Symphony Orchestra for Radio 2 with Helen Hobson as Guinevere, Robert Meadmore as Lancelot and Jason Donovan as Mordred at the Festival Theatre, Edinburgh.

Paul Nicholas & David Ian Associates now had very nice offices in Great Russell Street and were looking to do more producing. I heard about a show at the Tricycle Theatre on Kilburn High Road called *Ain't Misbehavin'* (named after a song written by Thomas 'Fats' Waller). It had been produced on Broadway in 1978 and again in 1988 and was a Tony award-winning musical revue based on the 'Harlem Renaissance' of the twenties and thirties. The music was timeless with great songs such as 'Honeysuckle Rose', 'Ain't Misbehavin'', 'Black and Blue', 'This Joint is Jumpin'' and 'I've Got a Feeling I'm Falling'.

Here at the Tricycle Theatre in 1995, it had rave reviews. With a cast of five and hardly any set, it should have been easy to transfer to the West End; so we asked Robert if he'd be interested in producing it with us. Robert, like us, thought it was worth transferring.

So we did and it was a lesson learnt. Yes the show had great reviews at the Tricycle Theatre. Yes it had won a Tony. Yes the cast were great and audiences loved the show. But… this tight little musical revue that worked so well at the 300-seat Tricycle Theatre was now at the Lyric Theatre on Shaftesbury Avenue which had one thousand seats to sell every night. It was very difficult. We had West End theatre rent to pay, advertising costs, West End wages, PR and were competing with every West End hit show in town including *Grease* which was just up the road. *Ain't Misbehavin'* was a great show in the wrong theatre with not enough star interest for punters to buy tickets at West End prices. We had overcooked it!

It had a respectable run but it didn't make back its capitalisation. We were disappointed but that is part and parcel of being a producer. Every producer at some point gets it wrong and so a valuable lesson had been learnt.

We had another idea up our sleeve and once again Robert Stigwood was key. David and I fancied *Evita*. In 1978, I saw the show on its first night with Elaine Paige arriving as Elaine and leaving as 'Miss Paige', leading lady. Yes, we'd done *Grease* together, but *Evita* was Tim and Andrew's follow-up to *Jesus Christ Superstar*. They had gone down the 1976 cast album route again with Julie Covington making an impact with 'Don't Cry for Me Argentina' and Colm Wilkinson – my old Judas adversary in *Jesus Christ Superstar* – as Che.

On 18th June 1978, at the first night of *Evita*, it was Elaine who starred along with David Essex. David sang superbly and was brilliant in the role of Che. Of course, the night belonged to Evita; and from that point on Elaine became a star.

It was a wonderful production; but then it was directed by a master, the great American director Hal Prince.

There is one scene in *Evita* that really shows the brilliance of Hal Prince's direction. It's a very simple idea and it takes place when six generals are vying to be top dog. They are seated in six rocking chairs and during the song 'Art of the Possible' they stalk each other in a game of musical chairs. One by one each chair and the general are removed until only two generals are left with one chair remaining. Of course Perón sits in the final chair. All very simple but clever and precise.

I remember seeing *Phantom of the Opera* and thinking only a director with the class and perception of Hal Prince could have turned the show from being a rather hammy melodrama into one of the longest-running shows ever. Hal was pure intelligence and class. His work lives on.

We convinced Robert, who of course knew *Evita* was a real winner on tour, that it wouldn't be difficult; but of course it most certainly was.

Marti Webb was brilliant as Evita. She sang it beautifully, as did Chris Corcoran as Che and Duncan Smith as Perón.

*

Bill Kenwright is not only a prolific producer, but also very loyal and uses actors when the chips are down. Bill came to see me in *Camelot* and I let Bill know that I would be interested in doing some non-musical acting if he ever had anything. Not long after he offered me a new play called *The Mysterious Mr Love* written by Karoline Leach. It was about a real character called George Love. George was infamous for courting ladies, marrying them, drowning them in their baths and stealing their money. He murdered three women before he was eventually caught.

It was set in the Edwardian period and a two-hander. Susan Penhaligon co-starred. We toured and then went to the Comedy Theatre and we were very well received and ran for three months. *The Mysterious Mr Love* had all the elements that I loved because although it was a dark story, it was also a love story.

It was well reviewed, a terrific play and wonderfully satisfying to know that two people could engage an audience for two hours. It showed me the power of good writing. It also gave me the opportunity to show that I could do straight acting. I didn't have to be 'Mr Musical' all the time.

Mr Love worked well enough for me to be offered another couple of plays for Bill Kenwright whom I enjoyed collaborating with. I co-starred with Chris Ellison from the television series *The Bill* in *Catch Me if You Can*, and also the play called *The Dark Side* with Jenny Seagrove. That was an appropriate title, for there were some difficult times ahead.

My father had another son, called Richard, with his second wife, Jenny, in 1963. Oscar was a great guy in many, many ways but he was not the kind of parent who was 'hands on'. Richard went to a good public school but that didn't make things any easier for him.

It was great for me when he was born for although I was eighteen years old by then I had always wanted a brother or a sister. Our nan gave him the same kind of treatment she had given me.

Richard played football and he was good. He excelled at sport and I remember Oscar and me going to Richard's very smart school to see him play. Oscar could turn on the posh voice at the drop of a hat. Richard was fifteen and Oscar was talking to the teacher about Richard's impending mock O levels. Removing his glasses and adopting his poshest voice, Oscar whispered in the teacher's ear as if he were imparting some very important top-secret information.

'Look, I can assure you that he may not do terribly well with his mocks but when it comes to the real thing, he'll piss it.'

That just made me die. It was another example of how embarrassing he could be, even then. He was the kind of guy that, if he met a good-looking woman, he would remove his glasses so that she could get the full 'beauty' of his eyes. I took him on holiday to France with me in 1991. I'd hired a villa in Grasse in the south of France and it was wonderful for about three days but then, of course, he started to irritate. I remember him taking his glasses off one day to my then three-year-old daughter and saying: 'Carmen. Do you think I look better with or without my glasses?' The truth is he was very shy and the bravado was his way of covering it.

Oscar's saving grace was that he was aware of all his idiosyncrasies. It didn't, however, stop him behaving that way.

He was very interested in my business. He was always asking me for tickets, and people always told me that he was very proud of what I had managed to do; and I was proud of him. He was a very successful lawyer. Our telephone conversations were like a tennis match. We would invariably end up screaming at each other.

Oscar had married three times: first my mother, then Jenny, and finally a very nice lady called Ann Wadsworth. Oscar used to call her 'Worthwads'. Ann didn't stand for any of Oscar's nonsense and they too remained good friends. His second wife Jenny had married a man called Johnny Russell. Oscar had known him from the Jack Hylton days; Johnny used to produce shows for Jack. I was always very happy to talk to John. He was a nice man and we talked about the theatre. He was very knowledgeable.

Oscar had a flat in London. He had a very nice job as a consultant for Davenport Lyons, a very prestigious law firm in Savile Row. And at weekends he would go down to his house in Folkestone where Jenny and Johnny Russell also lived. On occasions they would go away on holidays together. It suited him perfectly. He had someone to do his washing and cooking, and people to talk to. He would visit us in Highgate, eat a rice pudding, read the newspaper, fall asleep and as he was leaving, if you were lucky, he would nod and say hello to his grandchildren.

Unfortunately, Johnny Russell had cancer and was incredibly brave about it. He knew that he was dying and yet he was always courteous and stood up when my mother and Linzi entered the room. He seemed to me to be very stoic and didn't complain about his condition. Oscar still had a soft spot for his ex-wife Jenny. I think he had thoughts of perhaps getting together with her again once poor Johnny Russell had exited stage left. He was still with his lovely girlfriend Corrine.

Oscar updated me on the current state of Johnny Russell's condition. He tried to conjure up his most grave, concerned face. Shaking his head he said, 'He doesn't look well. He doesn't look well at all.'

'Oh dear,' I replied.

Oscar continued, with just a hint of glee in his eye, 'He finds me irritating.'

I said, 'I'm not surprised with you standing at the foot of the bed holding a wreath.'

Poor Johnny Russell died and I believe Oscar was genuinely sad to see him go. They had known each other for fifty years. Johnny Russell certainly had the measure of Oscar. Oscar was happy. He was still working. He could still walk about the office, drive his partners mad and open their mail. He could go down and see Jenny at weekends. Everyone was in their place.

Oscar telephoned me and for once we didn't have the usual row. He had been away and I had not spoken to him for two weeks. It was nice to hear from him. I told him I had a bad back and he recommended a cure. It was an unusually nice conversation.

The next day, I was alone in my garden in Highgate. Linzi, my mum and Carmen were on holiday in the south of France. I was still appearing in Windsor in *The Mysterious Mr Love*. The phone rang; it was my brother Richard. He said, 'Hello Paul. I don't know how to tell you this but I think Oscar may have died.'

I said, 'What do you mean?'

He replied, 'Well, they found the body of a man on the Leas. They think it's Oscar.' Oscar used to love walking on the Leas in Folkestone. I got a terrible feeling in my stomach. I thought: it *is* Oscar.

After his Sunday morning breakfast he had gone out to get the news-papers and helped himself to his favourite Belgian chocolates. While Jenny was cooking his lunch, he decided to go for a walk. While walking he had a massive heart attack. It was the end of a remarkable life.

The next evening, I was on stage. Oscar's death hadn't yet hit me. He was seventy-seven years old and when your parents get to that age, you half expect the worse. Oscar was very philosophical about death. I wasn't sure how I was feeling. I had to work.

I got through the first half of the play. In the second half my character has a long speech reminiscing about his father. It is a sensitive and well-written speech and was not dissimilar to my own thoughts of my father. I began the speech and it seemed to me that I was talking about Oscar. I became very emotional and the floodgates opened. I began to cry.

Susan Penhaligon was very, very kind to me and helped me get through it. I suppose my crying wasn't inappropriate for the scene. After the show, Sheila Ferguson – my future fellow 'Marigold' – came backstage to see me. She told me how much she had enjoyed the play and how she had been particularly moved by my speech. She said, 'How do you do it? How do you cry like that every night?' Being the old ham that I am, I didn't tell her. I still haven't.

I had to arrange the funeral. It could have been in Folkestone but so many friends of Oscar's – from show business and the legal profession – wanted to be there so we held it at the Golders Green Crematorium. We had an overflowing church. Timothy Dalton and Richard Harris came along to pay their respects. Brian Wadsworth and my solicitor Barry Shaw – a close friend and colleague of Oscar's – gave readings. Sadly dear Barry died in 2019. Oscar always referred to Barry as 'the chipmunk'. Everyone was very kind and told me how proud he was of me. We talked about how full of life he was and how we all missed him.

Which, of course, brought all the memories flooding back...

Chapter Twelve

Back to the Future

'I have a sort of obnoxious fighting charm but I'm a softie underneath'
    – Oscar Beuselinck, 1995

O SCAR WAS IN THE ARMY during the war and working for MI6 when I was born. He was in Holland and I was four days old before he knew I had arrived. My mother Marjorie had left London during the Blitz and was living with relatives in Peterborough. She had been a WAAF (Women's Auxiliary Air Force) and stationed at Bletchley Park where the German Enigma code was finally cracked. Which I may say she always took full credit for. I was born in Peterborough on 3rd December 1944. We were there for three months before we returned to my grandmother Winifred's north London family home.

Oscar was always determined and a clever man which had made him useful to British Intelligence. He was self-educated, smart and good at languages. He never talked much about the war but he was there for the Allied landings. His attitude was that he had a 'good war'. He had lived through it and he had survived it.

He was born in Endsleigh Gardens, just off the Marylebone Road, London in 1919. He was the eldest of four children. His father was a

Belgian seaman and a cook who served on the first convoys to Russia during the Second World War. He was also called Oscar. My grandfather spent most of his life at sea, sailing between South Africa and England as head chef for the Union Castle Line. My mother Marjorie was born in 1918, in the same hospital as my father in Endsleigh Gardens. Her father was a docker and when she was three, the family moved from Somers Town, Euston and went to live on the Isle of Sheppey in Kent. Oscar's family home was in Millman Street, Bloomsbury.

Oscar had always wanted to be a lawyer and when he was fourteen he got a job as a tea boy with a firm of solicitors called Wright & Webb in Bloomsbury Square, London. His thinking was that there was only one way to go and that was up. He was working there when the war started and living with my determined grandmother Winifred, who had now moved from Holborn to Burnt Oak in north London. It was one of the first and largest council estates to be built in the 1930s.

Oscar met my mother – he called her Peggy – at the Mary Ward Club in Queen Square, London. It was a place where young people could meet and exchange information, skills, ideas and experiences. After they married they went to live with his family – including his sisters Yvonne and Lucy and brother Alfonse – at my grandmother's in north London. That was the first home I knew.

When Oscar returned from the war he didn't have any money so he went straight back to work. He hadn't gone to university and was self-taught. He was caught in a difficult situation and a cramped one at that. I grew up in a busy household. There were three bedrooms and seven people living there, plus my grandfather when he came home from sea. The estate was relatively green and although the house we lived in was rather cramped, I was happy there. As an only child and being the baby, I got a lot of attention and felt secure and loved.

Things started to change when I was six and Oscar decided to buy his first house. It was a little semi-detached just off the Edgware Road in Colindale. It was a soulless, dreary place. Oscar couldn't afford the whole house, so my parents had 'vacant possession'. This meant we had to share it with an old woman called Mrs Mears and her daughter who were already living there. There were three bedrooms, two living rooms and a kitchen. We had to share the kitchen and had one bedroom and the use of one of the living rooms.

One night old Mrs Mears suddenly died. Unfortunately, she died in the bedroom next to ours. That night we went to bed knowing that next door there was a dead body. We slept with the lights on. Oscar wasn't the bravest man in the world. The woman's daughter decided to sell up, so Oscar bought her out. Suddenly, we had more space; but it was nowhere near big enough for Oscar's personality. He was studying to become a lawyer and doing it the hard way: working as an articled clerk by day and studying at night. There was a small park nearby where he used to take his law books and revise. By now my mother was working for the Board of Trade as a typist. There were all sorts of pressures.

Oscar was thirty years old when he qualified and went to work for the impresario Jack Hylton who was very much a 'Mr Showbusiness' at the time. As a pianist he'd played in big bands and then formed his own. He would be photographed conducting with his back to the audience and the slogan was 'Jack's Back'. He introduced the big band 'symphonic sound' to British dance music, imported from America. Jack Hylton and his Orchestra were the first British band to broadcast to America in 1931, and two decades later he became a great impresario, dominating London's theatreland and much of British light entertainment. He managed the Victoria Palace in London and presented a string of variety and comedy acts including the hugely popular 'Crazy Gang'. The Gang comprised three comedy double acts – Flanagan and Allen, Naughton and Gold, and Nervo and Knox – plus 'Monsewer' Eddie Gray. King George VI had been a big fan. My father took me to see them at the Victoria Palace in 1952. Little did I know at the time that some thirty-five years later, I would be starring in that very theatre with Cyd Charisse in *Charlie Girl*. Jack Hylton was a powerhouse.

For Oscar it was the start of what was to become a very successful legal career in entertainment. He was young and had lots of energy. He didn't drink or smoke and he had no hobbies. He would never cut the grass. It was like a jungle. Our neighbours used to organise coach trips and Oscar took great delight in telling them that what they were doing wasn't legal. If we ever got stopped by a policeman, he would remove his glasses and say: 'I think you should know that I am a solicitor.'

Oscar started work at Messrs Wright & Webb at the age of fourteen and ended up running the firm. He became a leading and well-known show-business libel lawyer, representing many famous artistes including Sean Connery, Richard Harris, John Osborne and the Beatles. Oscar could be very charming. He wasn't pompous and had a theatrical personality they could relate to. Both of my parents had the ability to laugh at themselves; something they passed on to me, for which I am grateful.

In 1950s Britain, you needed a sense of humour. It was drab and seemed like one long, wet afternoon with ration books. Occasionally, we went on family holidays to visit our Flemish relatives in Bredene, Belgium or to see my my mum's father Joe and his wife Jean who lived in Sheerness, Kent.

Listening to the radio was a great source of entertainment. After school, I would listen to *Children's Hour* on the Home Service, with programmes such as *Toytown* featuring Larry the Lamb and Dennis the Dachshund. My first recollections of popular tunes are of when I was five years old listening to 'The Harry Lime Theme' played on a zither from the film *The Third Man*, and 'Music, Music, Music' by Teresa Brewer.

On occasional Saturdays I would stay with my nan and visit my friend Colin who lived round the corner. We would listen to *Saturday Night Theatre*. I always looked forward to the radio plays and I think my interest in drama began there. There was of course *The Archers* which was 'an everyday story of country folk'. To this day, it is still the longest-running serial on radio. However, I stopped listening, like lots of fans, on 22nd September 1955 when Phil's wife Grace Archer was killed in a stable fire. As a ten-year-old I was very upset, as was half the nation who sent wreaths to the BBC. The BBC had scheduled the episode to coincide with the first-night broadcast of ITV, the new commercial television station. Comedy shows I enjoyed were *Life with the Lyons*, *Take it From Here*, and *The Goon Show*. Drama serials were *Dick Barton: Special Agent*, *Paul Temple* and *Journey into Space*. Sunday afternoons were spent listening to *Two-Way Family Favourites* and *The Billy Cotton Band Show*. Popular singers at that time were Alma Cogan, Dennis Lotis and

Lita Roza who had a UK number one hit with the novelty song 'How Much is that Doggie in the Window':

> *'How much is that doggie in the window?*
> *The one with the waggly tail*
> *How much is that doggie in the window?*
> *I do hope that doggie's for sale.'*

It was sixpence for Saturday-morning pictures where all of us kids would sing:

> *'We come along on Saturday morning*
> *Greeting everybody with a smile.*
> *We come along on Saturday morning*
> *Knowing it is well worth while.*
> *As members of the ABC club,*
> *We all intend to be*
> *Good citizens when we grow up*
> *And champions of the free.*
> *We come along on Saturday morning*
> *Greeting everybody with a smile, smile, smile,*
> *Greeting everybody with a smile.*

I liked the cartoons and the *Flash Gordon* serials (although even then they looked dated), the cowboys Hopalong Cassidy and the Cisco Kid. I found Laurel and Hardy very slow and they never made me laugh. Comics at the time were the *Beano*, the *Dandy* and the *Eagle* featuring Dan Dare and his heroic struggle against the evil Mekon.

But what I loved most of all was when my mum took me to the big pictures. Suddenly my eyes were opened to a world of sunshine, music and dancing. I loved the Hollywood musicals *Guys and Dolls*, *The King and I* and my all-time favourite, *Singin' in the Rain* with Gene Kelly, Debbie Reynolds and Donald O'Connor. These films had great warmth and made me happy. I used to go home and try and imitate them by tap dancing on the lino on our kitchen floor. Later, of course, I learnt how to tap dance and fulfilled a lifetime ambition by appearing in *Singin' in the Rain* on stage as Don Lockwood, the role immortalised by the great Gene Kelly.

The one really spectacular event I can recall, as a child of eight, was the show that Britain does better than anyone: pomp and ceremony. I was taken to the Queen's 1953 Coronation. We stood in the pouring rain watching the procession, waving our Union Jacks. My most vivid memory is of the Queen of the Polynesian Island of Tonga who was riding in an open-topped carriage despite the rain, waving and smiling to the crowds. She was without doubt the hit of the Coronation. She was a large woman, dressed in a very glamorous dress, wearing a feather in her hair. Sitting next to her in the carriage was a rather small man. When asked who the small man was, the 'Master', Noël Coward, was heard to answer, 'Her lunch.'

My mother loved Frank Sinatra, my aunt was into German tenors and my father had a passion for Beethoven and Mozart. Oscar was very musical. He played the piano and the violin and he used to sing naughty words to Gilbert and Sullivan songs. There was a piano in my grandmother's house and at Christmas he would play the piano and sing one of his favourite lyrics to Verdi's *Aida*: 'Celeste Aida, Paul is a silly bleeder.' I always felt comfortable when my parents were at my nan's because they seemed to relax.

I first heard rock 'n' roll at the age of ten when Bill Haley and the Comets released 'Rock Around the Clock'. I remember singing in the playground of my local primary school.

My nan took me to see Bill Haley in the film *Rock Around the Clock* at the Gaumont, Burnt Oak. This was post-war 1950s Britain: the days of Teddy Boys, drapes, sideburns and crêpe-soled shoes. Their clothes were inspired by the styles worn by 'dandies' in the Edwardian period. What amazed me was that every time Bill Haley started singing, all the 'Teds' got up and started jiving in the aisles. I'd never seen or heard anything like it before. The beat and rhythm was so infectious, it was impossible to keep still.

The Teddy Boys even had their own dance called 'The Creep', which was also a Top Ten hit record in 1954 for the Ken Mackintosh Band. I heard it for the first time when someone played it at a party. I was dancing with a girl and holding her in my arms. I was ten and not old enough to be a 'Ted' but I was still very taken with it.

Music was becoming more and more a part of my life. I was listening to rock 'n' roll records by Elvis Presley, Jerry Lee Lewis and Gene Vincent. I was glued to the radio as we didn't have a television. It was all very American. The first record I ever bought was Guy Mitchell's 'Singing the Blues' which was a number one in the UK in 1956:

> *'Oh, the moon and stars no longer shine*
> *The dream is gone I thought was mine*
> *There's nothin' left for me to do*
> *But cry-y-y-y over you (cry over you).'*

Tommy Steele's version of 'Singing the Blues' also made number one in the UK Singles Charts for one week in January 1957. The hit West End shows at that time were *West Side Story* and *My Fair Lady*. I was listening to modern jazz musicians like Gerry Mulligan and Chet Baker. I was a musical mongrel.

In those days, London was like a village and everybody knew everybody. Oscar was very much a part of that world. He was by now a young solicitor, making a name for himself and moving in literary circles.

In John Osborne's 1991 autobiography *Almost a Gentleman*, he wrote of his first meeting with Oscar:

> I asked Oscar Lewenstein (the renowned theatre and film producer) if he could recommend a solicitor. He knew someone he thought was just the man for me. 'You'll like him,' he said. 'He's rather like you, in fact he's rather like Jimmy Porter [Osborne's character from *Look Back in Anger*]. His office is in Ludgate Hill and his name is Oscar Beuselinck.'

Osborne goes on to list Oscar's sexual conquests of that day. Oscar appeared quite flattered when the book was published, although he reluctantly conceded that Osborne had somewhat spiced up his exploits to make them appear more salacious. *Private Eye* thought them entertaining enough to devote a full page to my father's adventures as penned by Osborne, and wrote in their 'Grovel' column:

> John Osborne gleefully informs me that he has issued a libel writ against the *Daily Mail*.

However, I fear the great playwright himself may soon be on the receiving end of one of these disagreeable objects. For his next volume of memoirs, *Almost a Gentleman*, contains a disgusting libel of one of London's most eminent solicitors, Mr Oscar Beuselinck, chief legal adviser to Mr Robert Maxwell. In a typescript of the book, which has come into my hands, Osborne recalls that in one of his many divorces he employed Beuselinck's services and recounts their first meeting.

Private Eye then went on to reprint the extract from Osborne's book of his first meeting with Oscar. Oscar had represented *Private Eye* and a conversation with him over lunch appeared in 'Grovel':

To lunch at the Gay Hussar with my old friend Oscar Beuselinck, famous for being the father of TV's Paul Nicholas and incidentally for being London's most sexually active lawyer.

'The reason I sued the *Mail on Sunday* over the Angela Levin interview was that I was clearly defamed,' the old shagger confides in me. 'It did not go far enough,' he continues, reminding me that when he occupied the old law firm offices of Wright & Webb Syrett, he had a different girl in every room, keeping his own office sacrosanct. He only used his desk for Ugandan purposes in his very last week there.

Oscar also passes on some advice: 'Never marry. I reckon my cock has cost me £100,000 per inch.' With only three marriages behind him, poor Oscar must be peculiarly under-endowed.

Osborne and Oscar were close friends for many years and both enjoyed a fondness for the irreverent. The last paragraph of Osborne's narrative about Oscar reads: 'You can't help liking him (Oscar); like Max Miller, no inner life to hinder.

As far as Osborne's reference to 'inner life' is concerned, Oscar had a lot. He just didn't want anyone to see it. He was an enigma. He once told me, 'At the end of the day, relatives are boring.' He made no pretence of being a family man and my parents' marriage wasn't a happy one so they decided to call it a day. I was twelve at the time.

Oscar decided to sell the house and my mother and I went to live in a two-bedroom flat in St John's Wood. My mother was going through an incredibly depressive time. Her man had left her. She was trapped within herself. Although the relationship didn't work, it was still a relationship. They had driven each other mad for fifteen years but without him, she was stuck.

Oscar sent me off to a progressive private school in Swiss Cottage. It was a very cosmopolitan establishment and suddenly I discovered a whole new world. There were American, Chinese and Indian kids and they all seemed very sophisticated, something I wasn't used to. Here was I, this kid who had lived on a council estate, and I didn't feel that I belonged with these rich kids whose parents all had large houses.

I had one good friend at the school, a boy called Peter Hoenig. The first day we met, he took the mickey out of my cockney accent. I didn't like it and we had a fight in the playground. It was a draw and afterwards we became friends. His parents were German Jews who had managed to escape Hitler's Germany prior to the Second World War. His father was a psychiatrist. At weekends, I used to go and stay with Peter at his house in Kilburn. I think his mother thought of me as a bit of a lost soul, for they invited me to stay quite often.

Peter and I would have midnight feasts with the boys who lived next door – the Cockerell family. There was Lolly, David and Michael who went on to become a very successful television journalist; at last count, he had interviewed eight British Prime Ministers.

They seemed to me a very bohemian family. Their mother belonged to a group called 'The Progressive League', and Peter and I joined the family on the very first CND (Campaign for Nuclear Disarmament) March in April 1958. I was thirteen. It was a four-day march from Aldermaston, the site of the Atomic Weapons Establishment, ending in Trafalgar Square. There were thousands of people marching, and overnight we slept in schools. Traditional jazz was becoming very popular and there were lots of trad jazz bands and dancing. At night we cooked sausages and spuds on a bonfire and had lots of laughs all in the name of a good cause. Or so it seemed.

The Cockerells were quite a musical family. They had a skiffle group and even some recording equipment. They had a microphone and a large tape recorder and occasionally they'd let me sing and they'd record me and I rather enjoyed it. My interest in music and singing was growing. I couldn't play any instruments so I began to sing more and started to learn how to keep time and sing in tune. I'd found something I really enjoyed. I had new friends, and music and singing.

But then my father had another plan.

Oscar decided to try for a reconciliation with my mother. They hadn't divorced. Nevertheless, I was to leave my private school in Swiss Cottage and we were all going to live together as a family again in a semi-detached house in Edgware. What a great idea dad! Thankfully the reconciliation didn't last long. The marriage was finally put to rest by my mother as Oscar was up to his irritating old tricks again and she had finally had enough. That was it: the absolute be-all-and-end-all, no turning back, nail in the proverbial, do not resuscitate, dead as a dodo. Thank God for that…

Oh and arguably, the beginning of my life as a performer.

I was thirteen years old and I was to continue my education at the local secondary modern. I had been wearing short trousers at the private school and on the first day at my new school, I had them on. I noticed that kids were looking at me like I was a little odd. Then I twigged: you don't wear short trousers aged thirteen, not in a mixed north London secondary modern. I told my mum and in a couple of days she bought me some long trousers.

After a few weeks I began to feel more comfortable. I was with working-class kids again and didn't feel overwhelmed by the situation. However, being a new boy and relatively sporty I decided that I would try and do well in my first cross-country to make an impression. I came second and that got me noticed by the games master, Mr Barnes. I liked sport and as a kid I'd always played football in my local park. Mr Barnes saw something in me so I was picked for the school's football and rugby teams. I wasn't terribly good at, or interested in, the academic stuff. I never understood what they were talking about. Even practical lessons like woodwork and metalwork didn't interest me.

One morning during school assembly, I was playing with a dead fly and got talking to a boy called Stuart Taylor who was very friendly. It turned out that he played lead guitar in a band called 'Gene White and the Phantoms', and Stuart invited me to see them. They were playing at a local youth club dance so I went along and I was very impressed. Gene White was a good singer and Stuart was an excellent lead guitarist. I thought, I'd like to do that.

Things were about to start looking up. Stuart and I had formed a little group at school; I was the singer and we used to rehearse occasionally in the school's hall. The powers that be got wind of it, so we were asked to play a short set at the school's end-of-term dance. I was still a little shy and self-conscious, and other than sport hadn't really made much of an impression. I was the new boy who turned up in short trousers. Now, without fanfare, I was the singer in the school band. It was 1959, I was fifteen and this was my first time. I was going to sing on a stage, in public. I sang Elvis's 'Blue Suede Shoes':

> 'Well, it's one for the money, two for the show
> Three to get ready, now go, cat, go
> But don't you step on my blue suede shoes.
> Well you can do anything, but lay off of my blue suede shoes.'

The number finished and to my surprise the kids applauded. We were a success. Suddenly, I became quite popular. Suddenly kids I didn't know were speaking to me. One or two girls even smiled at me. I liked that and maybe I had found something that made me a little bit special. I liked being that. I have never been interested in fame for its own sake but fame can open doors and helps make things happen. This was an early, small lesson in the power of the performer, a way to stand out from the crowd.

I was fifteen and soon it would be time to leave school or stay on and try and get some O levels. Not much chance of that, I thought. What was the alternative? I would have to leave and get a job. I didn't fancy that either. The school careers master suggested I get a job in a greengrocer's shop. I remember feeling a little offended that he hadn't seen my hidden potential.

To be fair he didn't have a lot to work with but time was moving on and the security of being at school was about to be stripped away.

CHAPTER THIRTEEN

Jack the Ripper

'There's a man who walks the streets of London late at night'
   – Screaming Lord Sutch, 1961

I WAS NEARLY SIXTEEN YEARS OLD when quite suddenly the lead
singer of the Phantoms left the band, Stuart asked me to replace
him and we became 'Paul Dean and the Dreamers'.

While I was still at school, I was travelling to gigs all over the country.
We were a covers band and played all the big hits of the moment; songs
by Chuck Berry, Elvis, and Cliff Richard who had recently released his
big hit 'Living Doll'. Cliff was just breaking through ('The Shadows' were
still 'The Drifters'), and 'Living Doll' was one of the songs written by
Lionel Bart for the 1959 movie *Serious Charge*. Cliff got a small role in
the film, and part of his contract stipulated that one of the songs would
be released as a single. When he was told it was 'Living Doll' he point
blank refused as that song didn't go with their image. They'd already had
a big hit with 'Move It' which was a good solid rock song of the period;
but it was in the film's contract, so they had to compromise. They
changed the way the song was performed in the film. Cliff felt it was fake
rock 'n' roll and gave it a slower, country and western feel. It was a good

choice as the song went to number one and was the biggest-selling UK record of 1959.

That sort of negotiation was a little beyond Paul Dean and the Dreamers, so if we could play it and it was popular, we performed it. Still, it was an early illustration of Cliff knowing his worth and standing up for it. Most performers know when a song or a role is 'right' for them.

I was fast approaching sixteen and had decided that I didn't want to stay on at school and take O levels. Stuart and I looked at all the options available that would allow us to keep the group going and avoid having to get a 'proper' job. Stuart came up with a plan to take a three-year catering course at Hendon Technical College. My grandfather had been a chef, so maybe I had a natural gift too and could do the same. The problem was, I wasn't that interested in food. I'd grown up on eggs and bacon and the odd meat pie. The other problem was that we had to take an exam to get in. I had never passed an exam in my life. If they were giving out an A level for looking out of the window, I'd have passed with an A*. Still, we had no other option. It was worth a punt.

On the basis that you can fool some of the people some of the time, we both passed. I was quite chuffed with myself. I still don't know how I did it. They have since renamed Technical Colleges; so whenever I drive past the old Hendon Tech building, l have a little chuckle because it's now called 'Middlesex University'. Who'd have thought it?

I was still living with my mum in Edgware and travelling around the country as Paul Dean and the Dreamers. We now had a manager – a nice guy called David Oddie, who ended up managing Status Quo. They originated as 'The Spectres' and were formed by Francis Rossi. Like us, they started as a school band. Status Quo is a great band, still rocking all over the world.

We were playing for fifteen pounds a night and if it was a really good booking we'd get thirty pounds. After we'd split it five ways it still wasn't very much, but it didn't bother me as I was living with my nan who looked after me. I used to arrive home from a gig in the early hours and not get up until at least midday.

The band was doing quite well so we had enough money for a down payment on a slightly bigger second-hand Bedford van.

We tried to keep up with the records that were in the charts, like Elvis's 'A Fool Such as I' and Chuck Berry's 'Sweet Little Rock and Roller'. We rehearsed the latest hits and played them when we gigged. As the singer I'd learn the tune and the words and we set the key. Stuart and I had achieved our goal. We played in the band at night and made rather flat soufflés during the day when we were at college. We were obliged to dress as chefs – white jackets, checked trousers, aprons and chef's hats. I realised early on that this wasn't for me.

My father Oscar gave me a job exchanging contracts on houses and serving writs which, being risk averse, I didn't like one bit. I once served a writ on a singer called Vince Eager (Roy Taylor) who was performing at the Orchard Ballroom in Purley. He was one of the Larry Parnes stable of singers which included big names like Billy Fury (Ronald Wycherley), Duffy Power (Raymond Howard) and Johnny Gentle (John Askew). Parnes was money-orientated and the first of the British rock 'n' roll managers. His nickname was 'Parnes, Shillings and Pence'. Parnes was famous for giving his singers surnames that reflected their personality; so, Vince 'Eager' and Johnny 'Gentle'. The writ I served to Vince Eager was for non-payment of bills. Vince was a very big guy and none too 'eager' to receive it.

'I've paid that fucker!' he protested. I didn't wait around. I slapped the writ in his hand and got out of there.

Vince Eager was an excellent singer and did a great version of Roy Orbison's 'Running Scared'. Paul Dean and the Dreamers backed him on a few of his gigs. He didn't remember me and I never did mention that I'd served a writ on him.

Oscar never asked me what I was going to do with my life. He knew that I was neither interested nor had the capabilities to be a lawyer. He never badgered me about getting a job. That was the great thing about my parents; I was allowed to find my own way. I was a free spirit. Oscar was irascible, but he was a unique man and clients enjoyed being around him.

In 1976, the *Sunday Times Magazine* carried a profile of him and called him 'unorthodox, flamboyant, the delight of almost everybody in the world of entertainment'. People impersonated him. The late John Thaw (Inspector Morse), who was a friend and a client, had a good take on Oscar. Another client, the playwright John Osborne (the best man at Oscar's wedding to Jenny), was inspired by Oscar to write his celebrated play *Inadmissible Evidence* in 1964, with the central role of the unconventional solicitor, Bill Maitland, created on stage and on screen by the actor Nicol Williamson.

In the late 1950s the work ethic was very much nine-to-five and getting a steady job. Being a singer in a band wasn't regarded as a stable occupation. Yet, all I wanted to do was sing in the band. At least on stage I was able to express myself. In person I was still quite shy, particularly around girls, so being in a group was a perfect way of meeting them. I wasn't good at chatting up girls. I couldn't walk across a dance floor to ask a girl to dance as the fear of rejection was far too great. However, as a singer in the band the girls would come to me and that was very helpful. I was up on stage belting out the songs while at the same time watching to see if any girls were showing any interest in me. I wasn't the most popular member of the group but luckily one or two thought I was okay.

My sex life began at fifteen. She was a very nice person of my own age, although she did look twenty-seven. I do not think, I must say, it was her first time. She was a friendly girl and more than willing to give a young lad a good start. I was grateful for the tuition and this girl liked to practise a lot. Sex was not readily available when I was a teenager, so I felt lucky to have someone introduce me to it. I am a patient man. I had been trying for two years.

After my first sexual encounter, things got better. Particularly with the girls who hung around after each gig. We didn't call them groupies but that is what they were. Sadly there weren't enough girls to go around and, as the band travelled in one van, if you didn't pull, you had to sit around and wait for that particularly band member to return. Not only would you get irritated by having to wait, you would be extremely pissed off that he had pulled and you hadn't so it became a bit of a competition between the lads. Rarely did we all get lucky at the same time; there were always one or two poor sods who had to sit around and wait for the others to return. It was usually George the road manager. Although not ugly, he had no teeth on one side. To disguise this he spent most of the time talking out of one side of his mouth so it appeared that he had a good set of teeth. We could never understand a word that he said. On the road there was never enough time to formulate a proper relationship with a girl. There was barely time to get their names.

I was eighteen and as the band lived in north London, I had moved in with my nan on the Watling Estate. Oscar was by now married to his second wife Jenny and living in Hadley Wood in Hertfordshire. They had a baby boy called Richard. A brother at last. That was all fine, everyone was happy. The group was working four or five nights a week so we decided to go professional. This meant there was no pressure to get a proper job. I was now singing full-time.

We gigged constantly but we had the odd night off. One night we decided to go to a dance hall in Harrow to see another band. The band performing that night would take me in a completely different direction and introduce me to a different kind of act.

That night in Harrow was the first time I saw 'Screaming Lord Sutch and the Savages' and believe me I'd never seen anything like it. Up until then we'd been doing Cliff Richard numbers – safe, boring, reliable pop – and now I was watching the Screaming Lord. He was completely original and dangerous. I had never seen a wild man with hair down to his shoulders, let alone on stage doing rock 'n' roll. He wore a lavatory seat round his neck and large buffalo horns on his head. He would wave a long pole, with a tuft of black hair dangling on the end, at the audience. This was, as I was later to find out, affectionately referred to as 'the minge pole'.

The Savages consisted of a lead guitar, bass guitar, piano and drums. The sound they made was loud, raunchy, hard rock 'n' roll. The Savages were very much a part of Screaming Lord Sutch's performance. He had always had great bands: fabulous guitar players like Ritchie Blackmore, who went on to play with Deep Purple and Rainbow, and Nicky Hopkins, who was a terrific piano player who ended up playing for the Stones. On drums was Carlo Little, an old friend of Sutch's and, at that time, the best drummer I had ever seen; and completing the line-up was a great bass player called Ricky Brown.

The Savages were mean, moody and very charismatic. I was an instant fan and as much taken with the theatricality of Sutch's act as I was by the music. At the start of the 1960s you never saw men with hair down to their shoulders. The Screaming Lord would come on stage with his hair pinned up under his hat; halfway through the opening number, he'd flip the hat off and shake his long, black shoulder-length hair into the faces of the girls who were gathered around the front of the stage. The girls would scream with terror at this long-haired, apparently raving lunatic who had by now lit a fire on stage as part of his 'Great Balls of Fire' routine. He would then produce a large axe and chase the Savages around the stage trying to smash them with it.

It was 1961, and it was 'blinding'. My band was used to people dancing to the music. They certainly didn't group round the front of the stage to watch a show. It was a revelation. This was a pulsating, hard rock 'n' roll act with a great shock horror routine. Sutch was completely over the top and funny. It was insane. The crowd was totally involved. They screamed, laughed, cheered and applauded. They couldn't believe what they were seeing: a madman wearing buffalo horns and his band wearing leopard skins. They'd never seen anything like it and neither had I. I thought, I'd love to be a part of that. Sutch's act had captivated me. It might have looked and sounded crazy but it was completely original and entertaining. Screaming Lord Sutch knew what he was doing.

Sutch – David Edward Sutch, the self-ennobled 3rd Earl of Harrow – ran as a Parliamentary candidate for the Official Monster Raving Loony Party thirty-nine times, wielding a loudspeaker and wearing a manic grin and leopard-skin top hat. He was a celebrity in those early days of celebrity. He had never had a hit record but packed dance halls and never stopped working. He was a master of self-promotion and always found a way to generate publicity. He was earning two to three hundred pounds a night. In 1960 that was a fortune. Sutch was no mug.

Much of what happened or did not happen was dictated by chance as much as talent. We were all becoming bored with Paul Dean and the Dreamers. We didn't have a record deal and were gradually drifting apart. Then, out of nowhere, Stuart Taylor had an invitation to join Sutch as lead guitarist in the Savages and he took it.

I was still a singer but I was bored. I had begun to teach myself to play the piano in the style of Jerry Lee Lewis. I was half hoping that at some point Stuart might put in a word for me with Sutch. By happenstance, Freddie 'Fingers' Lee, who was the piano player for Sutch, was leaving. It was a hard act to follow. Fingers, who had lost an eye in an accident with a dart, was quite a character and an excellent piano player. Stuart told me he was leaving and encouraged me to audition.

I went to meet David Sutch at what seemed to be a mansion in Harrow; a big, mock-Tudor place where he lived with his mum. We talked and I played the piano and sang a little. Sutch was happy. Stuart had put a good word in. I was to become the new Freddie 'Fingers' Lee. And I was in the money. We worked six or seven nights a week and I was paid a fiver a night. This was good money at the time, although sometimes we used to make more from people throwing pennies at us than what Sutch paid us.

It was a dangerous business working for the Screaming Lord, and being Freddie 'Fingers' Lee had its moments. One night we were doing a gig in Oxford and I got a message that some bloke wanted to see me. This big, strapping guy came round and said, 'Are you 'Freddie "Fingers" Lee?' I proudly announced that, yes, indeed I was. I thought that fame had finally come to me.

He said, 'Yeah, well I'm so-and-so and you've got my sister pregnant.'

I replied, 'Pardon?' I was tempted to say, not on this occasion. 'What's her name?'

He said the name and I said, 'No, no, no.'

'When you were here before,' he persisted.

Light dawned. 'No,' I explained, 'I was never here before. You've got me muddled up. The Freddie "Fingers" Lee that you want is the previous Freddie "Fingers".'

He was livid. He thought I was messing him around. 'What do you mean, the previous guy?'

'He only had one eye,' I said. 'As you can plainly see, I have two. Why don't you go back to your sister and ask her if her Freddie "Fingers" Lee had one eye or two eyes.'

He must have got the correct answer as I never saw him again. I had little time to dwell on it for Sutch kept us on the move.

The Savages would do a set before Sutch made his entrance; I would introduce him and then become his stooge. I was earning good money and paying rent to my grandma. Most nights of the week, I was a Savage being brutalised by Screaming Lord Sutch. What a wonderful life. I didn't think it could get much better. And subliminally, without knowing it, I was learning about performance and stagecraft. It wasn't RADA but it taught me a little about performing and creating a persona that wasn't my own. The audience didn't come to dance when Lord Sutch and the Savages were on. They came to watch, and we were part of the show.

As 'Paul Dean', I had worn traditional suits and jackets with a little bow tie, very straight and boring. With Sutch everything in excess was success. As well as our leopard skins we had another outfit: bright orange shirts, black trousers and white cowboy boots all topped off with our hair dyed a very tasteful shade of peroxide blond. Nothing was too much and we were part of a big attraction. People were paying good money to see Sutch and, we mistakenly thought, us. We felt like stars. We loved it and I loved the fact that it was crazy and different and about the music.

Sutch was a showman. He used to do a song called 'Jack the Ripper'. The lights would dim and a spotlight would find him as he entered through the crowd like a Hammer Horror Dracula with white face, black cloak, top hat and a medical bag and start to sing:

'There's a man who walks the streets of London late at night,
(The Ripper, Jack the Ripper),
With a little black bag that's oh-so tight,
(The Ripper, Jack the Ripper),
He's got a big black cloak hangin' down his back
(The Ripper, Jack the Ripper)
Well, that's one big cat I just hate to fight,
(The Ripper, Jack the Ripper),
When he walks down the streets
Every girl he meets he says: Is your name Mary Blood?'

I would dress up as his victim. I wore dodgy old wigs and dresses. Stuffed inside my dress were a large plastic red heart and a set of rubber lungs. About half way through the number, Sutch would grab hold of me, throw me on a table, produce a very large, dangerous-looking knife and plunge it into my chest. Then, slowly, accompanied by a ripping sound effect on the guitar, he would slice me open, thrust his hand inside and produce the pair of rubber lungs which he would wave in the faces of the audience – who would scream in terror. He would then repeat the action and produce the plastic heart. The girls – and the boys, although they didn't like to admit it – were terrified. They loved it and, happily, so did I.

Sutch began to try and make the scene even more horrific. He would visit the local butchers and started using real animal hearts. I said, 'Dave, I don't think the audience are as amused by the real animal hearts as much as the plastic ones. Plus they're ruining my dress.' He agreed and went back to the plastic hearts and lungs.

Musically, things were changing and Teddy boys, skiffle, Tommy Steele and the fifties were being left behind. There were new stars around in the late fifties/early sixties such as Cliff Richard, Billy Fury, Marty Wilde and Adam Faith. American acts like the Everly Brothers, Bobby Darin and Elvis were having big hit records. TV shows like *Oh Boy*, *Juke Box Jury* and *Boy Meets Girl* were the rage. Sutch never had a hit record but most people knew of him because he was so good at organising publicity stunts.

My first recording experience was with Sutch and the legendary Joe Meek. Joe Meek was a tall, gentle man from the West Country who had managed to create a unique sound, and I was somewhat in awe of him and the whole process. Meek was a genius; difficult, strange but a genius. He had been a BBC sound engineer but earned money from writing the 'B' side of a Tommy Steele hit record. He started Triumph, his own record company. His first hit was 'Angela Jones' by Michael Cox, and he had a number one with John Leyton singing 'Johnny Remember Me'. John Leyton was managed by Robert Stigwood whom I didn't know at that time but who was later to play a big part in my life.

Cliff Richard and the Shadows were massive. The Shadows had a string of instrumental hit records and Meek wanted some of that action. So he created 'The Tornados'. They had backed Billy Fury and then put out their own records. It was at the end of 1962 that their instrumental 'Telstar' was an enormous success. It was number one in Britain and the Tornados were the first British group to get a number one hit in America, before the Beatles. My pal Stuart Taylor and a fellow bandmate from the Dreamers, Ray Randall, joined the Tornados a couple of years later. They played with the group's original drummer, Clem Cattini. Joe Meek was also recording a group called 'The Outlaws' who later became Chas and Dave.

Meek was one of the first independent record producers and was a powerful man by the time I turned up with Sutch and the Savages at his studios. He had two rooms above a leather shop on Holloway Road where we recorded 'Dracula's Daughter' and the old Coasters hit 'Hog For You Baby'. Sutch was not the greatest singer in the world and Joe was very patient and kind until the point when he felt the Screaming Lord was never going to sing in tune. Then he would become very agitated and annoyed and let Sutch know it.

Joe Meek was a trailblazer and a very talented producer with his own original sound, not unlike Phil Spector. Sadly, on 3rd February 1967, Meek shot himself dead after murdering the woman who ran the leather shop below his studio. No one really knew why but he'd become obsessed with communicating with the dead, something that was thought to be a result of his anxiety and depression. It was coincidence but it was also the eighth anniversary of Buddy Holly's death in a plane crash. Such was Joe's impact on the music scene that there is still an appreciation society dedicated to him more than fifty years on, called the Joe Meek Society. Working with Joe was for me a very interesting and helpful introduction to making a record.

'Dracula's Daughter', like Lord Sutch's other recordings, wasn't a chart success; but Sutch was never intimidated by his lack of Top Twenty success. He didn't need a hit record. He lived and breathed publicity.

Although I'd only been with Sutch a couple of years it felt like I'd been doing it a long time. When you are a teenager every step of your life seems like forever. I had been singing professionally for three years – that's a century when you're nineteen. I was living with my grandma and running around the country with Screaming Lord Sutch. I was arriving home in the early hours of the morning and staying in bed until the afternoon. My grandmother had a very piercing voice and used to shout up the stairs, 'Come on, Paul,' to get me out of bed. She had a budgie called Nelson and he would imitate her: '*Come on Paul, come on Paul.*'

I escaped to Germany. In June 1963, Screaming Lord Sutch and the Savages were booked to play the famous Star Club on the Reeperbahn in Hamburg which was open 24/7. It was there that I first heard about a group called the Beatles – John, Paul, George... I can't recall if Ringo had taken over from Pete Best as the drummer at that point. They were the big stars of the Star Club. There were prostitutes advertising their wares in the windows along the Reeperbahn, and guns could be bought in shops as easily as buying a cup of tea.

I found the whole German scene as strange as the audiences found us. They loved the British bands, and the Beatles and Tony Sheridan were the kings of the Star Club. Sutch's wild-man act went okay but the crowds were more interested in drinking when we were on and didn't really 'get' the act.

That's when we, the Savages, decided we'd had enough of Screaming Lord Sutch. It was the usual thing that happens in bands. The Savages started to suffer from delusions of grandeur. We thought that we were just as important as Screaming Lord Sutch so we decided we would leave Sutch, use the Savages' name and present ourselves as 'The Savages'. How stupid! Of course – quite rightly – the Screaming Lord wasn't having any of it. The Savages was the name of his group and would remain his, so we left Lord Sutch without the name.

I did meet Sutch again, in 1985. I hadn't seen him for twenty-two years. I was playing Prince Charming in *Cinderella* at the London Palladium and, on my way in through the stage door, I saw him across the road in Carnaby Street. I think he was doing some sort of publicity stunt. He had put on a bit of weight and looked, I thought, a little tired. He was dressed the same in his top hat and leopard-skin coat.

'Hello Dave,' I said, 'great to see you, do you want a cup of tea?'

He said, 'Yeah, okay,' so he came to my dressing room and I made him a cup of tea. We chatted for a little while and then he left.

I saw David Sutch one last time in 1991. I was the subject of *This is Your Life* and he came on the show and presented me with a leopard skin as a reminder of my 'Savages' days.

I knew that David suffered with depression and that his mother whom he lived with died in 1997. Two years later at the age of fifty-eight, David Sutch hung himself.

A report in the *Guardian* dated 31ˢᵗ August 1999 read:

Recording a verdict of suicide, William Dolman, the Hornsey coroner, described the maverick politician and rock musician as 'a comedian with tragedy in his heart'. He added: 'The public saw the public face, a cheery outgoing character, yet in the privacy of his room, his true character, his true sadness, appeared.'

The 45-minute reconvened hearing provided an insight into the reality of life for Sutch, 58, who was found hanging at his late mother's home in Harrow, north-west London, on June 16 by his fiancée Yvonne Elwood. Beneath the trademark wackiness during a 35-year career in politics, which made him Britain's longest-serving party leader, Sutch, who changed his name from David Sutch by deed poll in the 1960s, was haunted by manic depression. Ms Elwood told the coroner that her fiancé had been on medication for many years for his illness. 'It would affect him physically and he just couldn't cope; he had to cancel appointments and nothing would make him happy.'

He was living in the dilapidated house of his late mother, Nancy, and when Ms Elwood wanted a bath she had to go back home to Reading because of the lack of facilities.

The coroner also heard evidence from Cynthia Payne, who used to run a brothel and is now an after-dinner speaker. Sutch had lived at Ms Payne's home for several years after they met while campaigning for the 1988 Kensington by-election.

'He was like a little boy, he always called me mumsy,' she said. 'He never slept properly. He used to get up at three in the morning and go down to the kitchen and drink tea or cocoa.' The death of Sutch's mother in 1997 had a severe effect on his health, she said. Ten days before Sutch's death, a promoter had contacted him to make sure he would attend a gig. Sutch, according to Ms Payne, had told him: 'Don't worry about that, I shall be on the front pages of the newspapers next week.'

The inquest heard that the weekend before his death, during a trip to Wales with Ms Elwood, he had seemed happier. He had discussed forth-coming concerts in Belgium and Las Vegas. Ms Elwood found him at his house, after clambering over filing cabinets in the hallway. He had hanged himself with a multi-coloured skipping rope. He left two notes and, on a calendar, had also written a daily commentary on his state of mind. The last entry, for June 15, read 'depression depression depression is too much'.

The coroner said: 'His life was a tragic comedy which came to a sudden end, [which] he obviously planned. The entertainment and fun he brought many, in what one might call the sometimes unsavoury world of politics, I hope will be remembered longer than the events of this June.'

When I look back to the early sixties, I was never going to make it as a rock singer in a band. Without Sutch and the Savages I don't know what I would have done or where I would have ended up. I was very lucky to work for David Sutch and be one of his Savages.

It taught me so much. He was fearless and opened my eyes to the possible and for that I will always be grateful. You meet very few one-offs in life; he was one. David Edward Sutch was unique. RIP.

Having left Sutch we thought we'd call ourselves 'The Soul Savages': very cheeky really but not a bad play on words. However, the name helped and we were booked as a rock 'n' roll attraction. We still wore the leopard skins and did a bit of an act.

The music world was changing. 'Beatlemania' had started. Every-where people were wearing Beatles suits and haircuts. British bands were ruling the record charts. We were ever so slightly out of our time dressed in leopard skins, but we were different enough to get work backing Del Shannon when he came over from America to tour. We played different venues every night, usually cinemas where the audience could buy a seat. The Soul Savages would open the show and then we'd accompany Del Shannon who was top of the bill along with emerging British bands Wayne Fontana and the Mindbenders ('Um, Um, Um, Um, Um, Um'), Herman's Hermits ('I'm Into Something Good'), and the American girl group the Shangri-Las ('Leader of the Pack'). Unfortunately they didn't turn up and were replaced by the singer Dodie West.

Wayne Fontana and the Mindbenders were an excellent group. Their lead guitarist Eric Stewart was to find international fame later with 10cc. Herman's Hermits were currently riding high in the charts with 'I'm Into Something Good' and they were the most popular act on the bill. Peter Noone (aka Herman) was the epitome of the boy next door and the teenage girls loved him. The moment they were announced the girls started to scream and they didn't stop screaming until they left the stage.

Del Shannon had to follow Herman's Hermits, which wasn't easy as Del wasn't a teenage heart-throb. However, after a couple of numbers the audience appreciated his singing and he went down very well. Del was a lovely chap and particularly patient when it came to my organ playing. Invariably I'd bugger up the iconic organ solo in his most famous hit 'Runaway'. He'd just turn round and give me a slightly withering smile and continue.

Following our first package tour we did another, this time with The Who. It reunited me with one of the long-lost fans of Paul Dean and the Dreamers. He was a young chap who used to follow us around and watch us play. He had the sweetest face, big brown eyes and was as angelic as any sixteen-year-old kid could be. His name was Keith Moon and he was beating the hell out of the drums with The Who. I'd seen them once before at the Railway Tavern in Harrow. They were playing a lot of Tamla Motown at that time and hadn't had a hit record, but it was clear that they were destined for great things. They were very stylish and were dressed in the fashion that represented a whole movement of teens at that time – the 'mods' with their parkas, Fred Perry polo shirts and Lambretta scooters. The Who were the first mod band and were very loud, powerful and charismatic. Pete Townshend was using feedback on his guitar, Keith Moon was the wild man on drums, Roger Daltrey had a great rock voice, and amidst all this mayhem was bass player John Entwistle who stood stock-still, expressionless, and was affectionately known as 'The Ox'.

Now we were on the same bill as them. Every night I'd watch them. At the end of their act Pete would smash his guitar and amplifier, Keith would kick over his drums, and they'd wreck the stage. I never understood or asked how they managed to replace their instruments every night. They must have had great deals with the manufacturers.

The Who, like Sutch, were dangerous and didn't give a toss. Their rebellious disregard for convention and the establishment meant they really connected with young people. By now they'd had big hits with 'I Can't Explain' and 'My Generation' which was a mod anthem written by Pete. *Tommy*, the album and film, were yet to come and our paths would cross again.

Those tours working with acts like The Who were the highs for me. We were enjoying good times. We weren't the star attraction but we were working. We liked going to West End clubs like the Scene in Ham Yard where we listened to John Mayall and Eric Clapton. If we finished a gig near London on Saturday nights we'd go and listen to Georgie Fame and the Blue Flames down at the Flamingo in Wardour Street. It was open until the small hours. A lot of American airmen used to go there. They really rated Georgie and his band who had a very American sound: echoes of Ray Charles and Mose Allison. There was some great jazz as well. Ronnie Ross, Bill Le Sage, guitarist John McLaughlin and Jack Bruce playing jazz on double bass long before co-founding the supergroup 'Cream'.

Being the supporting band on the same bill as Del Shannon and The Who was okay but we still wanted more. It wasn't enough. We were doing prestige gigs but we were the opening act. We felt like the poor relation. We were the same age as the stars. The big difference was, we didn't have a hit record.

One night after a show, Peter Noone (Herman of the Hermits) said, 'Why don't we all sing our hits.' I was embarrassed as we didn't have any hits. The nearest thing we'd come to stardom was backing Screaming Lord Sutch; so we decided to lose the leopard skins and change our image to a more modern look. We also changed our name and became 'The Thoughts'. We were obviously doing a lot of thinking.

I was nearly twenty and I was getting old. We still hadn't made it. The nearest we got was in 1965 with a cover of Lesley Gore's 'You Don't Own Me'. I was miming to our version on *Thank Your Lucky Stars*, a pop show on ITV. The only thing I can remember about that show was seeing my future *Marigold* mate Bill Oddie, who was on the same show. I can't remember what he was singing but it wasn't the 'Funky Gibbon'; that was ten years down the road.

The Thoughts did a tour of Denmark where we were more interested in the Scandinavian girls than the music. We also played in Berlin, Germany, where we decided on our night off to visit East Berlin in the communist-controlled German Democrat Republic. East and West Berlin were divided by the Berlin Wall. The only way into East Berlin was via

Checkpoint Charlie. This was at the height of the Cold War between the West and the Soviet-controlled Eastern bloc countries. East and West Berlin's divided city was a graphic example. Many East Berliners had been shot and killed trying to escape over the wall to West Berlin.

Unfortunately that night we got lost looking for Checkpoint Charlie and found ourselves driving in no man's land, alongside a narrow canal with the Berlin Wall on the other side. Without warning we were hit with a blinding searchlight from a patrol boat on the canal and a voice shouting at us through a loudhailer.

We crapped ourselves. We started waving white handkerchiefs and shouting, 'English! English! Don't shoot!'

Luckily for us the boat turned out to be manned by a British patrol. They pulled alongside our van and shouted, 'You shouldn't be here,' told us to turn around and gave us directions towards Checkpoint Charlie. Phew!

When we finally crossed into East Berlin you could really see a difference. It was like going back thirty years. It was run-down and very drab; everything looked pre-1940. It was a real contrast to West Berlin although that still had bomb sites and bullet marks on buildings.

From there we went on to Finland where we played at a town a few miles from the Russian border. After our first set we took a break. To our surprise the locals wheeled a jukebox into the hall and started dancing. That said it all.

We'd been doing the same thing for what seemed a lifetime. We were an okay group but we didn't have a record deal now and it didn't look like we would be getting another one. We had nothing original to say. Groups in the south of England didn't get into songwriting like they did in the north. The Beatles and the Hollies wrote their own material, but we were still doing covers of other people's hits. We weren't going any-where and we knew it. We were winding down as a band and I was about to call it a day.

CHAPTER FOURTEEN

Father Figures

'Over the wall we go, all coppers are nanas'
– David Bowie, 1967

MY GRANDFATHER HAD RETIRED from the ships and my nan, who was also known as 'Fighting Win', took every opportunity to give him a regular ear-bashing. He had been at sea for forty-five years with only one week in six at home. She was making up for lost time. Her voice boomed and, very sensibly, he got a job at the local hospital as a cook to escape.

It was not an atmosphere ideally suited to creative activity. Here was I, a twenty-year-old singer, living with my nan and grandfather in a council house on an estate in north London, and a very noisy council house at that.

It was at this point that my father returned to further complicate my life. He and Jenny had married and, as usual, Oscar had a master plan. He was doing very well. For decades, he practised a unique branch of the law, specialising in litigation in the world of entertainment and the media. It was said of him: 'His colourful clientele respected his professionalism, while at the same time savouring his flamboyant, sometimes profane, approach.' The essence of that approach was always to negotiate and mediate, but if a fight proved inevitable, he fought and fought.

After John Osborne's *Look Back in Anger* had become a theatrical landmark, Oscar suggested that the play be produced as a film. It was the start of Woodfall Films – named after Woodfall Road in Chelsea where Osborne lived – with Oscar as a company director along with Osborne and the director Tony Richardson.

From this came some of the most critically successful British films of the 1960s: *The Entertainer, The Loneliness of the Long-Distance Runner, A Taste of Honey* and the huge money-maker *Tom Jones* with Albert Finney and directed by Tony Richardson from John Osborne's screenplay. These films introduced the world to actors like Finney, Tom Courtenay and Rita Tushingham as well as giving meatier roles to established names like Richard Burton, Rachel Roberts and Laurence Olivier. (The British Film Institute in London hosted a season of films, 'Woodfall: A Revolution in British Cinema', to mark the company's sixtieth anniversary in 2018.) Oscar was acting for two of the five major American studios and a host of artists. He flew to Hollywood along with Sean Connery's agent to negotiate the contract for Sean's return as James Bond. He was working with MGM Films and representing Connery, the ebullient Richard Harris and the Beatles, which at that time was a pretty big deal.

Oscar was financially sound enough to buy a large house in Letchmore Heath, a beautiful village in Hertfordshire. It had a big garden, a stable block and a cottage in the grounds. My father invited my grandparents and myself to move into the cottage and we did. My motive was clear: it was cheap and I was fed. The downside was that I was living with my father, his new wife, my grandparents and Ted – Oscar's driver – his wife and many children. Ted had lived next door to my nan for years and the benevolent Oscar had hired him as his chauffeur. A recipe for disaster as Ted and my nan had never got on living next door to each other on the Watling Estate. What a scene it was!

Of course, looking back I can see what a successful time it was for Oscar. I was a young guy wanting to get on in the pop world. I wasn't that fussed about what my father was doing. Movie stars were one thing but much more in my sights was the Top Ten so I was very open for Robert Stigwood to make his first and big impression on me.

Stigwood had an immense influence over my career. Born in South Australia on 16th April 1934, he was an impresario and already steaming ahead in show business when I met him in 1964. At the time, he was living in Regent's Park and had offices in New Cavendish Street. He belonged to that 'village' of artists and entrepreneurs who became part of the fabric of London and its music scene. I was twenty and trying to be a pop star. He was a supporter of mine from the off.

Robert, who was ten years older than me and a veteran of the business but still a young guy, was friends and business associates with Kit Lambert and Chris Stamp who were The Who's managers. Chris was the brother of actor Terence Stamp. He was a good-looking guy and nice and friendly. Kit, like Robert, had a great capacity for drink. Both could consume enormous amounts of booze and still function. Kit was the son of Constant Lambert who ran the Royal Ballet and was rather flamboyant and capricious. His godmother was the prima ballerina Margo Fonteyn, so he had aspirations and that was good for me. He persuaded Pete Townshend to write a rock opera called *Tommy*. The Who were big but it was the release of *Tommy* in 1969 that made them superstars.

In 1960s Britain, what made Robert Stigwood different was his ability to diversify and grow his business, from managing pop acts to music publishing, concert promotion and his big move as an independent record producer. However, there had been a few bumps along the road. He'd had problems while producing a show with the trouser-splitting singer P. J. Proby, and a couple of other poorly received tours which bankrupted him; but like all great entrepreneurs, he picked himself up and was very much back in business.

I met Robert through a mutual friend in a pub in Soho in 1964. He knew I was looking to make a record and he seemed interested. When I told him my middle name was Oscar his eyes narrowed and something seemed to click. That's how I became 'Oscar', his new protégé and singing star.

Robert had already had the number one hits 'Johnny Remember Me' by John Leyton (produced by Joe Meek) and 'Come Outside' with Mike

Sarne. Robert recognised that the record business was changing and that groups like the Beatles and the Stones, who wrote their own songs, were now in fashion. However, he still believed that young solo singers like Cliff Richard and Adam Faith could have a recording career. He obviously saw that in me and decided he wanted to manage me.

Robert was a true talent-spotter and always had very big plans for any artists he managed. In those days it was all predicated on having a hit record. So eventually we agreed that he would find me a song and we'd make a record. As Oscar I made four singles for his Reaction label. The first, 'Club of Lights', didn't do anything. Robert then asked Pete Townshend to write a song for me which was called 'Join My Gang'.

Robert was determined I was going to be a recording star and I was not about to argue. I was given every chance. We had promotional pictures taken, a PR man was hired and a record plugger called Brian Lane – who went on to become a major rock manager – was brought in to promote the record with the radio stations. Robert even went to the trouble of having plaster-cast busts of my head made for use as a promotional tool. They were presented to the radio stations and the media. The idea wasn't original; Robert had used it before with a singer called Simon Scott. 'Join My Gang' got played quite a bit and scraped into the Radio London Top Forty but wasn't a genuine hit record.

Robert was by now getting involved with Eric Clapton and beginning to build his music empire. He had a deal with Polydor to release Oscar's records. It had been very philanthropic of Robert to indulge me but two singles had been released and still no hits.

Robert was also managing a new group who had originally emigrated from England and grew up in Australia. They were the Brothers Gibb or, as we know them today, the Bee Gees. Robert had signed them and they had a big hit with 'New York Mining Disaster', but Robert still hadn't given up on me.

My next attempt was a Bee Gees song called 'Holiday' on which they sang vocal backup. I sang the verses and they sang the middle section: 'De, de de de de de, De de de de de de'. It was interesting when I listened to the recording. As soon as they started singing you could instantly hear what an individual sound the three brothers made. It was clear, as with most big stars, that they had something instantly recognisable and uniquely their own.

I desperately wanted a hit. I was willing to do anything to promote it. It was suggested I take the Queen Elizabeth to Cherbourg and get married on board to a girl who was to be part of this brilliant publicity stunt. Thankfully, that idea didn't take off. And neither did the record.

Robert tried again and my next record was a song written by David Bowie. I'd heard about this songwriter called David Jones who was managed by a music publisher at that time. So I went to meet him. He struck me as very contemporary and in touch with the fashion at that time. He was into Marcel Marceau (the French actor and mime artist) and liked the idea that mime was the 'art of silence'. I asked him to demonstrate some mime for me and he did the hands against the window thing. He was very good and convincing.

There was a sort of distance between us and he didn't strike me as a 'happy-go-lucky' type of person. He was probably checking me out. I thought he was quite serious for a young man and so I was surprised by the funny anti-Establishment song he'd written. There had been a string of jail breaks and prison security had become a national joke, especially following the escape of the spy George Blake in 1966. Bowie had written a song called 'Over the Wall We Go'. It was a clever song and captured the situation perfectly – 'Over the wall we go, all coppers are nanas'. It suited me because instead of trying to be a rock singer, this was more of a comedy song that required me to do different voices for each prisoner. It was fun. Bowie did the roll-call in the middle and a little bit of the dialogue – 'Err keep it up lads another chorus and we're out' and it worked really well.

I was pleased with the recording and so was Bowie. The record got me on television with appearances on variety shows like *The Ken Dodd Show*. It came out in early 1967 and there are still bootleg copies about.

'Over the wall we go
All coppers are nanas
Over the wall we go
Leave 'em a note saying "Happy new year"

I know all the best ways to break out of here
I helped a young laddie called Ivan
I bundled him over the wall last night
Then he climbed back and he grabbed me tight
He uttered some words that I can't say to you
'Cause he remembered that he was a screw...'

It was banned by BBC Radio because the lyric was considered disrespectful to the police. 'All coppers are nanas' didn't sit well with them. Not unreasonable I thought. Even the controversy surrounding the record didn't turn it into a hit for me. However, David Jones became David Bowie and, in time, Ziggy Stardust. His first big hit was 'Space Oddity' and we were all singing 'Ground Control to Major Tom'.

David Bowie became a rock icon. I never saw him live but after he died on 10th January 2016, I saw him on stage in a recorded concert and for the first time saw what a fantastic performer he was. He had a very good voice, a little like Anthony Newley, but nevertheless very distinctive. I could see what a massive talent he was with that combination of originality and talent he had demonstrated at our meeting all those years before. He took his work seriously; he wanted everything to be perfect. Bowie would never settle for 'oh, that'll do'.

Artists like McCartney and Bowie, as well as being great singers, had the songwriting talent which meant they didn't have to rely on anyone but themselves for material. Hit records were the key to their long-term success.

Having a hit isn't easy, whether it's a hit record, a hit film or a hit West End show. If you're lucky enough to have one it's the best feeling there is. We all fail at some point in our lives. We're all fallible. But success is addictive and if you've tasted it, you want more.

Robert Stigwood now worked with Brian Epstein as managing director of Epstein's NEMS Enterprises, which controlled his enormous stable of stars led by the Beatles, Cilla Black, Gerry and the Pacemakers and Billy J. Kramer. Success was all around me but I was no longer flavour of the month. I had a proper contract and four single records – 'Club of Lights', 'Join My Gang', 'Holiday' and 'Over the Wall We Go' – none of which were a success.

Robert had worked very hard to try and make me a recording star but now he had much bigger fish to fry. Eric Clapton and The Who were soaring and the Bee Gees were taking up all of his attention, but they found something for me. I was to sing in Belgium at the Knokke Festival Song Contest. It involved teams of artists from different countries performing against each other. I was on the British team put together by the Beatles' manager Brian Epstein, along with Gerry Marsden, who had great recording success with Gerry and the Pacemakers, and who sadly died on 3rd January 2021 aged 78; Roger Whittaker, a South African singer with a very distinctive voice; and two female singers, Lois Lane and Dodie West whom I worked with on the Del Shannon tour. I was still Oscar.

Brian Epstein and his assistant Peter Brown came over to see the competition. We won and Roger Whittaker won the overall best artist of the competition. Epstein took us all out for dinner. It seemed to me that he was drinking a lot. He was unsteady on his feet and fell over; for a man at the height of his success, he seemed a little out of control and not very happy.

When we returned to London, Brian invited me round to his home in Chapel Street in Belgravia and asked if I'd like to hear some songs from the soon-to-be-released new Beatles album. That was the first time I heard the *Sgt. Pepper* album. He played me some tracks and then asked what I thought. It wasn't what I was expecting. It was quite a departure from the records the Beatles had made up to that point. To be honest I wasn't sure if I liked it. It was so different from what had gone before. It had so many layers and was difficult to comprehend on one listening.

I told Brian that I liked it although I wasn't sure I did. We had a drink and then I thanked him and left. I never saw him again. *Sgt. Pepper* remains the Holy Grail of all the Beatle albums and I grew to love it.

In the brief time that I knew him, Brian Epstein had seemed to me to be a very sensitive, unhappy lost soul. It wasn't long after, on 22nd August 1967, that he died from a drug overdose. I was sad when I heard the news. He did so much for the Beatles and the UK music industry and he was only thirty-two.

In contrast Robert Stigwood was flourishing. The Bee Gees were a huge success and now Robert had put together 'Cream' comprising Eric

Clapton, Jack Bruce and Ginger Baker. At the same time, he was running his own record label.

Robert had tried very hard to launch me as a recording star but it hadn't worked. Now, at twenty-three, I was married and had to get a proper job; so I went to work for Mellin Music, a music publishing company run by Robert Mellin who was an American-Ukrainian song-writer (Israel Melnikoff was his real name). The company controlled songs like 1961's 'Stranger on the Shore' by Acker Bilk, but that was just one of a strong back catalogue of hits. Robert Mellin wrote the fondly remembered theme music for *The Adventures of Robinson Crusoe* which the BBC screened in 1965; he also had hits with Frank Sinatra ('My One and Only Love' in 1955) and Nat King Cole ('My One Sin' in 1955).

Oscar set me up with an interview at his office in Bond Street. It was a heavy-hitting company. They wanted more IP (Intellectual Property) and I was hired to find new writers and songs as well as exploit Mellin's existing catalogue of music.

I had a regular job as a budding music publisher. I was making reasonable money, and I had expenses as well so financially it wasn't a bad arrangement, but it wasn't what I wanted to do. I felt a bit like a door-to-door salesman, hawking tired old songs to record producers. I was no longer a performer, so I decided to find a new group. One I could record and promote.

In those days musicians used to send tapes of their songs to the office and one particular tape caught my ear, so I called the number attached with their tape and went to meet them. They were called Wainwright's Gentlemen and they came from Sudbury near Harrow. They were a four-piece band and the lead singer was a young guy called Brian Connolly. Their drummer was called Mick Tucker. I listened to them and thought they had something.

I played their tape to Robert Mellin and he was as enthusiastic as I was. They were my first and only 'discovery'. I signed them up to Mellin Music and we renamed them 'The Sweetshop'. I got them a deal with Decca Records. Now, all we needed was a hit.

The publicity man for Decca at that time was Les Perrin who handled a string of names. We needed to attract some publicity to combine with the release of their debut single which had been produced by Phil Wainman. Phil was also working for Robert Mellin. I knew Phil who had been an excellent drummer in a local band in North London. He went on to achieve great success as the band's producer as well as running his own recording studio, Utopia.

I had what I thought was a brilliant idea to attract publicity for the record's release and contacted a company in the north-west who made jelly babies. The Beatles had once spoken about a love of jelly babies and as a result this company had enjoyed great success. Unfortunately, the Beatles had now moved on to slightly more hallucinatory substances and the sweet manufacturers were looking at ways to improve their profile, so I spoke to a representative of the company.

'I want you to make me the world's largest jelly baby.'

'Really,' he said. 'How big?'

I replied, 'Eight feet!'

'Jesus,' he said, 'we'll have to make a special mould.'

'Great! Thank you.'

My idea was to go to a children's hospital with the world's largest jelly baby, plus packets of sweets for the kiddies, and invite the press. That was Les Perrin's job.

I began to worry that the giant jelly baby, plus the group, might not be quite enough to attract the world's press, so to cover myself I thought it would be a good idea if we could make the jelly baby in the image of a well-known celebrity. At that time, Simon Dee was the biggest celebrity on television with *Dee Time* as well as hosting *Top of the Pops*. I thought to myself, he's the man. I called his agent Bunny Lewis and told him of my plan, and to my surprise (and because it was for a charity) he agreed to do it.

I then called the man at the sweet manufacturers and said, 'You know that eight-foot jelly baby you're making me?'

'Yes.'

'Could you make it look like Simon Dee?'

There was a silence. He then said, 'I'll do my best.'

The big day arrived and we all trooped to Great Ormond Street Hospital. Accompanying me were The Sweetshop, Simon Dee, and the eight-foot jelly baby which was pink and looked nothing like Simon. Unfortunately, Les Perrin – the publicist – hadn't managed to excite the world's press. Nobody turned up except for one journalist from the *Confectioners' Gazette*, who was incredibly excited with the scoop of a lifetime. Nonetheless, the group and Simon Dee, to their credit, plus the eight-foot jelly baby, visited the children, who were delighted to see them and the packets of sweets.

I never did find out what happened to the eight-foot jelly baby, but later The Sweetshop became The Sweet. Their debut single 'Slow Motion' was produced by Phil Wainman and released in July 1968 on Fontana. It went nowhere. It is now a rarity and will cost you a few hundred quid if a copy ever comes up for auction. Of course, they went on to fabulous success throughout the world as a glam rock band. 'Funny Funny' was their first of thirteen Top Twenty hits during the 1970s along with 'Block Buster!', 'The Ballroom Blitz', 'Fox on the Run' and 'Love is Like Oxygen'.

Finding supergroups for record companies was all very well but I was twenty-three, losing weight, married and miserable doing what I was doing. If you are a performer and you're not performing you don't have a release for all your excess energy and neurosis. However, once again, something was about to turn up that would bring a little sunshine. It did in 1968 – *Hair*.

Oscar had left instructions that if there were to be a memorial service after his death, he would like it to be held at St George's Church, Queen Square, just three hundred yards from Millman Street, Holborn, where he grew up and where at fourteen he had become an altar boy. So with the help of Philip Conway of Davenport Lyons, on 3rd November, 1998, a memorial service was held.

The church was packed. Two very famous lawyer friends of Oscar's did the readings. George Carman QC read one and the actor John Thaw – famous for *Kavanagh QC* – read the other. A brilliant young violinist called So-Ock Kim played one of Oscar's favourite pieces, Massenet's 'Meditation', accompanied by my son Alexander on the piano. Tributes were paid by Jarvis Astaire, former Deputy Chairman of Wembley Stadium, Robert Stigwood, Peter Ash and Arthur Davidson QC who recalled: 'I must say up here I do feel a sense of nerves and fear because I'm thinking what Oscar's reaction would be to seeing me up here? I know what the reaction would be. He would say, what have you got him up there for? I could have got somebody much better than him. I could have got George Cole if you'd asked. And then of course he would have reacted in a predictable way. He would have shouted, he would have objected and then ultimately, offered his resignation.'

Finally, Peter Ash who had known and worked with Oscar for over forty years told of Oscar's inability to do the *Times* crossword. 'I remember one clue that he did which impressed him greatly. It was a five-letter word and it said, "He started with nothing but then left his mark" – and of course the answer was Oscar. Oscar started with nothing and he left his mark. I think that's an appropriate epitaph for him.'

Oscar received many obituaries, including magnificent half-pages in *The Times* and the *Daily Telegraph*, which is very unusual for a lawyer. Ned Sherrin gave his memorial service a wonderful review in *The Oldie*. I'm sure Oscar would have been delighted.

Oscar was a big part of my life and is irreplaceable. I loved him very much and I think about him a great deal.

CHAPTER FIFTEEN

Saturday Night at the London Palladium

'Here, this is dancing, not that Fred Astaire thing – I just move and strut, and that's dancing!'

    – John Travolta as Tony Manero, 1977

O SCAR'S WORDS ALWAYS RESONATE in my ear: 'Do not put your own money in a show.' Well, I had certainly ignored him with *Grease* and here I was about to do it again with *Saturday Night Fever*.

I had money in the show from the production company with David Ian, plus my own separate investment. I was doing the one thing my father never witnessed when I was a kid – being a little 'angel'. The odds on a return are, as we know, glum. Here was I, in for a penny... in for an awful lot of pounds. Character building, I told myself. It was a big commitment. Obviously, I was very keen to make sure my involvement was as hands-on as it could possibly be.

It worked! When *Saturday Night Fever* officially arrived at the London Palladium on 5th May 1998, it was magical. I had my moment when I sat in the theatre's front balcony watching the first preview performance of the show, which David and I had co-produced with Robert Stigwood.

On stage, a young man I had discovered in a dance line was gyrating and getting squeals from the girls as he belted out the Bee Gees hit 'Night Fever'. I felt as though *I* had a fever. I was glowing. In nearly forty years in show business I had never been so elated, happy and gratified – and I wasn't even on the stage!

I could feel tears rolling down my eyes as the audience began to applaud wildly and rushed towards the stage, dancing as they went. They were going crazy, waving their arms in the air, swaggering and discoing and singing along with the music. They were caught up with it and completely lost in it.

That night I felt vindicated, for the lad making such a success of the lead role of Tony Manero was my choice for the part. I had to fight hard to get him and coached him every step of the way. Now Adam Garcia had stamped his name and personality on this Palladium stage as much as John Travolta had in the movie version. It was proof of all the belief I had in Adam and in the show. It had involved a lot of tough, sometimes emotional and motivating sessions.

If I have learnt one thing over the years, it's that if you are going to satisfy audiences you have to give them quality and value for money, and that doesn't just happen. You have to work at it and we had. Our pay-off was the audience going absolutely bonkers over Adam Garcia and the cast of *Saturday Night Fever* in the most famous theatre in the world. We had a big hit on our hands, and playing the London Palladium was a wonderful bonus. It rolled back the years for me.

I was fourteen years old before my family got a television set, but four years earlier in 1955 *Sunday Night at the London Palladium* was the big hit on television. We watched the show at the home of our neighbours, who were very posh with their nine-inch black-and-white set. It was a very big deal and in those days nearly twenty million people tuned in. A colossal number, all gathered in groups around the TV just like us.

It had the audience participation game 'Beat the Clock', and Tommy Trinder as the master of ceremonies; and then Bruce Forsyth took over, making him a household name. It also introduced Norman Vaughan with his catchphrases 'swingin'' and 'dodgy'; but in 'Brucie' he had a hard act to follow, as did Jimmy Tarbuck.

I grew up watching acts like Frankie Vaughan, Max Bygraves and Ken Dodd headlining at the Palladium on television. Cliff Richard, Tom Jones... all the stars played the Palladium. There were the big American names too, like Jack Benny and Bob Hope. I told you how I worked with George Burns in Hollywood, but in those early days of ATV's *Sunday Night at the London Palladium* my ambitions ran to a little intrepid tap-dancing on a tea tray in my nan's kitchen in north London.

I first saw the movie of *Saturday Night Fever* when I was living in America in the late seventies. Robert Stigwood, who was the mastermind of the film, had screened it for me at a giant of a house in Beverly Hills. He was renting it from the Hollywood producer Freddie Fields, who had just had a big cinema hit with Diane Keaton in the movie *Looking for Mr Goodbar* which had made a lot of money around the world. Freddie Fields' success was reflected in his house which had all the superstar trappings: swimming pool, manicured lawns, vast, high-ceilinged rooms plus of course its own screening room. I enjoyed the film, particularly John Travolta and the songs by the Bee Gees.

I had met John Travolta through Bob and found him a nice, polite gentleman. He was then just twenty-three years old and about to become one of the biggest stars in the world, but he was quite shy which didn't prepare me for his performance on screen. There really wasn't much of a story but the movie came alive when he strutted his stuff.

But the element that struck me most was the soundtrack of songs which were all by the Bee Gees. Barry Gibb says that after the movie their feet did not touch the ground for four years. The Bee Gees had hit after hit, all on Robert Stigwood's RSO label. It sealed them as the huge artists they were to become, and the income they generated became an important part of Robert's vast fortune. The soundtrack of *Saturday Night Fever* became the biggest-selling soundtrack album in history.

I wasn't alone in being impressed by the music. It took me a few years but eventually we did something about it. It has always been my experience that in this business you can lose and lose and lose, but sometimes you win, and if you win big enough it can make up for all those times you lost. What is really important is that you stay in the game. You cannot deceive audiences in the theatre or on stage, television or film. If you try and short-change the public they will catch you out. It may not sound like a masterclass in entertainment but it has kept me going through the years. I also know now that trusting my instincts is usually the best course.

I always remembered the power of that music from the screening of *Saturday Night Fever* in Beverly Hills. John Travolta got a 1978 Oscar nomination; he lost to Richard Dreyfuss for *The Goodbye Girl*, but I had an idea which never died. So, when David Ian and I started talking about the follow-up to *Grease*, I was already keen on *Saturday Night Fever* as a stage show.

Robert Stigwood was also interested and had already hired Nan Knighton to work on the script with Arlene Phillips. They wanted to do *Fever* as a Las Vegas revue, using a band like Take That to supply the music with the actors working around it. Finally, Bob ruled out Vegas and, seeing the success of *Grease*, decided that *Saturday Night Fever* should be staged in London. At the beginning of 1997, our companies were officially producing partners.

That was when the hard work really started. I was full of excitement when I drove into central London from my house in Highgate for a meeting at the Grosvenor House Hotel. There was a draft script that Nan and Arlene had been working on for a year. I hadn't seen it until then. I raced through the pages. There seemed to be one big problem – the basic concept. I just couldn't see that it would work with a group playing and singing in the background while the actors acted. Why couldn't the actors sing? It seemed to me like a perfectly legitimate way to do it. I had looked at the movie prior to the meeting. When Travolta is walking down the street in the opening sequence to the music of 'Stayin' Alive', there is absolutely no reason why he shouldn't sing.

It seems the most obvious thing to everyone now, but they had been fooling around with the concept for years and hadn't actually managed to unlock that; so when I suggested that the actors sing there was a little bit of a 'eureka!' moment. Arlene said, 'Of course.' Robert, being Robert, wasn't so quick to say 'of course' but things started to motor from then on. I had no idea what I had started. The money was in. I couldn't change my mind.

Fever did not have the instant family appeal of *Grease*. It had fantastic songs and had been a huge hit as a movie, but it had strong language and quite a lot of sex. There were no guarantees of success. It also did not have a star. Here I was, a comparative newcomer to the production business, following my nose. There were to be times when I thought it was going to be bitten off. It was a testing experience and one that was to prove to me yet again that 'show' and 'business' are equal partners. It turned me into a star-maker. I felt obliged to be. My role as a fledgling theatrical entrepreneur about to co-produce a giant, £4 million London West End musical was one thing. The other was that a lot of my own money was going along for the ride…

When you are dealing with a man like Robert Stigwood who, like all great producers, has total self-belief and is most of the time right, you need to stay on top of the game. It's a good idea to see shows and movies to learn what's going on and what is current. It helps gives you the edge as a producer and as a performer. It was certainly an ethic that rewarded me with *Saturday Night Fever*.

The original 1977 movie is a dramatic film with a great soundtrack. It wasn't written as a musical, but by marrying the soundtrack to the dialogue we could turn it into one. We just needed to change things around a bit. In the movie, most of the songs are well positioned to suit the dialogue of the scene; all we had to do was incorporate the dialogue and the song so they gelled together.

I wanted Arlene Phillips to direct. Arlene had a wonderful record as a choreographer with shows like *Starlight Express* but had never directed before. I thought she should direct *Fever* because it was music- and dance-driven. A world she knew very well. The dancing would make the show stand out above others. The fact that it had fantastic songs was key. *Saturday Night Fever* is about a guy who works in a paint store whose chance to excel and be a star is on the dance floor, and the relationships that are built around that. The banker for me was the Bee Gees' soundtrack. *Saturday Night Fever* is packed with hit songs – 'Jive Talkin'', 'Stayin' Alive', 'You Should Be Dancing', 'If I Can't Have You', 'How Deep is Your Love', 'Night Fever', 'More Than a Woman', 'Boogie Shoes' and 'A Fifth of Beethoven'. It doesn't come much better than that.

My main thrust was to try and make sure that we did as good a job as possible. We had the concept, the director and the budget, but we needed a star: a guy who had the image of a young Travolta in a white suit. Someone who looked just as good, could sing the Bee Gees songs and could dance. You can't just conjure someone up. Given the vast pool of performing talent looking for work throughout the UK you might think they would have flooded through the door, but they didn't.

In 1994 I had been at a Variety Club dinner at the Grosvenor House and part of the cabaret was from the show *Hot Shoe Shuffle* which was playing at the Queen's Theatre in the West End. It was an Australian tap-dancing entertainment troupe and they were really very good. There were a dozen dancers and at the end of the line was a very handsome young guy with dark hair who was a fantastic tapper. We were then auditioning people for *Grease* and I thought he had star potential. I had my daughters with me and they were both seriously impressed by him. He was, as my teenage daughter would say, extremely 'fit'. This was my first encounter with Adam Garcia.

What struck me about him was that he looked like John Travolta. He had blue eyes and black kiss-curls along with charisma and charm. I was focused on *Grease*, but *Fever* as a stage show was always on my mind. I talked to David Ian and suggested Adam try out for the role of Doody in *Grease*. We asked him in for an audition; but instead of a fantastic, smooth, slicked-back Travolta type with shiny black hair, in shuffled this kid of about eighteen in an old overcoat with glasses on who looked about twelve. I had called everyone in for this audition and when Adam sang he did not sing terribly well. He didn't project himself. He was sort of laid-back and rather inexperienced, but there was something about Adam that had star potential. A couple of years earlier he was studying science at Sydney University and surfing in his spare time. He was more 'Beach Boy' than 'Bee Gees'. Robert Stigwood was at that audition and like me, he probably saw a Tony Manero down the line. Adam was very vulnerable and good-looking and although he didn't sing brilliantly, he sang well enough to get the part of Doody.

By the time we were preparing *Saturday Night Fever*, Adam had grown and he was number one in the frame in everybody's mind to play

Tony Manero. He knew this and had worked with Arlene prior to auditions. He had gone to Brooklyn to work on his accent and lost that natural, plain Australian. We all turned out at the Cambridge Theatre in London to watch Adam Garcia audition as Tony Manero. We were all there – everybody involved. Adam wasn't good. He gave a very poor audition. Yes, he looked fantastic and his dancing was good but Arlene had doubts about his determination to be exactly as she wanted him to be. She wanted more attack, but Adam didn't have that real punch that the show required. His singing was not his strongest suit and his acting, although it was okay, didn't reach beyond the front row.

Adam's first report card as Tony Manero was not good and I was a worried man. I suppose subconsciously I was expecting him to walk on stage and just wow everybody, myself included. Of course, that only happens in a Walt Disney world and this was the very real, tough world of musical theatre.

Adam left everybody with a certain amount of doubt, including Bob Stigwood. Arlene had great doubts, as did David Ian. I believed that Adam needed further work and had the potential within him to succeed.

It got worse. Here were all these giant talents questioning my judgement. Arlene had worked with Andrew Lloyd Webber and choreo-graphed more than a dozen movies and lots of hit shows, including Michael Flatley's *Lord of the Dance*. Stigwood had been a box office champion since the musicals *Oh! Calcutta* and *Hair* in the sixties. David Ian has a good pair of ears and was no mug. I had to be hard-headed about it myself for at that stage I was not entirely convinced. I suggested, after much haggling, that we should work on him, send him away and bring him back again at a later date to reaudition – whilst at the same time, being practical, continue searching for a Tony Manero.

Immediately there was a problem. Arlene could not work with Adam because she was contracted to go off and work on the show *EFX* which was the Michael Crawford extravaganza at the MGM Grand Hotel in Las Vegas. We needed to get him trained within four weeks and Arlene was committed.

I suggested we use a director that I had worked with to coach Adam, but Stigwood wasn't happy with that. It was simple behind-the-scenes politics. He thought bringing someone else in would undermine Arlene – be a bit, as he put it, 'too strong' for her – so he asked me to do it instead. It was like being in one of those Judy Garland/Mickey Rooney 1940s movies when all the kids jump up and down and decide to put on a show.

I planned to crack the whip. I set up a series of full-day rehearsals for three weeks at Pineapple Studios and at the Dance Works. I arranged for Adam to work on three numbers and about three scenes so that we could get him in good shape.

Although Adam's initial audition hadn't been fantastic, when he sang 'Night Fever' it worked. One of my fears prior to that was that, because the Bees Gees have such an identifiable high-voice signature, anyone else singing their songs in full voice might sound a bit odd. What had become clear to me at Adam's first audition, and which I found very exciting, was that it sounded perfectly natural for those songs to be sung in that way on the stage. That was a big moment and I realised that, musically, it was going to work. From then on my job was to make Adam work as Tony Manero. The potential was there. It just had to be rooted out.

I understood Adam and what he was going through. He had this wonderful laid-back Australian quality which is something I recognised in myself. Particularly as I started off as a singer and didn't know much about acting and performing.

When you are young, you believe you are being real and natural – being cool. Usually you are being anything but. The thing Adam lacked above all else was the ability to project himself beyond the first row. He had it all and he just needed to give it another seventy-five per cent. In other words, this wasn't a movie so you aren't in close-up on a large screen. This is stage acting and you have to project, be bigger, louder and stronger. It was simple really. It was a large two-thousand-seat theatre so your performance needs to resonate to the back of the stalls, dress circle and upper circle. If possible, extend to the end of Regent Street.

Adam understood. I spent three weeks working with him. I went in every day. We did scenes in which I directed him. We started about ten in the morning and worked through until about four o'clock. It was a long, physical day for him. I'm fit and used to doing eight shows a week but for him it was very hard work.

I worked on his singing and his acting. We ended up choreographing some material so he could sing and dance. He worked very hard and I kept saying to him: 'Adam, this is a fantastic opportunity for you. Big opportunities come along once in a lifetime. It's very important that you get this part. I think you're right for it. I know that Robert believes you're right for Tony. However, *you* have to know you're right for the part. Arlene certainly needs to be convinced because she's going to have to work with you.'

The reaudition day arrived. The creative team were all there – Robert, Arlene, the musical director and David Ian – to see what Adam could do. I was very nervous. I was beginning to feel like his father. We had rehearsed and rehearsed and this was it. Adam walked onto the stage. I'm saying to myself, be strong, you can do it. I was too nervous to sit with the others.

The backing tape started playing the intro to 'Stayin' Alive' and Adam started singing. Whoa! He was really giving it some. He sounded great, looked great and above all he dominated the stage. The others were bowled over; I was so proud the tears were welling up. I could see everybody was excited. Adam acted out a couple of the dialogue scenes which were confident and strong, and by the end of the audition he had 'smashed it'. He had morphed into Tony Manero.

Everyone was in shock at Adam's transformation. I was completely and utterly thrilled. Robert was so excited that he came up to me and said, 'I want you to co-direct this show. In fact, I'm going to get Arlene to get you to co-direct this show now.' Arlene took me aside and said how impressed she was and would I co-direct the show. I said, 'I think you need to go away and think about this. I think we are all riding on a high.'

And we were. We were all so relieved that we had found our leading man. Someone who had it all. I was willing to do anything to make the show work and I believed that Arlene should be the director. It was her gig. Robert embraced me. He felt the problem was solved. I was relieved. David Ian was convinced. My main doubt was Adam. I always felt we could get him to the previews and the first night, but would he then settle back into something else? Would he be able to sustain the performance every night?

My other concern was the script. Weeks before the show was to open, it still wasn't right. Nan and Arlene had done a good job but I didn't think it was in a good enough shape. I thought there were many things missing and the song placements weren't right.

They had worked from Norman Wexler's movie script but had diluted its rawness. I was very keen to get the structure right, to get the song placement right and put back some of Wexler's material. I said to Robert: 'I'm not going to co-direct it. What I'd like to do is work on the script because I don't think it is right.' Robert knew the script was not quite right so he said okay.

For the next six weeks, Arlene and I worked intensively on the structure of the script. We changed the opening and made 'Stayin' Alive' visually more representative of the opening of the movie. We added 'Tragedy' which wasn't in the original film. I found it fascinating restructuring the show with Arlene.

The problem with producing any show is that you are dealing with so many egos and, if things start to go wrong, people start looking for scapegoats. People don't tell the truth. They protect their own position rather than the product. My point of view is that you mustn't lose sight of the production. You don't manoeuvre for the next job, because if you mess this one up there won't be a next job. That was the reason I worked so hard with Arlene to get the script for *Saturday Night Fever* as good as we could get it. By the end of the process, I was in a situation where I thought, it will work. This is a show. What we had before didn't quite work but now we had a show.

With that we focused on the right theatre. Robert was very keen on the London Palladium but I had doubts. It's very big, 2,300 seats, and expensive both in rent and running costs. The Dominion, where we were presenting *Grease*, seated the same number but I always felt *Grease* was a more certain hit. I knew from my youngest daughter who watched the *Grease* video constantly that there was an instant market. She was not so aware of *Saturday Night Fever*. That's what made Robert the master producer that he was. He had a great instinct and a fantastic nose for a 'hit' and he had tremendous courage and was never afraid to back himself. He insisted: 'I want the Palladium.' I thought he'd overcooked it. My partner certainly did. The Palladium became free. Cameron Mackintosh was in there with *Oliver!* which was about to end its run.

We set an opening date. We had a theatre. We had a star. We had a script.

All we had to do was sell tickets. How? The first thing was a logo. Initially we had a not-very-good drawing of the famous Travolta pose in the white suit. It did not work. I had come up with the original *Grease* logo which was the word G-R-E-A-S-E shaped into the face of a quiff with glasses. For *Saturday Night Fever* I helped design the famous pose in the shape of the letters of the title. It took more than thirty designs to get the right shape. Then we worked on the colours. I wanted the image to be right as it is the first thing the public see. This was a trademark for our production around the world and I have learned that attention to detail is vitally important in any enterprise.

Robert was responsible for much of the production, and ultimately for the product, because it was based on his original movie; but he would not have given me a large financial share of the show if he had been totally confident. He needed me there to spread the risk, and share the load. I didn't need recognition as a producer. I have all the adulation I need through performing. People like Robert get it from being top dog. The most important job is making the show work.

As our female star we had found this wonderful Australian girl called Anita Louise Combe, who played Stephanie Mangano. But another problem emerged. We felt that the girl playing the second female lead, Annette, was not working out. She had a great voice but not the experience for the show. We wanted her understudy Tara Wilkinson to be Annette instead, which is how it worked out. It was a tough decision, and Robert made it; and to the girl's great credit she stayed with the show in another role. She understood that the show came first. That was the most heartbreaking moment during rehearsals.

I wanted to try out the script in a workshop on my belief that if it doesn't work in a room with six actors, it's not going to work on the stage. Forget costumes and scenery; if the piece doesn't cut it in a room with six actors, you might as well go home. I wanted to see how the script developed. When they opened with the first number, I saw it worked. I had helped create an opening where we could introduce the main characters and keep the music going. I felt that most of all in this show, the pulse of the music must never drop.

I had seen *Oliver!* at the Palladium. *Oliver!* is a traditional musical; there's a lot of dialogue followed by a song. Audiences' attention spans were far shorter than in the sixties, and people were used to instantly flipping TV channels if they got bored. It was vital that we kept them engaged, particularly as *Saturday Night Fever* was an adaptation with a thin narrative. It wasn't Dickens.

The first workshop had proved that the concept worked. We talked Robert into doing a second workshop and we were now able to use the actors that had been cast in the show. It was then that I knew that all the care and attention that we had paid to the project for more than a year was worth it.

I had not performed as an artist for more than eighteen months.

We were now into rehearsals but there were still doubters. Arlene had a lead actor she wasn't totally sure of and a script that people were unsure whether it worked. I believed! I had seen it work in the workshop. If there was any doubt it was over whether Arlene could make the dance as good as it needed to be. After a week of rehearsal I went to see a run-through of the first act with the full cast.

I had never been so excited in my entire life. It had worked. The dialogue worked, the scenes integrated perfectly with the dance and Arlene's choreography was sensational. Magic! I went berserk. I hugged everyone. I was the only producer there and I was completely thrilled. 'Adam is wonderful. Look at him!'

Arlene had worked with me over the past eighteen months and I think she trusted me telling her that we were better than okay. We were great! It filled her with renewed confidence. Robert came in later, saw the run-throughs and said it would run for ten years. We knew we had something.

We had to make sure the promotion was right. We needed as much profile for the show and exposure for Adam as we could get. I found out the name of the PR people behind the Spice Girls. They were a company called Brilliant and so we took them on which allowed us to market the show in a more contemporary direction. David Ian, my partner, remained a little nervous but that is part of David's careful nature. His caution is an asset.

David and I went to the first technical rehearsal. This is when sets, costumes, lights and sounds are put together for the first time. You block the scene, run it and move on to the next scene. It's a tedious process. It's like watching a bad performance in slow motion and can be very dispiriting. It's no way to judge a show. We sat up in the gods because I wanted to watch it quietly. As the disco spaceship was refusing to land for the third time, David leaned across and said: 'How much have you got in this?' It was a wind-up, but the whispers on *Saturday Night Fever* within the business at that point were iffy.

'Never put your own money in shows' was my old man's mantra. You limit the risk with lots of outside investors funding the budget for the entire show, which on *Fever* was four million. The investors capitalise the show once it goes into profit. The share is usually split sixty/forty between investors and producers, plus a management fee and an ongoing royalty.

One thing that I learned from Robert, who was a big gambler, is that if you believe in something, go for it. My father's advice conflicted with that. However, I had believed in *Grease* and that had worked, and now I thought we could do the same with *Saturday Night Fever*; and although it had a bigger budget than *Grease*, the show had far more hit songs. Robert's self-belief was contagious.

In the early days, when I was working for music publisher Robert Mellin, I met Clint Eastwood. He was doing *A Fistful of Dollars* and Mellin published the film's music. I was a callow youth with ambitions of being a star. I'm thinking, yes he looks like a star. He's really tall and handsome, so that's what it takes to be a film star. Those guys are very special. Michael Caine was another one. I met Michael Caine and I could not believe the size of him. They are big men. I know not all film stars are big – Tom Cruise isn't – but there is a certain presence, a star quality that sets them apart from the average actor.

Very few shows are critic-proof and you have to be able to take the criticism. Critics are a necessary part of performing and producing. A good review is very valuable. They help to publicise shows, and you can display the quotes outside the theatre and in print advertising. I don't believe a bad review can kill a show. However, if they are unanimously against it, they are probably right. Ultimately it's the public who decide if a show runs or not.

The worst thing about reviews if you're a performer is that you only remember the bad ones. You never believe the good. The only ones you take to heart are the bad ones.

When I'm doing a weekly tour, I do not let them put the reviews up. There's going to be the odd negative one for somebody in the cast, and the one thing you don't want to look at for seven days of a weekly tour is a rotten review. What's more important is that, before the critics come in, you have a reasonable amount of preview time which is usually two weeks. The audience's reaction will tell you what's working and what's not. Then you have time to fix it before the first night and the critics.

We were all very pleased *Saturday Night Fever* had sold out its first two weeks of previews. Selling out early means the word of mouth is always very good. The phones in the box office rang incessantly and our daily figures were excellent. Extra staff were called in to meet the demand. *Fever* was about to be a smash.

David and I had had a tough year producing *Saturday Night Fever*, but we had a hit show we were both proud of. Plus the audiences loved it which is the whole point of the exercise. We'd had hits, but both *Grease* and *Fever* were revivals. Well, *Fever* was a movie, but they both had hit songs which the public already knew.

However, when it came to the American production, things changed. Robert started to move the goalposts. We were suddenly not as involved. It seemed that now *Saturday Night Fever* was a hit, we were no longer joint producers. I still had a small royalty for my work on the script, and our company had a producers' royalty; but as for fifty/fifty producing partners – that was no more.

We weren't happy but there was little we could do. For Robert, *Saturday Night Fever* was his creation. It had been a movie and together we made it a hit show. He hadn't been sure it would work and our involvement, both artistically and financially, helped him. Now the show was a hit, he could do what he liked as the rights were his and we were expendable and unnecessary. The show had worked in the West End; it would work on Broadway. We were pushed aside, not completely but as good as.

It was a shame that we went to see it. It had all the same elements as the London show – set, costumes, music, the lot. However, the most important element, the ingredient without which the show was doomed, was missing...

The actor they had chosen to play Tony Manero couldn't dance. As one reviewer put it:

> Against all odds, James Carpinello gives a more than respectable and winning performance as the self-centred and difficult to like Tony Manero. His acting and singing talents are up to the challenge of carrying a major musical but it's his dancing that, you should forgive the expression, reveals his Achilles' heel. As hard as he seems to be working on the dance floor, he just misses projecting the flair and polish the role demands.

It was a silly mistake. Robert wasn't as focused as he once was. He was drinking and someone had convinced him that James Carpinello was a good idea, even though he couldn't dance and the main attribute the character Tony Manero had to have was being a great dancer. The show limped on but never recouped.

David Ian was considering going out on his own. On return from holiday in June of 1998 he called me and said he had decided he wanted to move on. He'd had a great offer to become managing director of Clear Chanel, a large American company which had bought all the theatres from Apollo Leisure who had produced my tour of *Barnum*. I said to him: 'Yes of course.'

Dave Ian has great persuasive powers and without David, I probably wouldn't have become so involved with that side of theatre. It wasn't my first love; I'm essentially a performer. We had a lot of laughs and our successful partnership meant it was great fun. David has gone from strength to strength and had learnt a lot from our involvement with Robert Stigwood. David is now up there as a major producer with the very best of them.

It was a very amicable end but I was quite sad because we'd had seven really good fun years together. There aren't too many people you choose to share a good portion of your time with. I'm so glad I was able to share mine with David. Thereafter David and I continued to tour *Grease*. We had offered Robert a partnership based on the same terms as London but he thought *Grease* had had its day so we continued to tour the show on and off for the next twenty years.

I went to Robert's sixtieth birthday party and the young assistant stage manager, who in 1968 had taken my name and announced me at my audition for *Hair*, was sitting next to me. Sir Cameron Mackintosh. How wonderful! At that time Cameron was yet to make the movie of *Les Misérables* which became a huge success. I have known and worked for Cameron for many years and felt comfortable winding him up. I said to him: 'The great thing about Robert is that he's done it all. He has been successful managing groups like Cream, Eric Clapton, the Bee Gees, Blind Faith and The Who, and he's had his own record label, so he has done that whole pop thing. Plus he's produced hit shows like *Hair*, *Evita*, *Jesus Christ Superstar* and *Saturday Night Fever*; and hit movies like *Gallipoli*, *Evita*, and the biggest grossing musical movies of the century, *Saturday Night Fever* and *Grease*.'

Cameron smiled and graciously nodded in agreement.

Robert Stigwood was a remarkable man. I can't think of anybody in show business who has encompassed the breadth of success in so many different areas as Robert. I had and have tremendous admiration for him. Robert was always a kind man, a generous man and very good to his friends which is why there was so much sadness when he died, aged eighty-one, in London in January 2016.

I went to his funeral which was a simple affair. Linzi and I sat next to Tim Rice, Sarah Ferguson and Adam Garcia. Tim spoke to the congregation, remembering the help and guidance Robert had given him and Andrew with *Superstar* and *Evita*; as did Patrick Bywalski, Robert's right-hand man for many years.

Robert had left instructions that a party was to be held at the Dorchester for his friends. Robert was a wonderful host. He used to throw wonderful parties at the Thatched Barn, his home in Stanmore.

Plenty of everything and nothing was off the menus. At the centre of it would be Robert, drink in one hand, fag in the other and definitely very pissed or stoned, whichever came first. He had enormous stamina and he loved having a good time. He had the constitution of an ox. I didn't go to Robert's party at the Dorchester as he wasn't there. I owe Robert a great deal of thanks. He was my friend and my life and career were better for having known him.

I wanted to be involved in a musical from day one: from formulating an idea right through to the finished production. I wanted to do something where, hopefully, I could be involved as a producer *and* a performer. It always helps to have a known and successful writer on board, especially one with a track record as good as Charles Dickens.

Chapter Sixteen

What the Dickens

'It is a far, far better thing that I do than I have ever done; it is a far, far better rest that I go to, than I have ever known'
   – Sydney Carton, *A Tale of Two Cities*

I T ALSO HELPS TO HAVE a talented friend like David Soames who was a very active writer in musical theatre. David co-wrote the show *Time* which starred Cliff Richard and, later, David Cassidy. David often brought ideas for shows to my attention, and with one of them I thought the songs were very good although I wasn't keen on the show. The songs were a great start though, so I asked David to adapt a musical around them from an existing book or play.

He worked with two Americans: lyricist Steven David Horwich and composer David Pomeranz. Pomeranz had enjoyed a few hit records, including 'Trying to Get the Feeling' and 'The Old Songs' for Barry Manilow and 'I Believe in Fairytales' for Cliff Richard. I asked David Soames to put my idea to Horwich and Pomeranz to see if they could come up with something.

It was the start of a long process which was not helped by them being half the world away in Los Angeles. That something was a musical called

A Tale of Two Cities. I liked the idea although I was aware that it would be a very complicated endeavour with such a classic story, set during the French Revolution. It is, of course, a love story which, like a lot of Dickens' work, started in a weekly paper and had all the elements of a nineteenth-century soap opera.

In many ways it was similar to *Jesus Christ Superstar.* Jesus martyrs himself as does Dickens' conflicted protagonist Sydney Carton. I fancied the part of Carton and I asked Pomeranz and Horwich to put a couple of ideas on tape. I liked what they came up with and, like that other popular Dickens character, I asked for more. When they had completed writing we flew them over, and David Ian and I met them at my house and listened to the six songs they had ready.

As Dave Pomeranz finished singing the last song, Carton's 'What a Man May Do', I looked at David Ian. He looked at me. We both had tears in our eyes. Mine were brought on by the beauty of the music and David's because he could see that I was about to spend the company's money.

We commissioned them to write a full-blown musical and they flew back to California. The tapes of the completed show arrived three months later. David and I made a conscious decision to listen to them separately. They had written, at my request, a sung-through musical in the style of *Les Misérables.* It had very little dialogue, and as I listened I had this sinking feeling. David was a terrific songwriter but telling the story through song rather than dialogue takes twice as long and recitative (sung narrative) is a very difficult musical form to pull off. It's vital that musically it's melodic enough to keep the audience hooked. If the audience switches off on a particular song they don't get the story, and *A Tale of Two Cities* has many characters and locations switching between London and Paris. David Ian agreed, so it was back to development and – with them in Los Angeles and this still the days of faxes not texts and emails – long-distance creative struggles between London and Los Angeles. Our own 'tale of two cities'.

A lot of David's recitative was very angular and had been difficult to listen to but, after a lot of hard work, they had addressed this problem. We decided to go ahead and do a workshop of the musical with twelve actors at The Laundry which is a rehearsal venue in Soho. After a week's rehearsal, they presented the musical to David and me. After only five minutes I thought it wasn't working. The songs were great but it wasn't enough. David Ian and I were a little dispirited because we had employed David Gilmore – the director of *Grease* – to direct it and give it some shape. It wasn't good. Quite rightly, David wanted to let it go; but I still had faith in the story and a love for the songs. David bowed out at that point. We had given it a fair shot and the company had invested quite a lot of money in it. We were about to lose our option and it would involve further expense not to.

Yet, I couldn't let it go. I decided to call Bob Tomson who directed *Blood Brothers* and *The Mysterious Mr Love*. Bob's a brilliant and hard-working director, a real award-winner, and I believed he was the right man to get *A Tale of Two Cities* into shape.

I played him the workshop tape and gave him the history of the show, and he almost immediately wanted to be involved. He got in touch with the writers who'd flown back to California, which meant more trans-atlantic back-and-forth and still the old-fashioned way with faxes and tapes. Bob and I would review the work as it came in. I had no contract with the writers by then. It was all done on a wing and a prayer and much mutual trust.

The show was now a traditional book musical and it got better and better; good enough for me to take it to the producer Bill Kenwright. Bill is a marvellous producer who does everything from musicals like *Joseph and the Amazing Technicolor Dreamcoat* to serious plays. He's always willing to give new writers a chance and keeps most of London's acting fraternity gainfully employed. He runs the Theatre Royal in Windsor where I hoped for a try-out. I didn't play him the workshop tape. I just let him hear the six songs. He liked them and the idea of the musical. I suggested he hear the whole score, so I flew Pomeranz and Horwich over from the States. They played the musical for Bill Kenwright on the piano in his office. Bill liked it.

Although *A Tale of Two Cities* has an epic quality, it is essentially a love story. The question was whether to do it big or small as the Theatre Royal has six hundred seats. Bill had the answer. 'We do it small, sixteen actors and a six-piece band;' but small didn't mean cheap. Bill had to invest £250,000 on a set and costumes for a six-week run at Windsor on the chance he got a show at the end of it. He had little hope of getting his money back. Not many producers would do that. Bill did.

At last we were in rehearsal and guess what? I got the part of Sydney Carton. Well, I certainly knew his character inside out by then. I was thrilled for the writers, and for Bob Tomson, for they had stuck with the show through turbulent times. They rarely got upset or grand and were always willing to try a different approach for the good of the show. They never lost sight of their goal.

That whole process from beginning to end had taken six years. The show was well received, but my great satisfaction was getting it on. Creating it from start to finish. In the final scene of the musical, as Sydney Carton is led up the steps of the guillotine to meet his fate, he delivers Dickens' famous line that ends the book. It was most appropriate: 'It is a far, far better thing that I do, than I have ever done; it is a far, far better rest, that I go to, than I have ever known.'

It's a historic line and it's a very fine line between something that works and something that doesn't. It's not enough to have a good show. It has to be a great show!

I think it's very difficult to go into a West End theatre with a brand-new show and expect to have it dead right. It's almost impossible. There are always a few small changes between the previews and opening night. You can tinker with a show but it is very wearing for the cast to try and do more because they are performing at night and that leaves limited time during the day. Actors have a battle to learn words, for example, so you have to run through the show as often as possible. You have to make the actors feel as secure as possible. There's also no point in doing any of this unless you can have a laugh. You've got to have a sense of humour. When you work with a director that doesn't have a sense of humour it's difficult. Some directors bully actors and pressure them. I've seen that and I don't like it. I always recommend workshopping a new show before you spend £4 million doing it. It takes a very brave man not to. As I can't stop repeating to whoever is listening out there: 'If it doesn't work in one room with six people and a piano, it won't work anywhere. No matter how many millions it costs.'

*

I optioned the rights to Christine Keeler's autobiography (*The Truth at Last*, republished in 2019 as *Secrets and Lies: The Trials of Christine Keeler*) and developed it into a stage play. I hired Gill Adams to write the script and, in time, it was one Christine approved of ('Gill Adams's play is brilliant. She tells it like it was').

Christine's book reveals the inside story of the infamous 'Profumo Affair'. In 1963, the Secretary of State for War, John Profumo, was forced to resign after it was established that he had lied to the House of Commons about his relationship with Christine. She was also involved with a Russian spy, Eugene Ivanov, during her affair with the Secretary of State. The scandal was, in part, responsible for the resignation of the then Prime Minister, Harold Macmillan, one of the last grandees of the Conservative government, and the suicide of the man who introduced Keeler to Profumo, Dr Stephen Ward.

I was a young man when the story broke. A young lad trying for a pop career. It was really the first time that the upper classes had come under any kind of public scrutiny in my lifetime. The newspapers were full of it on a daily basis. It had the lot: drugs, the upper classes, Russian spies, politicians and of course sex – with the added ingredient of sex between young girls and older men. The world then was so unlike the #MeToo environment of the twenty-first century, which is why Christine's story is forever relevant.

I tried *Keeler* first at a small theatre in Highgate, north London, called Upstairs at the Gatehouse (beautifully run by a lovely couple called John and Katy Plews) with Alice Coulthard playing Christine. The play was well received and, with me tinkering away all the time, went on a UK tour in 2007 and 2011. It also went into the Charing Cross Theatre for a West End premiere in December 2013 which was terrific. We opened on the eve of the first night of another show: *Stephen Ward*, a very lush version of the same events created by Andrew Lloyd Webber and his team. It was a big production at the Aldwych with all the benefits of expensive publicity and, of course, with Andrew's magical name attached. David and Goliath. Well, you know who was cast as David.

I never saw it as a competition but the newspapers, particularly given my past history with Andrew with *Superstar* and *Cats*, were able to have some fun. I think most reviewers thought we were trying to capitalise on the Lloyd Webber musical. Not so. We already had it booked due to it being the fiftieth anniversary of the Profumo Affair. Andrew's show was sympathetic to Dr Ward, who killed himself while standing trial for living off immoral earnings. I don't think Ward was a pimp, but I think having access to young girls gave Ward a certain kudos amongst his high-society friends.

Christine Keeler was eighteen and Mandy Rice-Davies sixteen and they loved being the centre of attention around rich, older men. They were certainly along for the ride. However, Christine had to live with it for the rest of her life and I think she found it very difficult, certainly in my dealings with her. There were a couple of nasty unflattering shots of her shopping. She was by now an older lady and not overly well off or in particularly good health. I always enjoyed speaking to her. Her memory of the events of those days was as vivid as ever.

I managed to find an account of Ward's trial which was pretty much a verbatim record of the court proceedings. It was written by Ludovic Kennedy, who attended the trial every day, and we used his transcript as the climax of the play.

It was too much for Ward to bear. The public humiliation and the desertion by his so-called friends left him isolated and alone. It helps to explain how Ward must have felt prior to committing suicide. Our play didn't take a point of view. It's a pretty honest and straightforward version of events, and we left it to the audience to make up their own minds.

Critics are a necessary part of performing and you have to live with the good reviews as well as the bad. If you're lucky enough to get five-star reviews across the board, it can do a lot to promote the show. Sometimes, though, reviewers differ quite sharply, and *Keeler* is a good example of this. Below is a two-star review from the *Evening Standard*; but first, a four-star review from the *Sunday Telegraph* which is, in my opinion, spot on! Although, to quote Mandy Rice-Davies: 'He would say that, wouldn't he?'

★ ★ ★ ★ ☆

Little boys like to believe that they will one day be defined by great acts. All too often, when they grow up, alas, it is silly, trivial little things – not uncommonly taking place between the sheets – that ensure their name makes it into the history books.

Stephen Ward wanted so much for society to take him seriously with the famous friends and clients that he'd assiduously accumulated as an osteopath in the Britain of the Sixties, but one of the girls he used to bait them turned out to be his undoing. *Keeler* by Gill Adams purports to tell the truth about the woman who, 50 years ago, precipitated both John Profumo's resignation from Harold Macmillan's government and Ward's suicide.

With the two principal victims of the saga now dead, the truth doesn't matter that much – and, goodness knows, Christine Keeler's version of events has changed over the years. It has to be conceded, too, that generations have since come up who neither know nor care about the affair.

Keeler has to be judged purely as drama, and as such it works admirably. Miss Adams, with her director Paul Nicholas – the one-time straggly haired star of *Jesus Chris Superstar* – and the designer Charlie Camms, could very easily just have contented themselves with a cheap and cheerful spoiler ahead of Lord Lloyd Webber's musical *Stephen Ward*, which opens next month.

In the event, with Sarah Armstrong in the title role and a superb ensemble, this straight play gets to the heart of the story: how a group of bored, naive individuals, in trying to add some excitement to their lives, inadvertently brought down upon themselves the wrath of a hypocritical society.

Keeler, Ward's 'lodger', was accused of two-timing Eugene Ivanov, a Russian naval attaché (played by Alex Dower), and Profumo, the Secretary of State for War – which to the *Daily Mirror* (at the time a ruthless and powerful newspaper) meant she was trading pillow talk.

This story – as Richard Davenport-Hines communicates so well in *An English Affair*, the definitive account of it – cries out for people to feel compassion, if not pity, for just about everybody it ensnared. Rightly, therefore, *Keeler* is depressing theatre.

It is true there is not a lot of depth to Armstrong's portrayal of Keeler, but I make no complaint about that as there has never been a lot of depth to the woman. Michael Good makes a wonderfully emotionally stunted Profumo, but it is Nicholas – no longer the pretty boy of the Sixties and Seventies, but a proper grown-up actor as well as director – who gives the performance of the night as the seedy Ward.

The actor may be a couple of decades older than his character – Ward was 50 when he took his own life – but, bewigged and bespectacled, he captures the tragic man's increasing sense of despair.

Here's the *Evening Standard* review:

★★ ★ ★ ★

We British do love a good sex scandal and none has enjoyed the enduring fascination of the Profumo Affair.

It's 50 years now since nightclub dancer Christine Keeler was revealed to be sleeping with both John Profumo, the Secretary of State for War, and Russian spy Yevgeny Ivanov, at a time when the world was poised on the brink of nuclear catastrophe. We've had the film *Scandal*, of course, and Andrew Lloyd Webber's musical on this subject, *Stephen Ward*, opens in the West End next month. First up, however, we have to endure *Keeler*.

One of the many dispiriting things about this play is the fact that, although it was based by writer Gill Adams on Keeler's own autobiography, we glean nothing about what drove any of these characters, least of all Keeler herself, to do what they did. The script is lumpen and the acting flat and there are few glimpses of the thrilling dashes of beau monde and low life, power, politics and class that have intrigued down the decades. It's mightily frustrating, given that Keeler's story has the classic hubris-nemesis axis of all good tragedy.

What is fascinating, though, is how, despite the play's title, it is Stephen Ward, the so-called 'society osteopath', who becomes the central character. Paul Nicholas, who also directs, makes him a chillingly creepy panderer, although I got no sense at all that Ward had even the faintest predilection for women. Sarah Armstrong's Keeler swishes her hair and floats about in a silk dressing gown a lot. Mandy Rice-Davies barely figures until the final tumult of short scenes; various other characters flit, inadequately explained, on the periphery of the drama. This has set the bar low for Lloyd Webber and his team.

I think the 2020 BBC television series *The Trial of Christine Keeler* took our viewpoint; it showed very clearly how in the end the Establishment set up Stephen Ward and, indeed, Christine. I spoke to Christine a number of times while I was developing the play, always on the phone as we never met. She was using a pseudonym, Christine Sloane, as her own name fifty years on was still recognisable to many and a burden she was still carrying. Unfortunately it was her only source of income, and people like me were still fascinated by her story and willing to pay to tell it.

I sent the play to Mandy's solicitor and she asked me to remove some of the strong language that the author had attributed to her. Other than that she was fine with it and didn't ask for any money. Christine wasn't overly fond of Mandy whenever she came up; there was never profanity but she was somewhat dismissive. Christine met with the author Gill Adams once it was written and I was pleased she approved of the play. I invited her several times to come and see it but she never did. When I think of Christine and Mandy I see them as they were in the early sixties: two young girls, young and alive, with their whole lives in front of them. Now they have both gone.

Keeler was a project where I had total control. I produced and directed and played Stephen Ward. It wasn't an ego trip, but it became something that I wanted to see through. I offered it to Nigel Havers as I thought he was perfect for Ward but he declined. I had a couple more thoughts and, even though I was really too old for the part, I felt that I could still do it. The bonus was that we made a profit on the production. Andrew's *Stephen Ward* didn't do so well and came off after a short run. It was quoted that the show lost around £20 million. I suspect that's a rather inflated figure. I get no satisfaction from something like that because if a show is a hit, everyone benefits.

We could have come a cropper with *Grease* or *Saturday Night Fever*, and I've had bad moments as an 'angel' investor in shows; but we've been lucky with profitable tours of *Grease* in America and South Africa over the years. There are no guarantees, no matter how good the reviews are for a show. I invested in *Tootsie* on Broadway, an adaptation of Sydney Pollack's 1982 film starring Dustin Hoffman. The show opened at New York's Marquis Theatre in April 2019 to much fanfare. It got great reviews, plus Tony awards for Lead Actor in a Musical (Santino Fontana) and Book of a Musical (Robert Horn), and was expected to run and run; but there wasn't a strong enough 'name' to attract big audiences to the Broadway production and it finished in January 2020, after twenty-five previews and 293 regular performances. Ultimately the best reviews are word of mouth and the public buying tickets. Sometimes even a really good show doesn't make it, and *Tootsie* is a good example.

While *Tootsie* was saying goodbye to Broadway, another show, *Hadestown* – based on the Greek myth of Orpheus and Eurydice –

celebrated 2020 as the first musical of the 2018-2019 Broadway season to make back its initial investment of $11.5 million. That's a lot of money to recoup before you go into profit. It's an expensive business producing a show, and always a fine line between it working or not.

Being a producer carries a different pressure from performing in that you are risking other people's money and, sometimes, lives. On stage, it's usually only you that can come a cropper. As a performer, you receive great satisfaction from making people happy, be it on television, film or theatre. Yet there's nothing like the buzz of performing in front of a live audience.

I'm pretty much a shy person, and playing a character gives me a tremendous release and a sense of freedom. On occasions I ask myself why I need to go to a party, when on stage I can get music, dancing, beautiful girls and always be the centre of attention? Oh and get paid for having so much fun? There's great satisfaction when you finish a performance and you know the public were entertained. The only way I can get that feeling is when I do a musical because it has everything: music, dance, songs, humour and drama. It was very therapeutic for me, in my late forties, to add extra physical elements such as learning to walk a wire, juggle and tap dance. It did confirm that the only limitations we have are the ones we put on ourselves.

Nowadays the standard of musicals is so high. There is no divide between the West End and provincial tours. The show has to be as good in Manchester or Edinburgh as it is in the West End. Playing a new town each week keeps you fresh. Every one is different so there's no sense of tedium because you have to convince each audience, each set of critics that you're the best thing to come into their town for at least a week.

I have more enjoyment doing a show than anything else I do in my life. For me, the fun and enjoyment of life comes with performing. It's my biggest kick and when I feel most happy and relaxed.

I was very lucky that my mum took me to see *Singin' in the Rain*, because when I looked at the big screen and saw the magic of Gene Kelly, I knew then what I wanted to do. And, now, all these decades later, I'm as enthusiastic as ever. One reviewer when I was touring as the title role in *The Exorcist* in 2019 wrote: 'He's an old-school trouper to his bones and an infectiously happy man.' I think that's true because I love what I'm doing. I'm blessed with a happy family life and work is fun – which brings me to *Fiddler on the Roof*.

'You pulled it off.' This was said to me by an enthusiastic audience member who'd just seen me perform as Tevye in *Fiddler*. I suppose you could say that it was one of my best reviews ever. A Jewish man telling me I did okay for a non-Jew in this most Jewish of Jewish musicals. What he didn't know was that I had a good teacher in Oscar, who spent most of his life having to convince everyone he wasn't Jewish.

The truth is, of all the shows I've done, *Fiddler on the Roof* is the one that I have loved the most. Why? It has life, joy, sadness and humour. You don't have to be Jewish to know what it is to have a family – a wife, daughters, suitors, religion and of course... tradition. As Tevye says:

> A fiddler on the roof. Sounds crazy, no? But in our little village of Anatevka, you might say every one of us is a fiddler on the roof, trying to scratch out a pleasant, simple tune without breaking his neck. It isn't easy. You may ask, why do we stay up there if it's so dangerous? We stay because Anatevka is our home... And how do we keep our balance? That I can tell you. In one word... Tradition!

And off we'd go for the next two hours, living our lives as family and all that that means: good times, bad times, weddings, funerals, rows and celebrations, everything a family goes through in their lives – and again, you don't have to be Jewish to relate to that.

It does of course have great songs: 'If I Were a Rich Man', 'Sunrise Sunset' and my personal favourite, 'Do You Love Me?' which is lyrically the most perfect description of a long marriage. Tevye starts the song and keeps asking his wife Golde the same question:

'*Golde... do you love me?*'

She initially mocks him for asking such a thing after twenty-five years of an arranged marriage, but he persists...

Tevye: *Golde, I'm asking you a question: do you love me?*
Golde: *You're a fool*
Tevye: *I know... but do you love me?*

Eventually, a little reluctantly, she ponders the question:

Golde: *Do I love him?*
For twenty-five years I've lived with him
Fought him, starved with him
Twenty-five years my bed is his –
If that's not love, what is?
Tevye: *Then you love me?*
Golde: *I suppose I do*
Tevye: *And I suppose I love you too*
Both: *It doesn't change a thing, but even so*
After twenty-five years, it's nice to know.

Golde was played by the beautiful and talented Sara Weymouth. Every night I looked into her deep blue soulful eyes and every night I could feel my own eyes begin to fill with tears. She made me feel that we had been married for twenty-five years and no matter what, we would always be together. I think that's one of the show's main strengths. A lot of couples in the audience could identify with that song.

Sadly Sara died in 2010. Performing that simple song with her is a moment I will never forget. It was the most genuine I've ever felt on stage with any character I've ever played. That was because of a great song and because of her.

UK Productions' Martin Dodd and Peter Frosdick, the producers, had done a brilliant job with *Fiddler* and the show had done really well. I was keen to work with them again and suggested the musical *Jekyll and Hyde*. It had played Broadway and had toured with David Hasselhoff. It was composed by Frank Wildhorn, with book and lyrics by Leslie Bricusse who as a lyricist is right up there.

I found playing the dual lead roles a challenge, especially the point when Dr Jekyll is about to take the potion that changes him to Mr Hyde, in the musical number 'This is the Moment' which has a key change and is a big sing. The part requires great vocal stamina, which is best demonstrated towards the end of the show when Jekyll and Hyde battle together in the 'Confrontation' between them where vocally the actor has to alternate between the darkness of Hyde and the lightness of Jekyll. It's the climax of the show and a marvellous piece of writing by Wildhorn and Bricusse. Hyde was perfect for me because I was able to use my baritone voice.

Something had to give on eight shows a week, and it was usually Dr Jekyll around the key change in 'This is the Moment'. Eventually I learned to control my vocals so that I wasn't shot by show six of the week. We had two very fine ladies in the show, Louise Dearman and Shona Lindsay, who kept the show flying vocally. The show has loyal fans and it had a cult following. Its original Broadway production ran for four years and the leading man had an alternate which meant he only did six shows rather than eight per week. That gave him time for his voice to rest and recover. Having done eight a week for five months on the trot, I think that's a very good idea. Pass the throat sweet.

The next Leslie Bricusse show I did was playing another doctor, only this time it was the far more congenial Dr Doolittle. I was the 'alternate' to Phillip Scofield who starred in the show.

Phillip has always had a great TV career and still has. David Ian was producing the tour of *Doctor Doolittle* and Phillip was asked to present the National Lottery show on BBC One on Saturday nights. David called me and asked if I'd mind doing two shows a week on the Saturday. I said okay and had two weeks of rehearsal and a dress rehearsal with the cast. It was a little odd as every Saturday I was parachuted in (not literally) so Phillip could do the Lottery programme. I can't remember much about the show other than 'Talk to the Animals' and Jim Henson's animatronics which meant there were lots of mechanical animals in the show. I managed to shave three minutes off the show and it became a bit of a competition between us. Phillip would try and do it even quicker. I think it ended in a draw. The only thing you need to remember if you're a performer reading this and you are ever asked to play Dr Doolittle is that the 'Pig' is the STAR.

With *Blockbuster the Musical* I got to mix pop music and the stage, which in 2014 seemed a good idea following the success of *Mamma Mia!* and Queen's *We Will Rock You*. We used all the seventies/eighties classics from Sweet, Suzi Quatro, Smokie, Tina Turner and Mud – hits like 'Ballroom Blitz', 'Block Buster!', 'Tiger Feet', 'Devil Gate Drive', 'Hey

Mickey' and 'Living Next Door to Alice'. These songs were written by the very successful Nicky Chinn and Mike Chapman.

David Soames – who worked with me on *A Tale of Two Cities* – wrote the book. Soames had met David Howells, who at one time managed Nicky Chinn; Howells told Soames that he wanted to put a show together using Chinn and Chapman's catalogue of songs. Soames saw the potential because the songs are great. He wrote a script and brought it to me with the idea that I might want to produce it.

I read it and saw the potential in the songs, but the script wasn't right. I said yes, I was interested, but we needed to work on the script. We met with David Howells and we agreed we would produce the show fifty/fifty and Howells would secure the songs from Universal Music. Soames and I worked on the script and we decided to workshop it. I directed it and Rebecca Howells choreographed the workshop.

Nicky Chinn and Mike Chapman both turned up to the workshop having not spoken for years. I don't know why, but by the end of the workshop they were both smiling. We had a show and half the money. My half. Soames and Howells didn't come through with their half so we elected to do a limited tour of three venues to see if there was any appetite for a seventies musical.

I played the part of Crazy Max who helps out Mickey Block (played by Aaron Sidwell), a young busker singing in Soho. He's borrowed money to buy a car and a loan shark is after him. He hides out in Crazy Max's Retro Record Shop and I tell him he can turn his life around if he performs two selfless deeds within seven days. Max tells Mickey to hide in the store's record booth and as the loan shark enters the shop, Max starts the booth spinning and transports Mickey back in time to London, 1975… at which point Suzanne Shaw joins the show. She made her name as part of the pop group Hear'Say on ITV's *Popstars*.

The songs were terrific; for me it was like being in the Tardis and going back to my pop-star days, and the show enjoyed a short UK tour. With such a limited run it was difficult to judge if the songs and story were strong enough to fill theatres. One day we may find out.

Meanwhile David Ian was producing *The Sound of Music* with Andrew Lloyd Webber and as part of that they came up with the idea of a TV search for Maria called *How Do You Solve a Problem Like Maria?* Andrew and David were both judges on the TV panel and it proved a very popular show. Eventually they found their Maria, a newcomer called Connie Fisher who went on to star in the show.

Thereafter David set up the same format with NBC in LA, called *You're the One that We Want,* for our production of *Grease.* Eventually a Danny and a Sandy were chosen and in 2007 the show opened on Broadway. Directed by Kathleen Marshall, it was a new version which was okay but didn't have the element of fun that the London production had. It received a Tony nomination and closed after a two-year run.

Following the success of the search for Danny and Sandy in the States, Simon Cowell's company decided to use the same format to cast a new production of *Grease* in the UK. This time the TV show was called *Grease is the Word*; David was again on the panel and I was the coach. This meant that each week I would work on the songs and dialogue with the remaining contestants before they performed on the live show, when they would either survive for another week or be voted off.

Eventually we came down to our four finalists and, on Saturday 9th June 2007, the public voted for Danny Bayne and Susan McFadden to play the roles of Danny and Sandy in the new West End stage production of *Grease the Musical,* which opened at the Piccadilly Theatre on 25th July. Danny and Susan were terrific. The show enjoyed a very successful run at the Piccadilly and they later toured the show.

I hadn't performed for some time because of my producing commitments so I was ready to do a show. As it happened, I received a call from Martin Dodd and Peter Frosdick of UK Productions. They asked if I would be interested in doing a tour of *42nd Street* to play the leading role of Julian Marsh who just so happened to be – wait for it… A producer!

I said, 'Yes. Who's directing?'

'Mark Bramble, who adapted the film version.' Mark and I had worked together before. He co-wrote *Barnum* and had been hands-on when I toured the show all those years before.

I was excited at the thought of doing *42nd Street*, based on the classic 1933 movie of the same name. It's the 'musicals musical' – the ultimate

Broadway musical comedy. It's also one of the biggest shows in terms of production value, with big sets and a very big cast.

The story concerns a naive young actress named Peggy Sawyer who arrives to audition for the new Julian Marsh extravaganza, set to open on Broadway starring ageing leading lady Dorothy Brock. Dorothy breaks her ankle so she cannot perform. Peggy takes her place and becomes a star. It's a classic backstage story. *42nd Street* is a delightful throwback to the time when musicals had a simple story and big production numbers and everything turns out fine in the end.

Mark Bramble knew what it took to make *42nd Street* work, having directed the 2001 Broadway revival which ran for over fifteen hundred performances. He later brought the show back to London's West End, at the Theatre Royal, Drury Lane, where it had played more than thirty years earlier when Frankie Vaughan starred as Julian Marsh. It returned as big as ever with fifty-five performers, lavish sets, fabulous costumes, full orchestra and was of course a smash hit.

I loved playing Julian Marsh, and shows like *42nd Street* were my inspiration and fuelled my ambition to be part of that world. Mark Bramble, who died in 2019, wrote a speech for Julian Marsh which pretty much sums up what it takes to put on a show:

> You're gonna work days and you're gonna work nights. And you're gonna work between time when I think you need it. You're gonna dance until your feet fall off and you're not able to stand up any longer. But five weeks from now, we're going to have a show!

I hadn't been away from television as I'd had guest leads in two episodes of *The Bill, Doctors, Heartbeat* and *Holby City*. I had to learn how to showjump for the BBC's Sports Relief show *Only Fools on Horses*. I'd never done a reality TV show and this was for a good cause. Also in the show were Jenni Falconer, Suzi Perry, Diarmuid Gavin, Josie D'Arby, Nicki Chapman, Ruby Wax, Matt Baker, Anna Ryder-Richardson, Sally Gunnell and Sara Cox.

The premise was simple: we would learn to showjump and then compete against each other. I'd seen showjumping on the telly for years. You wear nice outfits and there are great horses so it all looked pretty straightforward. You even get to learn how to ride a horse. I explained to the production team that I was sixty and I couldn't ride but I was happy to have lessons. The idea was that, once I'd learnt how to ride, they'd start filming us learning to jump.

So I started with the basics in an indoor riding school in Hatfield. Walking, followed by a bit of trotting. It was all going fine but I noticed how easily spooked my horse was. He seemed very nervous but I continued and we went for a little hack. Once again my horse recoiled at a little piece of paper that blew in front of us.

I was due to film the following week with my son Alex as he rides a bit. Again I'm in the indoor riding school doing a brisk trot and gaining confidence when suddenly my horse pulled up but I continued. I'm flying through the air and I was thinking, this is going to be fine as I won't be landing head first. I will land on my left buttock.

Well, that is what I did. I have never felt such pain. I couldn't move as I was in agony. The horse was standing over me dribbling. The trainer rushed over. I told her I couldn't move. I needed to keep still. After about seven minutes, I tried to stand but I couldn't straighten up.

I slowly walked to the edge of the arena and sat down. I was still doubled over but I eventually made it to the reception area where again I had to rest. I explained what had happened and, after about twenty minutes, I decided to drive home. It wasn't easy getting in the car but I made it home. Linzi was at work so I went upstairs and got on the bed. I called the show's doctor and told him I had had a bad fall. He asked me if I could wiggle my toes and I said yes. He thought that I was probably bruised and told me to take a Neurofen. I knew that I was due to film with my son Alex in a week's time so I stayed in bed for the week. Every time I moved, my back hurt.

A week later I went back to do some filming where I told the director that I couldn't do much other than sit on the horse. I thought I could manage to walk the horse so that's what we did. Over the coming days my back started to ease a little, although I was still in pain, so we began to learn how to do small jumps. I resolved above everything else that no matter what, I wasn't going to fall off because if I did, I might not be able to walk again.

I was given a horse to ride called Funtime. Apparently he was supposed to be gentle with an even temperament; but on one of the training sessions in an outdoor paddock, he took off and I couldn't stop him. Round and round we went. Luckily for me, the paddock was fenced. People were jumping in front of us, waving their arms about trying to stop us but to no avail. I held on but Funtime kept going round and round. Eventually he slowed down and I was able to rein him in. It was close but I survived.

We were all living together, just like in *Big Brother*. I shared a room with Matt Baker and Diarmuid Gavin. The first night's competing arrives in an arena with an audience and TV cameras. Funtime and I are on. I saw the fences in front of me and the bell rang and off we went. Funtime and I had a rush of blood so we tore round the course and didn't knock anything down. At the end of the first night's competition Funtime and I had won the first round. We had the fastest time and had an all-clear. Everyone was in shock as I was clearly the worst rider and Funtime was considered to be a bit tame. Funtime and I survived the next few rounds as various celebs got eliminated and had to go home. I heard on the grapevine that Funtime's owners were worried about him as they thought it might all be too much for him.

It came to what was to be my last night competing. I was prepared and ready, but no Funtime. Where is he? I was told he had gone lame. Oh dear. So they brought me another horse that I didn't know. I climbed on and off we went. It was a disaster as we were not in tune with one another and so knocked a few fences down. For some reason (and I can't remember the format exactly), Diarmuid Gavin – the gardening celebrity – had to choose who should be eliminated, Suzi Perry or me. He chose me. I was very close to shouting 'Rhubarb' at him but in truth, it was probably just as well as my back was still in pain. I checked on Funtime and was told that he was okay.

A couple of nights later, we all stayed and watched the final round. Everyone thought that Matt Baker would win but Jenni Falconer rode beautifully and deserved to win.

One month later I was still in pain so I went and had a scan. The doctor returned with the results. He told me that he wasn't surprised I had pain as I had fractured three vertebrae in my spine. There was at least some compensation as we raised £250,000 for Sport Relief, and I haven't ridden a horse since. I had every chance of doing some really serious long-term damage to myself.

My agent called. 'Gillian Lynne wants to see you for *Dear World*, the Jerry Herman musical she's putting on at the Charing Cross Theatre. It's for the part of the Sewer Man.' I later met Gilly and we chatted and it occurred to me that she was auditioning me. I didn't sing or read. She just wanted to get a feel of how I was. I hadn't worked with her for thirty-five years so it was understandable. I went to meet her again at her home and we discussed the musical and the part of the Sewer Man.

Eventually I was offered the part and we all turned up at Her Majesty's Theatre to rehearse in the large rehearsal room. Gilly choreographed *Phantom of the Opera* which was still going strong at Her Majesty's Theatre where it had been since 1986. I arrived and who should also be in the cast but Annabelle Leventon who had played Sheila to my Claude in *Hair* in 1968. It's always the same when you meet actors; you pick up forty years down the line and it's as though you last saw them yesterday.

Gillian was as focused as ever and drilled me in my dance number until she thought I was passable. Of course she had an eye like a hawk and she knew all my weaknesses and strengths.

Dear World is a mixture of fairytale, comedy and drama. It's a show about capitalistic injustice in post-war Paris. The music and lyrics are by Jerry Herman, who wrote the massive hits *Hello Dolly*, *Mame* and *La Cage aux Folles*. The problem with *Dear World* was that the narrative was odd and there wasn't really much to satisfy an audience other than to be charmed by the quaintness of the characters. I think the producers were hoping for a transfer. Cameron Mackintosh came in to see it as did various others but it wasn't meant to be. It was perfect for where it was: a small theatre with a lovely cast headed by Betty Buckley. We were billed as the 'three legends'; Gillian Lynne certainly, Betty Buckley maybe, Paul Nicholas, don't be ridiculous.

It was lovely to work with Gilly again and Peter Land, her husband of many years. They complemented each other and were a team. Gilly and

I had some laughs and the odd glass or two when Peter wasn't looking. Unfortunately after *Dear World* closed, I didn't see her again.

In 2018, I was invited by Andrew Lloyd Webber's office to the New London Theatre as it was to be renamed the Gillian Lynne Theatre, but I was out of the country so couldn't be there. Gilly certainly was.

Sadly, three weeks later she died aged ninety-two. Linzi and I went to her memorial service at the Actors' Church. It was beautiful and I'm sure Gilly would have approved. Now every time I drive down Drury Lane past the Gillian Lynne Theatre, I see her name up there in lights, where it belongs.

My old producer friend Peter Frosdick called.

'Do you fancy directing *Tommy* at the Winter Gardens, Blackpool?' I knew the theatre well. It's where David Ian and I had staged our first concert of *Jesus Christ Superstar*. He said: 'You played Cousin Kevin in the movie so you know it well.'

'Who's playing Tommy?' I asked.

He said, 'I don't know yet.'

'Okay,' I said.

I started to think about what I could bring to the show. My first thought was the choreographer Rebecca Howells. Rebecca had worked with me on *Blockbuster* so I knew she would be great. *Tommy* had run in the West End in 1996 directed by Des McAnuff who had also adapted the script with Pete Townshend. I read it and thought they'd adapted the movie very well for the stage. A week later Peter called to say he'd managed to get Joe McElderry as Tommy, and Anthony Costa to play my part in the movie, Cousin Kevin. Joe won *The X Factor* in 2009 and Anthony had been with the very successful band Blue.

We started rehearsals and what was clear from day one was that both Joe and Anthony were genuinely good singers. *Tommy* is not an easy sing but Joe sang it effortlessly. Anthony too had no trouble with Cousin Kevin's number. We had a great set and we used a lot of film and still projections. I also introduced a character who had never appeared in the show before, 'Pete Townshend'. There are so many iconic guitar moments so I thought it would be nice to feature them. I found a great guitarist who looked like Pete, dressed him in sixties clothes and featured him throughout the show. It really worked. The audience loved the show. Every night we had standing ovations and the show was nominated for an entertainment award which wasn't bad as it only had a short run. *Tommy* is one of the best shows I've ever directed.

Six months later I was back at the Winter Gardens for a Christmas season of *A Christmas Carol*. It started life as a TV adaptation starring Kelsey Grammer but had been adapted for stage and played Radio City every Christmas since 2012. The music is written by Alan Menken who wrote *Little Shop of Horrors* and *Beauty and the Beast* and has won numerous Oscars and Grammy awards for his work with Disney.

I loved playing Scrooge. Having reached seventy, I was ready for it. It was marvellous to play a character that was the same age as me. It felt more comfortable.

Another of those more mature roles had me playing the former Prime Minister, Neville Chamberlain, in the film *Masaryk* which was also known as *A Prominent Patient*. The film was set a couple of years prior to the Second World War. It was a Czech-led production, screened at the Berlin Film Festival in 2016, on the life of Jan Masaryk and starts with the death of his father, Tomáš Garrigue Masaryk, who had been the first and hugely popular Czechoslovak president. Now his son, played by Karel Roden, is the Minister of Foreign Affairs to the United Kingdom. Czechoslovakia is up against it with Nazi Germany claiming that German Sudetenland – a part of Czechoslovakia – should be returned to Germany. Chamberlain negotiates the Munich Agreement of September 1938. Chamberlain thought that letting Hitler occupy the Sudetenland would appease Hitler's ambitions. Of course it didn't. Six months later the Germans occupied all of Czechoslovakia and, in September 1939, Hitler invaded Poland. England declared war on Germany and the rest is history.

Physically at seventy I wasn't unlike Chamberlain, although I could see a little of Harold Macmillan as well. As Jan Masaryk, the star of the movie was Karel Roden, a very good actor who starred in *Hellboy*.

Although *Masaryk* was a Czech film, my scenes were in English. We shot some of them in the Prague State Opera House which is beautiful, as is Prague. It was a strong film about a pivotal time in all our history; serious times that didn't end well for Chamberlain, Hitler and much of the world. The film won twelve Czech Lion Awards and Karel Roden won Best Actor and Julius Sevcik, Best Director. Bravo!

CHAPTER SEVENTEEN

EastEnders

'Hello, Princess'
   – Gavin Sullivan, *EastEnders*, 2017

E astEnders has such a cult following. I was Gavin Sullivan, a truly bad guy. I'd played Jesus in the past and now I was pretty much playing the devil. It was great, because I don't particularly look like a thug but there was definitely an element of Gavin being a psycho. One minute he was fine and you think he's normal, and the next he's trying to blow you up.

One of my favourite movies is *Strangers on a Train* (1951), the Hitchcock thriller about two characters who meet on a train and agree to swap murders so there is nothing linking either of them to their victim. Robert Walker was great as Bruno Anthony, who is an absolute psycho, so if I got anywhere close to what he did in that role, then I'm happy.

Gavin wasn't going to be pushed around by anyone and it was very satisfying to leave people – even real hard men like Steve McFadden's Phil Mitchell – in a gibbering mess.

It was like joining an ever evolving process. *EastEnders* is a great big pulsating machine that never stops. The thing that surprised me about it was that I didn't have to read for the part. These days people want to check you out for most jobs, particularly at my age. They wanted me for the character of Gavin Sullivan, the real father of Sharon who's played by Letitia Dean. She told me I was her favourite actor when she was sixteen years old! I'm not sure she felt the same way with a seventy-year-old playing her dad.

Dominic Treadwell-Collins, the producer, had mapped out who and what the character of Gavin Sullivan would be. It wasn't just a question of turning up on the first day and reading your lines. They give you a real insight into your character and where he fits within the context of the *EastEnders* family.

I arrived on the scene after my on-screen wife Kathy, played by Gillian Taylforth, turns up alive almost a decade after she was apparently killed off. As the Albert Square residents dealt with the shockwaves caused by her return, Sharon was seen getting close to solving the mystery of her biological dad's identity. The young Sharon, whose real dad abandoned her, had been adopted by Angie and Den Watts. Den, the original landlord of the Queen Vic, was killed off in 1989 but famously returned from the dead in 2003 and greeted her with the words 'Hello, Princess.'

History repeated itself when Sharon discovered that it was Gavin who abandoned her to Den and Angie's care when she was a child. The phrase 'Hello, Princess' had actually come from Gavin all those years ago. It's something Sharon's aware of in the back of her mind, so when he said it to her at the end of an episode, she recognised it straight away. That expression was the connection between them.

It's a massive shock for Sharon to have this guy turn up and then to realise he's her dad. He looks a little off-centre. Gavin was a contemporary of Den Watts and they were both slightly on the wrong side of the law and would talk about bank jobs and things like that. So there was a history there that went way back. Gavin was a villain like Den.

When you join *EastEnders*, they don't give you your whole storyline. They don't tell you that you're going to end up killing your sister. They don't tell you when you're going to go. I was in *EastEnders* for a year before Gavin was finally dragged away by the police and I'm afraid my desperate plea of 'But I need this job...' went unanswered.

However, you never know; maybe Gavin will return – from the dead. In March 2021, during a double bill of episodes, Kathy tells Sharon that Gavin has died. She's not that bothered but ends up going to my, sorry, Gavin's funeral with Kathy. The wake is interrupted when a stranger, Zack, makes a scathing toast, where he brings up many of the nasty things Gavin did throughout his life. Kathy and Sharon can't help but agree with Zack's sentiments and the funeral ends with Sharon tossing the urn with Gavin's ashes into a nearby rubbish bin. A little harsh I thought. Still, it's all set up for Gavin's return and we may yet again hear him whisper his immortal catchphrase: ''Ello, Princess.'

Playing Gavin was timely. I'm at an age where I can no longer play romantic leads, although dirty old men is an option. Over the years the fans waiting for me at the stage door have grown older with me. I used to get seventeen-year-olds waiting for me, then it went to twenty-some-things, then ladies in their thirties, forties and fifties.

Now if I am lucky, I get much older ladies shuffling up to see me after a show. However, I do have a stalker; I just have to walk very slowly.

EastEnders was great fun and they gave me a strong character with a storyline that got the audience's attention. I loved it. It's very good to be involved in an iconic show that was watched by millions. I take my hat off to the regulars in *EastEnders*. It's a punishing schedule and when you're not filming you're learning lines. It takes over your life, but it's a great regular job and the number one TV show. That's the upside, and of course the actors are doing what they love to do and they are excellent at doing it.

It got even darker than *EastEnders* at the theatre when I toured as 'The Exorcist'.

It was a faithful adaptation of the book on which the cult movie was based, about a twelve-year-old girl possessed by Satan. After she starred in the film, Linda Blair received death threats from religious fanatics and was given bodyguards. The special effects which made that one of the creepiest films of all time – the head-swivelling, projectile vomiting, bloodied writing on walls – are a tough ask in live theatre but they were all there.

I was costumed in a cassock and zucchetto (a Roman Catholic cleric's skullcap) as Father Merrin, the title character. It gave me a chance to work with my fourth knight although I never actually saw him. Sir Ian McKellen played the voice of the Devil. Every night we did battle and every night Father Merrin vanquished the Devil and drove him out of Regan, the young girl he had possessed. It was futile of course because Satan returned every night at 8:00pm and twice on Wednesday and Saturday matinee days.

Sir Ian brought plenty of colour to the part. He was very powerful as the voice of the Devil. It was interesting to hear the different nuances he brought to each speech. Sean Mathias, the director, didn't hold back on the effects and the audiences were stunned.

I saw Hitchcock's *Psycho* when I was sixteen and had not watched a horror film since, not even *The Exorcist*. I have never been very good with things that make me jump. I've been performing for more than half a century and I've never done anything that dark. I had never played a priest and the intensity of the play was something I had never experienced before. The mix of religion, good versus evil, had a palpable effect on the audience; as was evidenced when Father Merrin finally exorcises the Devil from the young girl Regan – the audience demon-strated their relief with wild applause and cheering.

In collaboration with the Cheltenham Theatre Royal, David Ian and I produced the Ronald Harwood play *Quartet*. The film starred Maggie Smith, Pauline Collins, Tom Courtenay and Billy Connolly. Guess which part I played? Yes of course, the Maggie Sm... no, the Billy Connolly part of Wilf. It's a touching and very funny play about four retired former opera stars who decide to have one last sing at the annual Christmas do at their care home. They realise of course that they no longer have the voices to sing their original parts to Verdi's *Rigoletto* so they decide to mime to the recording they had made many years before.

At the end of the play, fully costumed and in character, they sing along with themselves from a recording they made together years before. It was a wonderful moment in the show because as actors you really feel like opera singers and the audience applaud as an opera audience reacts with bravos and cheers. I noticed on our individual bows that the lead soprano, Cissy, got the biggest cheer. I sang the baritone part which was way behind Jeff Rawle's tenor who received many more bravos than me.

I enjoyed the company of my fellow actors who were superb on the tour – Jeff Rawle, Sue Holderness and Wendi Peters. My character, Wilfred, is a bit of a dirty old dog and not exactly PC. I loved playing him because he had some funny lines and if you're in a comedy that always helps.

I particularly liked Wilfred's opening speech. It was quite long and provided me with a couple of the best opening lines I have ever had. Wilf enters the care-home lounge where Cissy is seated wearing headphones listening to music so she can't hear him. Wilf tries to engage her but she waves him away and indicates the headphones. Wilf turns to Norman who is reading and in turn waves Wilf away.

We think that Wilf is about to exit to the garden, but he stops and stands behind Cissy's chair as she continues to listen to music on her headphones. Wilf speaks. 'May I say Cissy in all honesty that you have the most beautiful tits I've ever seen?' He continues: 'I'll tell you what I'd like to do to you. I'd like to take you from behind when you're bending over to put on your surgical stockings. You'd like that, wouldn't you?'

It never failed because here's an old man with a stick who can barely walk. An absolute banker!

At seventy-six, the urge to tour is finally abating but perhaps now I should be more selective rather than taking the next thing that comes along. It's what I like to do more than anything else. It's good for older people to get enjoyment from their work for as long as they can, to stay involved with the younger generation.

I'm beyond leading man these days but there are plenty of roles for older people, as I keep reminding my agent. I thought about doing the play *On Golden Pond*. It was Henry Fonda's final film in which he plays a man of eighty. I sent the play to David Ian, who left me a message. He said: 'I read the play my darling. You're too young of course. You'll have to age up.' Now that's a miracle!

CHAPTER EIGHTEEN

The Family

'Come and check me out,
Here I'm standing with my crew, yeah'
  – 'Bad Bad Rapper', Paul Nicholas recording 2020

I STARTED AS A SINGER and tried to become a recording star and from there I moved into musical theatre and all other forms of entertainment. I think you have to look forward. The past was great. It was brilliant but the future should be too. I think you've got to try and keep moving forward.

Aled Jones has a radio show and he asked me what my favourite Christmas song was. I think he was expecting me to say Mariah Carey or Slade. I said 'Rudolph the Red-Nosed Reindeer', which was originally recorded in 1949 by Gene Autry. I was five years old and I heard it on the radio.

It was a world where you had to use your imagination. A world of powdered eggs and ration books. Of bomb sites and disused air-raid shelters. It was a time when you had to create your own entertainment. It was a grey world just after the war. There seemed to be no colour. Everything was in black and white. The vivid colours, music and dance

I found in the MGM musicals I saw at the cinema. It made me realise that there was another world out there and I wanted to be a part of that.

I loved my mum and dad as they did their very best for me despite their problems. As individuals they were great but together it didn't work for them. My mum was talented. She had rhythm, she could sing and had a great sense of humour and could, I think, have been a performer. My dad liked to create drama. He was clever, charming and had a great instinct coupled with a wry sense of humour... So when I think about what a wonderful life I've enjoyed as a performer, it's partly down to them for letting me find my own way. Thank you mum and dad. It's been spectacular and never boring with lots of laughs which for me has been one of the greatest gifts.

When we moved into our house in 1978, we had our coach house converted and my mother came to live with us. For the first time in her life she had something approaching a warm and secure environment. She enjoyed a settled existence with the family. My mother was sixty-five when she moved in with us. She died in 2001 aged ninety-two so she had nearly thirty years of living with us being content and happy. Linzi and mum were very good friends. I see a lot of myself in my mum and when I look at my brother Richard, I see a lot of Oscar in him. He's a lovely man Richard. He lives in Ireland with his wife Martina and their children David and Maria and his mum Jenny.

Oscar's great facility, one of his finest attributes, was that he really knew how to get under people's skin. As a lawyer it's a wonderful quality to have as inevitably he always arrived at the truth. He was a very good lawyer, fearless and wasn't afraid of a fight. He wasn't pompous; neither of my parents were. They were generous, honest and hard-working. Neither of them had it easy growing up but they always did the best that they could. I've tried to do the same. I have kids in their thirties, forties and fifties. I have ten grandchildren and three great-grandchildren. Every year we have to add an extra chair around the Christmas dinner table.

I didn't see *Four Weddings and a Funeral* and for the moment I'd rather not go to the last one. A wedding is a great opportunity for family and friends to get together and celebrate as we did at the end of 2019, when our youngest daughter Carmen married Blake. I felt very proud to be able to walk our daughter down the aisle. I have to say that the production was spectacular. A fabulous location, fantastic music, fine food, great company and everyone had a wonderful time. It was a sensational production put together by a brilliant producer. It was of course all down to... yes you've guessed it... my wife Linzi.

I've been very lucky to have enjoyed performing for the past sixty years. The thrill of never knowing how it will turn out has always kept it exciting. Sometimes it did and sometimes it didn't but then there was always the next one... 'Cos you never really know what's around the corner. Thanks for reading my story.

Postscript

It's September 2021 and for much of the last year and a half or so my wife Linzi and I, along with the rest of the country and indeed the world, have been in Covid-19 lockdown. Having had our double doses of vaccine we are now beginning to emerge into the light.

For the last fifty-plus years I've been constantly on a treadmill of either working or looking for work. However, the enforced break has allowed me to take a pause from my never-ending pursuit of a gig and write this book. Douglas Thompson, whom I worked with on my 1999 biography *Behind the Smile*, thankfully agreed to help me. Douglas did a great job and recorded hours of my recollections and then fashioned a structure before returning it to Linzi and me for a final edit.

Thereafter I had to find a literary agent and then a publisher. My now literary agent Guy Rose sent it to Dexter O'Neill at Fantom Publishing; Dexter was enthusiastic and here we are. I'd like to take this opportunity to thank Dexter, Phil Reynolds and all at Fantom for their tremendous help. My thanks too to Martin Dodd at UK Productions for permission to use the photos from *Fiddler on the Roof*; and to David Clews, Anna Collins and everyone at Twofour for the *Real Marigold Hotel* photos.

Special thanks go to Elaine Paige, Sir Tim Rice, David Essex and David Ian for taking the time to read the book and being so generous with their quotes. It was a great pleasure to work with them all and I have treasured memories of our time together.

In tandem with writing the book I've had the time to pursue writing and recording new songs. These, combined with a number of show tunes, pop songs and romantic ballads I've recorded over the years are assembled on my new three-CD album called *Paul Nicholas Gold* for Adrian Sear at Demon Records. My old friend Marcus Savage who was our MD for *Saturday Night Fever* and who is currently the MD on the West End production of *Mamma Mia!* arranged and recorded some of my recent songs, and we had an enjoyable (masked) and productive time. Both the book and the *Gold* album will be available online and in the shops from October 2021.